BOSNIAN HAJJ LITERATURE

To all the Bosnian Hajjis, who lived on and from hard Bosnian soil,
yet maintained the strongest link to the Hijaz: one of the heart.

BOSNIAN HAJJ LITERATURE

Multiple Paths to the Holy

Dženita Karić

EDINBURGH
University Press

Edinburgh University Press is one of the leading university presses in the UK. We publish academic books and journals in our selected subject areas across the humanities and social sciences, combining cutting-edge scholarship with high editorial and production values to produce academic works of lasting importance. For more information visit our website: edinburghuniversitypress.com

© Dženita Karić, 2023, 2024

Edinburgh University Press Ltd
The Tun – Holyrood Road
12 (2f) Jackson's Entry
Edinburgh EH8 8PJ

First published in hardback by Edinburgh University Press 2023

Typeset in 11/15 Adobe Garamond by
IDSUK (DataConnection) Ltd

A CIP record for this book is available from the British Library

ISBN 978 1 4744 9410 6 (hardback)
ISBN 978 1 4744 9411 3 (paperback)
ISBN 978 1 4744 9413 7 (webready PDF)
ISBN 978 1 4744 9412 0 (epub)

The right of Dženita Karić to be identified as author of this work has been asserted in accordance with the Copyright, Designs and Patents Act 1988 and the Copyright and Related Rights Regulations 2003 (SI No. 2498).

CONTENTS

List of Figures vii
Acknowledgements viii
Note on Transliteration xi
Timeline xii

Introduction: Writing about the Hajj through the Centuries 1
Layers of Mediation 9
The Bosnian Hajj through the Centuries 14
The In-betweenness of the Bosnian Hajj 23
The *Manāzil* of the Book 26

1 The Meanings of the Sacred 29
Bosnian Scholars in the Ottoman Empire 33
The Universal Values of the Holy Places 36
The Eternal Protectors of the Holy Places 41
Mediating Worlds through the Black Stone 46
The City and the Prophet 50
Loving the Prophet 53
Living and Dying in Medina 56
Conclusion 59

2 The Roads to Mecca 61
The Habitus of the Hajj 65
Setting Off on the Voyage 71
On the Journey 73
Pious Visitations 77

Places of Highest Importance 81
Places and Senses 83
Conclusion 92

3 Change 94
Interwar Debates on the Hajj 95
Transforming the Hajj 100
The Hajj on the Marketplace of News 104
The Hajj as a Modern Curiosity 109
The Hajj between the Local and the Global 113
The Significance of the Pilgrimage 126
Conclusion 133

4 Dis/Connections 135
Promoting Yugoslavia: Postwar Hajj Delegations 140
Mecca in the Postwar Imaginary 148
No Angels in the Desert: Zuko Džumhur in the Hijaz 151
Against Empty Form: 'I Do Not Kneel to You, Nor Do I Worship Thee' 158
Modernist Disconnections: Objections to Sufism 164
Kissing the Prophet's Tomb with One's Heart 167
Conclusion 172

5 Bosniaks between Homeland and Holy Land 174
Bosniaks on the Hajj with their President 181
Maimed Bodies on the Hajj 186
Places without God's House 192
Rites and Close Encounters 198
Traversing the Distance: The Hajj and the Self 202
Conclusion 206

Conclusion: The Persistence of Devotion 208
Writing about the Hajj 210
The Hajj and the World 212
The Possibilities of Mediation 214

Bibliography 216
Manuscripts 216
Printed Books and Articles 217

Index 233

FIGURES

2.1 A detail on the walls of Mišćina džamija depicting Medina 66
2.2 A detail on the walls of Mišćina džamija depicting al-Baqīʿ graveyard 66
3.1 Muhamed efendija Krpo 98
3.2 Muhamed Krpo on a camel in the shadow of the pyramids 103
3.3 Muhamed Krpo and his fellow Hajjis on the way back, in front of the steamship *Romanija* 110
3.4 Modern young Egyptian girl 112
3.5 Hajj stones denoting a Hajji's name, birth date and the year of pilgrimage have been popular throughout the twentieth and into the twenty-first century 114
4.1 Hajjis on a construction site in Medina 142
4.2 Hajjis on the steamship *Romanija* 143
4.3 'Our Hajjas on Arafat' 159
5.1 The title page of the bi-weekly *Preporod* in 1994, announcing the first wartime Bosniak Hajj 182
5.2 Bosniak Hajjis on pilgrimage in 1994 189
5.3 'Our Hajjis in Mecca await the rituals with longing' 205
C.1 The title page of *Preporod* announcing the Hajj at the time of the pandemic 209

ACKNOWLEDGEMENTS

Life is, indeed, not only a journey, but also a pilgrimage. And as such, one is not just uniquely inspired, but also helped and supported by companions along the way. This book is the product of a decade-long challenging struggle, which would have been impossible to finish without the kindness of many people I was lucky to encounter in my life.

The PhD research from which this book emerged was generously supported by the Yamani Charitable and Cultural Foundation. In that regard, I remain grateful to Professor Ekmeleddin Ihsanoglu for his recommendation and continous interest in my work. The Oriental Institute in Sarajevo was my first academic base and a place where my first ideas about Bosnian Hajj literature originated. In the years that followed, I benefited from the kind staff of academic and research institutions such as the Bosniak Institute in Sarajevo, the Historical Archives of Sarajevo, Gazi Husrev-bey's Library in Sarajevo, Mediacentar, Süleymaniye Library in Istanbul, İstanbul Üniversitesi Nadir Eserler Kütüphanesi, Istanbul Şehir University, SOAS (University of London), The British Library, and the University of Tübingen.

My doctoral supervisor, Dr Yorgos Dedes, remains an inspiration. In academic settings beset by neglect, I can only wish that every student had the opportunity to encounter someone as open-minded, supportive and resourceful like Dr Dedes. Professor Hugh Kennedy and Dr Mustafa Shah offered useful advice in the early stages of my PhD. As my examiners, Dr Helen Pfeifer and Professor Ian Netton provided not only much needed criticism, but also encouragement.

This book belongs to multiple spaces and the people who made those spaces special. In my hometown Sarajevo, many colleagues and friends were generous with their advice and time. I am thankful to Belma Adžamija, Ikbala Ćatić, Emina Ćerimović, Elma Dervišbegović, Professor Kerima Filan, Nenad Filipović, Dr Sabaheta Gačanin, Dr Fazileta Hafizović, Mubera Bavčić, Vasvija Kapo, Lamija Hatibović, Đermana Kurić, Amer Maslo, Ena Mulaomerović, Dina Nadarević, Sadžida Tulić and Dr Asim Zubčević. Sarajevo was the backdrop to many conversations I had with Enisa Alomerović, Olimpia Dragouni, Florence Graham, Darryl Li, Piro Rexhepi and Nir Shafir.

In London, I am grateful that I crossed paths with so many inspiring people. Eyad Abuali, Yakoob Ahmed, Ebru Akçasu, Zahra Ali, Omar Anchassi, Alyaa Ebbiary, Dena Fakhro, Taylan Güngör, Aurangzeb Haneef, Ayşe Kara, Najah Nadi, Amina Khatun, Simon Leese, Paula Manstetten, Dominique Oliver, Fatima Rajina, Chinmay Sharma, Farrah Nazh Sheikh and Walaa Quisay shared some of the graduate student struggles. Professor David Waines painstakingly read every single line of my thesis as it came to fruition and offered much needed wisdom (and I am sorry about all the extra 'the' that I added in my texts as native Bosnian speaker!). I keep learning from Michael Noble, Yossi Rapoport, Sajjad Rizvi, Liana Saif and Nur Sobers-Khan. And my time in London would not be the same without Usman Ahmedani, Talha Ahsan, Laila Alabidi, Doğukan Atmaca, Iskandar Ding, Nasfim Haque, Ozan Huseyin, Yahya Nurgat, Sabina Pačariz and Fatima Spahić. The Yunus Emre Institute in London showed interest in my work from its early stages, and I remain grateful for that.

During my time in Istanbul, Professor Yunus Uğur was immensely helpful in ensuring that I would have a temporary academic base at Şehir University. I am very grateful to Professor Zişan Furat and Professor Hatice Aynur for their help and research advice. I thank the Pašić family for their care and support. Alp Eren Topal never complained when I asked for help with convoluted Ottoman phrases and always patiently resolved the issue.

My current academic path took me to Germany. In Tübingen, Professor Lejla Demiri was my academic host for a year. I am grateful to Nora Ateia, Bilal Badat, Soumaya Belhadj, Hiroaki Kawanishi, Kübra Kısa, Mujadad Zaman and Amina Nawaz, Lea Schlenker, Blanca Villu, Selva Yıldırım and Ali Zaherinezhad for their kindness and friendship.

In Berlin, the Berlin Institute for Islamic Theology at the Humboldt Universität has been a perfect space for completing this book. I am grateful to Dr Mohammad Gharaibeh for having faith in my work and ideas. It has been a wonderful experience to learn from my colleagues at the BIT. While not physically present in Berlin, Amra Čović has been extremely supportive as I was navigating the murky lands of German bureaucracy, and in Berlin, Eyad Abuali has been a great comrade during the plague.

In the meantime, through the spaces created by conferences, summer schools and workshops, as well as through our increasingly online world, I had the opportunity to meet and benefit from the knowledge of Cemil Aydin, Björn Bentlage, Marjo Buitelaar, Sohaib Baig, Marko Barišić, Ammeke Kateman, Daria Kovaleva, Nadirah Mansour, Umar Ryad and Zacky Umam.

I feel very lucky for having met Leyla Amzi-Erdoğdular, Harun Buljina, Edin Hajdarpašić, David Henig and Ana Sekulić. You all inspire me in unique ways, and this book has been shaped by your feedback.

I cannot think of a better venue for my book than Edinburgh University Press. Nicola Ramsay has been supportive from the beginning of the book project, and Eddie Clark, Louise Hutton, Caitlin Murphy, along with copy-editor Nina Macaraig and indexer Katharine Kent, all helped bring this book to its completion. I am grateful to Elvir Jusufović and his creative drawing of Bosnian women on the Hajj. Needless to say, all shortcomings are mine and only mine.

Far from academic venues and professional spaces, I was inspired by the Hajj experiences of the 'common' people, who generously shared their impressions with me, showed me their photographs and videos and spoke about their ancestors and the objects they brought from the pilgrimage. I will never forget the cold autumn day when my grandfather Sulejman (a triple Hajji!) and his friend, Učitelj Abid, took me on a Hajj tour of Bužim, a tiny town in northwestern Bosnia. We saw Hajj stones, visited the oldest wooden mosque in the region and met the oldest Hajji in the city at that time. Rather than being a distant ritual performed thousands of miles from Bosnia, the Hajj was ever-present in this border town, giving flavour to the daily rhythms and devotions of the people. Realising that was a blessing in itself.

Finally, the love of Mubina, Merjema, Said and Sara is a persistent source of light in my life. I am eternally grateful for the love and care of my parents Ajiša and Enes, whose prayers I felt every step of my way.

NOTE ON TRANSLITERATION

The first chapter, which deals with Arabic texts, follows the IJMES transliteration style. The second chapter, which deals with Ottoman Turkish source material, follows the transliteration of the critical edition of the text in question (Menderes Coşkun, *Bosnalı Muhlis'in Manzum Seyahatnamesi: Delîlü'l-Menâhil ve Mürşidü'l-Merâhil,* Isparta: Fakülte Kitabevi, 2007). In both chapters, I have usually transcribed the titles of works, as well as names, according to the IJMES transliteration style. Some of the more frequent Arabic terms related to the Hajj are given in their more common Bosnian forms, e.g. *ikrar* and *ihram* instead of *iqrār* and *iḥrām.* The last three chapters, which deal with works written in the Bosnian language, contain phonemes characteristic of the Bosnian language. I apologise for any inconsistencies that might arise, especially where all three languages intertwine.

TIMELINE

1463	The Ottoman conquest of Bosnia and the fall of Bosnian Kingdom; Islamisation process which lasts several centuries.
1878	Austro-Hungarian occupation of Bosnia.
1882	Austro-Hungarians appoint the first *Raīs al-'ulamā* of Bosnia; the establishment of what will be later known as the Islamic Community as the representative body of Muslims in Bosnia and Herzegovina.
1908	Austro-Hungarian annexation of Bosnia.
1909	Statute for autonomous administration of Islamic religious *waqf* and educational affairs approved; more freedom and autonomy for the Islamic community.
1918	The end of World War I and the establishment of the Kingdom of Serbs, Croats and Slovenes; from 1929, the Kingdom of Yugoslavia. Bosnia divided into administrative regions without regard to its historical contours.
1930	The seat of the Islamic community transferred to Belgrade; the Community is officially known as the Islamic religious community; the seat later returned back to Sarajevo.
1945	The end of World War II; the establishment of the Federal People's Republic of Yugoslavia (later Socialist Federal Republic of Yugoslavia); in the postwar period, Muslims in the new Yugoslav state faced a series of challenges, including bans on face veiling and closure of *tekke*s.
Mar. 1992	Bosnia and Herzegovina declares independence.
Apr. 1992	Bosnia and Herzegovina receives international recognition.
1992–5	Serbian aggression on Bosnia and Herzegovina; the war ends in November 1995.

INTRODUCTION
WRITING ABOUT THE HAJJ THROUGH THE CENTURIES

In the hot summer of 1981, two Bosnian women decided to go on the Hajj, driving a Volkswagen Beetle all the way to Mecca. One of them, Hidajeta, was a housewife, and the other, Safija, worked for Energoinvest, a gigantic energy corporation and the pride of the socialist Yugoslav state. The two pilgrims were friends; however, they were also bound by a subversive link: in their youth, both of them had been members of the women's branch of the Young Muslim Movement, and in the late 1940s Safija had even spent several years in prison, for her political and social activities that were deemed unacceptable by the new post-World War II communist rule. By the time they decided to go on the Hajj, the Yugoslav communist leader Tito was no longer alive. The purges of the early decades seemed to belong to a different era. Yet, Safija thought it would be wise to keep quiet about her journey in order to avoid troubles at work: 'We won't hide but we won't spread the news either', she said. The journey by car – and not by plane or bus, as Yugoslav Hajjis were by then accustomed to – meant to mask their true intention and to present the trip as any other tourist adventure across the Middle East.

More than three decades later, Hidajeta's children wanted to publish the diary in which she had jotted down the impressions and descriptions of her journey. Hidajeta was no longer alive, and Safija – in 2014 a lively octogenarian – decided to write an introduction and add photos to serve as documentation and means of remembrance. Hidajeta's family printed the diary in several copies. Since the community knew me as a person working on Hajj narratives, I was given a copy which I reviewed in *Preporod*, a local religious biweekly newspaper, published in Sarajevo and distributed across Bosnia and the Bosnian diaspora abroad. The review stirred great interest in the diary, which was not readily available to readers. Moreover, over the ensuing years, various stories about local pilgrims and curiosities regarding their travels continued to appear in the media, presenting a most popular topic especially during the Hajj season.

Hidajeta's diary consists of a series of entries which were written at different points of the journey, describing the trip and also the Hajj ritual itself. The diary reads as instructions for future pilgrims, the account of a very unique embodied experience placed in a concrete time and place, as well as a narrative that signals the Islamic ethical virtue of unity in diversity under one God. In all these aspects, the Hajj is revealed as a central event over the course and entirety of a believer's life, and as main motivation for the specific and in many ways unprecedented act of writing. While the former remains bound to the singularity of Hidajeta's life, the latter concerns everyone who read, heard, saw, or engaged with the text, often transcending Hidajeta's original intention. After all, the diary was published posthumously, mediating her religious experience to readers unbeknownst to her, while simultaneously rendering her present beyond the limits of human mortality.

As far as we know, Hidajeta never wrote anything even remotely resembling her Hajj diary, but she was certainly not alone in this once-in-a-lifetime endeavour. As part of a global phenomenon manifest across vastly different Muslim societies throughout history, many Bosnian Hajjis wrote about their pilgrimage experiences in a range of forms and genres, mediating them to even larger audiences of Muslims and non-Muslims without access to the holy places of Mecca and Medina. Writing about the Hajj is arguably the ultimate democratic medium, allowing both highly educated and semi-literate, rich and poor, women and men, to instruct, show, or share different facets of knowledge about the Hajj. At the same time, this medium served devotional purposes, thus connecting individual believers vertically with God,[1] while also expanding their religious experience beyond the performance of the pilgrimage to include interactions with people and places.

This book is about Hajj writings as a medium between the pilgrimage and the world, between striving for the transcendent and material demands of Bosnian Muslim[2] lives shaped by a range of factors. It investigates the ways in which such textual practices reflect the influence of the socio-cultural circumstances on religious experience, and, in turn, the effect that the Hajj (as a ritual and a journey) has on conceptions of the world itself. Writing about the Hajj encompasses different genres, by no means unified by any formal criteria except for the central focus on the pilgrimage and the holy places of Mecca and Medina. Pilgrimage, in textual sources and as living, embodied practice for its participants, includes travel. Where possible, the extension of the pilgrimage to include both the journey and the ritual in the context of a vast Hajj literature allows for a detailed observation of the dynamics between the relationships to different spaces, as well as for showing how the lines between the mundane and sacred are blurred.

By focusing on the Hajj literature created by Bosnian Muslims over the span of five centuries, this book examines socio-cultural influences and changing observations of holy places and the pilgrimage, in order to demonstrate the overwhelming importance of the Hajj as a multi-faceted experience, motive and symbol. The analysis turns to two aspects that affected the rise and ongoing importance of Hajj literature throughout the long period between the sixteenth and twenty-first centuries. Firstly, where possible, it observes the

[1] Juan E. Campo argues that mediation brought by different media operates on three planes: connecting viewers horizontally with each other; vertically with higher beings and the cosmos; and temporally with past, present and future. Juan E. Campo, 'Visualizing the Hajj: Representations of a Changing Sacred Landscape Past and Present', in *The Hajj: Pilgrimage in Islam*, ed. by Eric Tagliacozzo and Shawkat Toorawa (Cambridge: Cambridge University Press, 2016), p. 269.

[2] This book uses the terms 'Bosnian Muslim' and 'Bosniak' interchangeably, recognizing the self-determination of contemporary Bosniaks, as well as keeping in mind that historically these terms had different connotations. In general, when using either of these terms, I refer to people who are Muslim and have a connection to the historical and geographical region of Bosnia and Herzegovina.

socio-material predispositions in terms of mobility, literacy and ideological pressures in order to see how they shaped the pilgrimage, in terms of both experience and expectation. Secondly, it evaluates the inner structures of religious expressions about the Hajj and shows how they participate in constructing an Islamic discursive tradition. Both of these overlap in the question of writing, which falls under both the influence of socio-cultural factors (such as the fact that the choice of a language or script is often predetermined by education) and the workings of a discursive tradition with its own genres, expectations and mechanisms for adaptation and change. A wholesome view of both intertwined perspectives indicates that the Hajj was never an isolated, atemporal practice devoid of external – even non-Muslim – influence; rather, it simultaneously retained a particular discourse inspired by Islam, which shaped the way in which Muslims saw and experienced the pilgrimage.

Thus, the study of Hajj writings needs to investigate two interrelated perspectives. The influence of political and socio-cultural circumstances on the religious expression of the Hajj presents the first, and potentially more visible, part of the equation. Hidajeta and Safija went on the Hajj under specific conditions dictated by a nation-state's control of its subjects' mobilities, by technological advancements that offered an array of transportation means (buses, airplanes, cars) and by interstate surveillance that manifested itself in the form of passports, visas and international driving licences. Their own personal history of breaking the ideological boundaries of the socialist regime influenced the journey and caused them to play hide-and-seek with the authorities, by hiding the journey's purpose from Safija's employer. Hidajeta and Safija's Hajj was also affected by their gender which framed the way in which their mobility was seen during the pilgrimage, as well as in the way in which the diary was later received. Their pilgrimage also highlighted underlying cultural links of the Yugoslav region with the Middle East: the journey of Bosnian Hajjis often took them through cities such as Istanbul or Damascus where they could reconnect with *muhajir*s, Balkan emigrants settled in various locales after the disintegration of the Ottoman Empire. The microhistory of Safija and Hidajeta's pilgrimage was embedded in these larger currents.

Furthermore, the simple example of Hidajeta's diary tells us a great deal about how literacy, language, genre and publishing media influence the expression of the Hajj experience. While elite women had limited access to both religious mobility and writing prior to the modern age, the twentieth century brought tremendous changes in terms of general access to education and the public sphere. As this book will explore further, language also played a significant role in allowing a greater number of pilgrims to share their experiences, and it also accounted for the emergence of a variety of genres employed by different actors. That Hidajeta was able to convey her impressions in the form of a diary speaks about a particular writing and reading culture that was at first confined to the family circle. Its subsequent history, however, reveals how such text becomes public and further shapes ideas about the Hajj, especially when performed by women.

Over the last decades, the socio-cultural shaping of the pilgrimage, its imagination and expression have been part of the unsteady focus of Hajj studies. It is manifested in the emphasis on the influence of last century's technological transformations, as well as studies on pan-Islamic tendencies in Hajj travelogues. This often led to 'mining' Hajj literature for studies on other historical phenomena; while valuable, the overt centring of this specific dimension threatens to leave out the crux of the issue: why did so many Muslims write about the Hajj, and sometimes only about the Hajj, during their lifetime?

While Safija and Hidajeta's journey and performance of the Hajj was shaped by specific political and socio-cultural frameworks, their faith, their feeling of attachment to the holy places and their attention to the rites, in fact, transcended these frameworks and even went counter their dictum. Investigating how the Hajj is experienced and understood by pilgrims and what it *does* to the creation of religious experience through their writing is arguably a more complicated task. It is, however, a necessary one if we are to overcome the reduction of the expression of the pilgrimage to the crude reflection of and determination by material circumstances. The shaping of the experience and understanding of the Hajj does come with a set of influences framed in and around a distinctive Islamic discursive tradition, which 'consists essentially of discourses that seek to instruct practitioners regarding correct form and purpose of a given practice that, precisely because it is established, has a history'.[3] As such, it is inseparable from the textual tradition of

[3] Talal Asad, 'The Idea of an Anthropology of Islam', *Qui Parle* 17/2 (2009), p. 20.

the Qur'an and the sunnah; however, depending on the genre, as well as the innovation and personal sensibilities of the authors, it also goes beyond them.

But how does pilgrimage reflect on the world? Hidajeta's night under the Arabian stars provides some insight:

> We slept outside, got into our sleeping bags and thus spent our first night in the desert. It is a special experience, the sky is full of stars and is close, the desert makes you think only of Allah, and I had a feeling that the whole *dunya* was left behind us, and that I am here with my life account in front of Allah. I could not sleep for a long time and that is when I realised the purpose of the Hajj.[4]

Pilgrimage affects the imagination of space, separating the ordinary from the special and, in the context of the Hajj, it involves not only Mecca and Medina as primary sites of devotion, but the entire journey. As we will see throughout this book, Bosnian Hajjis have imbued their pilgrimage itineraries with religious meaning, making Istanbul, Damascus, Cairo and Bosnia a part of the Islamic geography as much as Mecca and Medina.[5] The Hajj literature is thus important for deconstructing the idea of the Muslim World with a fixed geographic centre and points to the immense diversity of Muslim experience. Furthermore, the assumed centrality of Mecca and Medina is destabilised by taking into account the multiple belongings that Bosniaks feel and cultivate. What does it mean to place Mecca and Medina at the centre, then? What is the centre? And what happens when these holy places lose their centrality? The Hajj brings all these relations to the fore: as a journey and a ritual, it highlights the entanglements of the world and the faith and their mediations.

[4] Hidajeta Mirojević, *Putopis sa hadž-a, 1981. god*, [n. p.]: [n. d.], p. 39.

[5] In her work on Moroccan pilgrims from the beginning of the twentieth century, Ammeke Kateman has shown the persistence of the importance ascribed to the Hajj and the Hijaz even in colonial times. By using the term 'sacred Islamic geography' (Annemarie Schimmel), Kateman shows how other places on the way to the Hajj 'were Islamic and carried ritual meaning'. Ammeke Kateman, 'In Moroccan Pilgrims' Own Words: The Hajj Journeys (1321 AH [1903–4]) of Muhammad bin ʿAbd al-Kabīr Al-Kattānī and Muhammad bin Jaʿfar Al-Kattānī in an Age of Steam, Imperialism and Globalization', *Qira'at* 13 (Riyādh: King Faisal Center for Research and Islamic Studies, 2020), p. 19, passim.

Hajj writings, especially those from the twentieth century, show numerous variations in the conception of spiritual and imaginative centres.

The spatial imagery in the Hajj literature is mediating in several ways: horizontally by connecting members of the same community, or different communities; vertically by establishing a link with God, the prophets and God's friends (*awliyā*); and temporally with the past, present and future.[6] In the special context of the Hajj journey, Hidajeta felt alone in the space that made her focus on God *and* connected with other people whom she idiosyncratically characterised as the true 'brotherhood and unity' at an earlier point in the diary. This phrase is Hidajeta's Islamic appropriation of the Communist slogan '*bratstvo i jedinstvo*', used to refer to the imperative of harmony between the different peoples of Yugoslavia. Hidajeta's subversive rendering reflects her awareness of different communities of belonging, and her decision to embrace the *umma* on her own terms. Furthermore, being in what she termed 'the desert' focused her thoughts on Allah and brought her in a specific position to temporal relations that were annihilated for at least a short period ('the whole *dunya* was left behind us').

However, apart from a particular spatial context that mediated several horizontal, vertical and temporal relations, Hidajeta's description of the night in 'the desert' also relays another important perspective. The understanding of the ritual as 'account in front of Allah' transcends socio-cultural and institutional dependencies, and while in close relation, it is not reducible to them. The conceptualisations of the Hajj – meanings and images given to them by authors of the Hajj literature – are part of Islamic discursive tradition in its role of forming 'moral selves'. By evoking the sense of responsibility ('account') in front of God, Hidajeta was evaluating her life in a moral framework in relation to past, present and future. Framing the ritual as a moral account was not a simple verbal expression utilised for the purposes of genre or the readers' expectations, but the articulation of values instilled through the community and Islamic institutions and enhanced by personal piety. Moreover, the tradition through which Hidajeta shaped her conceptualisation of the Hajj was not a closed one: it received as much as it exuded, which is why she was able to compare the *umma*, the idea that all Muslims are

[6] Juan E. Campo, 'Visualizing the Hajj', p. 269.

one collective and one body, to 'brotherhood and unity', the oft-proclaimed Yugoslav socialist slogan.

The focus on the Hajj writings of Bosnian Muslims like Hidajeta and those before her, who throughout history have lived on the fringes of two empires and often presented a religious minority in later nation-state constructions, is especially important for the global history of Islam. Throughout the twentieth century, Bosnia was portrayed as a historically pivotal place of fraught multi-religious coexistence and a complex space of intersecting religious differences and commonalities. At the same time, the religiosity of Bosniaks in the twentieth century was frequently tied to academic readings of nationalism, thus placing it in the subordinated dialectics of reflection and reaction to narrowly defined historical circumstances.[7] Bosniaks, however, have been living at the perceived peripheries of both the Muslim world and Europe, complicating any quick generalisation about belonging or religious practice. The connections between Bosnian Muslims and the traditional centres of the Muslim world such as Istanbul, Damascus or Cairo enabled continuous exchanges of different forms of knowledge that continued deep into the modern period.[8] These exchanges, as well as the unique views produced by Bosnian Muslims throughout the centuries, offer an insight into the ways in which Islam has 'come into life' and how it was sustained, often under harsh historical circumstances.

Its specific geographical location and turbulent historical periods marked by imperial and state formations certainly affected the Hajj as a journey, yet the Hajj experiences also challenged entrenched conceptions of belonging in the world. The specific location of Bosnia at the perceived margins of the Muslim world and Europe, respectively, allows for a closer look at how socio-historical circumstances influenced the way in which the Hajj was imagined and experienced. At the same time, the Hajj literature from Bosnia can tell us how the very concepts of 'Muslim world' and 'Europe' can be brought

[7] For a sustained critique of this academic tradion, see David Henig, *Remaking Muslim Lives: Everyday Islam in Postwar Bosnia and Herzegovina* (Urbana: University of Illinois Press, 2020), pp. 9–10.

[8] David Henig, 'Crossing the Bosphorus: Connected Histories of "Other" Muslims in the Post-Imperial Borderlands of Southeast Europe', *Comparative Studies in Society and History* 58/4 (2016), pp. 908–34.

into question, through the Hajj as a differentiating as much as integrating medium. In other words, the Hajj affected the way in which Muslims saw themselves *locally,* as well as how they situated themselves *globally.*

Layers of Mediation

In this book, I wish to trace the significance and multiplicity of meanings ascribed to the Hajj. My goal is not to establish *the one, unique meaning* of the Hajj, but to look at how the pilgrimage was understood and experienced by Bosnian Muslims throughout the centuries. In that regard, Hajj writings (be they travelogues, treatises, essays, or poems) are crucial as mediating channels – the forms through which the mediation between the world and the pilgrimage is carried out. Analysing Hajj writings as mediating channels comes with an awareness that the Hajj itself is a multi-layered medium between the believers and the transcendent, the community of believers (as well as those outside of it), and the believers and the sacred space. While the rites themselves do not change (standing on Arafat, *saʿy*, or *ṭawāf* do not change over time as normative requirements for Hajjis), the attitudes, ideas and experiences related to them do vary for pilgrims across different periods. These are observable from the Hajj literature, among other textual and visual material.

This book is not a historical account of the Hajj in Bosnia with an emphasis on imperial and state actors and their regulations of the Hajj. The political and social formations indeed had a tremendous impact on the Hajj, but the primary focus of this study is on the voices of those who participated in the pilgrimage and who, through the creation of the Hajj discourse, mediated that experience for others. Many of these voices were 'ordinary people'[9] whose only written output would be their Hajj travelogue. Naturally, the appearance of voices and the channel through which they expressed, imagined and conceived their ideas on the Hajj was itself socially conditioned: women were especially underrepresented in writing about pilgrimage before the twentieth century. Still, by including the widest possible amalgam of writings about the Hajj – some also from anonymous or quasi-anonymous sources – I intend to show the variety of modes that the Hajj discourse could

[9] Lale Can, *Spiritual Subjects: Central Asian Pilgrims and the Ottoman Hajj at the End of Empire* (Palo Alto: Stanford University Press, 2020), p. 31.

assume, and its ultimate openness that continues today. Pointing to the close connection between socio-historical context and the ever-evolving textual tradition of writing about the Hajj, as well as fleshing out the mechanisms of this intertwinement, is of importance to studies on the religious mediation of normative rituals in a variety of geographical and historical contexts.

Hajj literature, and especially Hajj travelogues, have attracted some academic attention over the past few decades. Apart from being unavoidable source material in different studies on historical, economic, cultural and other aspects of the Hajj, the travelogues have also been examined for their sociological and literary value, albeit less often. Although dealing with the Hajj travelogues, these studies have subordinated them to the study of different phenomena, such as conversion,[10] transnational connections[11] and Pan-Islamism,[12] all the while showing intense preoccupation with authenticity.[13]

Less frequently, Hajj travelogues have been studied on their own merit. Hajj travelogues appear as parts of anthologies of travel writing,[14] and Hajj literature is often meticulously classified in a variety of genre categories.[15] In line with Barbara Metcalf's injuction that twentieth-century Hajj travelogues reflect the shaping and centring of the Hajji persona more than the Hajj itself,[16] some of the critical literature has focused on the self-fashioning

[10] Umar Ryad, 'On his Donkey to the Mountain of ʿArafāt: Dr Van der Hoog and his Hajj Journey to Mecca', in *The Hajj and Europe in the Age of Empire*, ed. by Umar Ryad (Leiden, Boston: Brill, 2017), pp. 185–216.

[11] Umar Ryad (ed.), *The Hajj and Europe in the Age of Empire* (Leiden, Boston: Brill, 2017).

[12] Homayra Ziad, 'The Return of Gog, Politics and Pan-Islamism in the Hajj Travelogue of Abd al Majid Daryabadi', in *Global Muslims in the Age of Steam and Print*, ed. by Nile Green and James Gelvin (Berkeley: University of California Press, 2013), pp. 227–47.

[13] Ulrike Freitag, 'Heinrich Freiherr von Maltzan's "My Pilgrimage to Mecca": A Critical Investigation', in *The Hajj and Europe in the Age of Empire*, ed. by Umar Ryad (Leiden, Boston: Brill, 2017), pp. 142–54.

[14] Michael Wolfe, *One Thousand Roads to Mecca: Ten Centuries of Travelers Writing about the Muslim Pilgrimage* (New York: Grove Press, 1997).

[15] Menderes Coşkun, *Manzum ve Mensur Osmanlı Hac Seyahatnameleri ve Nabi'nin Tuhfetü'l-Harameyn'i* (Ankara: Kültür Bakanlığı Yayınları, 2002).

[16] Barbara Metcalf, 'The Pilgrimage Remembered: South Asian Accounts of the Hajj', in *Muslim Travellers: Pilgrimage, Migration, and the Religious Imagination*, ed. by Dale F. Eickelman and James Piscatori (Berkeley, Los Angeles: University of California Press, 1990), pp. 85–107.

role of the travel literature.[17] On rare occasions, the Hajj accounts have been examined in terms of the ways in which they articulate the pilgrimage in a long-term perspective.[18] In that context, the focus has recently shifted to closer observations of the mediating role played by Hajj travelogues among Muslim reformists,[19] which merits further comment.

While discussing the Hajj travelogue of scholar Rashid Rida (1865–1935), Rainer Brunner remarks on its eclectic nature that encompasses a variety of literary genres.[20] Without reducing the travelogue to a 'political or reformist testimony', Brunner shows how it actually shapes the 'personality profile of its author', 'an elucidation of the underlying motivation that made the author wield the pen'.[21] Yet, despite such an ambitious aim, the author still avoids to discuss 'the timeless religious and spiritual experience'[22], rather turning his attention to the Hajj as an event with political and economic ramifications, revealing their profound 'contemporaneity'.[23] This excision of religious and spiritual experience (the sweeping categorisation itself necessitates further clarification) indicates a relegation of the most commonly proclaimed motivation to the background. This is amplified by the timelessness ascribed to it: vague and undefinable characterisation puts this experience beyond the pale of analysis.

[17] Ammeke Kateman, 'Fashioning the Materiality of the Pilgrimage: The Ḥajj Travelogue of Muḥammad Labīb al-Batanūnī', *Die Welt des Islams* (2020), p. 3 (including n9).

[18] Virginia Matheson and A. C. Milner, *Perceptions of the Haj: Five Malay Texts* (Singapore, Institute of Southeast Asian Studies, 1984); for recent examples, see Danielle Ross, 'Retelling Mecca: Shifting Narratives of Sacred Spaces in Volga-Ural Muslim Hajj Accounts, 1699–1945', *Religions* 12 (2021), p. 588; Christopher Mark Joll and Srawut Aree, 'Images of Makkah and the Hajj in South Thailand: An Ethnographic and Theological Exploration', *Studia Islamika* 27 (2020), pp. 205–37.

[19] Rainer Brunner, 'The Pilgrim's Tale as a Means of Self-Promotion: Muḥammad Rashīd Riḍā's Journey to the Ḥijāz (1916)', in *The Piety of Learning: Islamic Studies in Honor of Stefan Reichmuth*, ed. by Michael Kemper and Ralf Elger (Leiden, Boston: Brill, 2017), pp. 270–91; see also Ammeke Kateman, 'Fashioning the Materiality of the Pilgrimage', pp. 384–407.

[20] Brunner, 'The Pilgrim's Tale', p. 271. Also, the author mentions works of 'secondary literary value' while not defining it; see Brunner, 'The Pilgrim's Tale', p. 270.

[21] Brunner, 'The Pilgrim's Tale', p. 271.

[22] Brunner, 'The Pilgrim's Tale', p. 271.

[23] Brunner, 'The Pilgrim's Tale', p. 271.

Marking ritual and spiritual experiences of the Hajj as 'timeless' (even if for the individual author only) reflects a common prejudice that ritual – as a set of rites with meanings – is unchanging. In this context, Catherine Bell identifies the problem of the static representation of rituals and suggests that, although 'ritual activities generally tend to resist change',[24] it is necessary to look at the meanings that they carry in different contexts over time.[25] While a ritual such as the Hajj does not intrinsically give any ready and fixed meaning,[26] its structure and form invites intense meaning-making processes. By looking at the variety of meanings given to the Hajj, as well as the mechanisms behind them, we can see not only the persistent significance that this ritual has in the lives of Muslims in a historical and contemporary perspective, but also the vital adaptability of the ritual to different geographical contexts and times.

In her study of Muḥammad Labīb al-Batanūnī's Hajj travelogue, Ammeke Kateman goes one step further and observes the author's 'fashioning' of the Hajj, with a particular focus on its materiality.[27] Like Brunner, Kateman uses the concept of contemporaneity, but pushes it forward to show al-Batanūnī's shaping of the Hajj through engagement with and contribution to debates of the time, which the author at the same time contrasts with the interpretation of his contemporaries, be they Muslims or non-Muslims. In this way, it is possible to observe the interrelation of the textual and contextual with the imaginings of the Hajj, as well as how individual authors shape it and further the discourse in dialogue with their contemporaries. Thus, Hajj writings simultaneously are a product of their habitus that consists of different discourses, and they also push beyond contextual confines. For example, Hidajeta and

[24] Catherine Bell, *Ritual: Perspectives and Dimensions* (Oxford, Oxford University Press, 2009), p. 211.

[25] Bell, *Ritual*, p. 211 and further.

[26] For a summary of debates on the meaning of the Hajj and whether it can be ascertained, see Marion Holmes Katz, 'The Ḥajj and the Study of Islamic Ritual', *Studia Islamica* 98/99 (2004), pp. 95–129, as well as A. Kevin Reinhart, 'What to Do with Ritual Texts: Islamic Fiqh Texts and the Study of Islamic Ritual', in *Islamic Studies in the Twenty-First Century: Transformations and Continuities*, ed. by Léon Buskens and Annemarie van Sandwijk (Amsterdam: Amsterdam University Press: 2016), pp. 67–86.

[27] Kateman, 'Fashioning the Materiality'.

Safija formed their expectations of the Hajj based on the literature that they had read and listened to in formal and informal settings, including other people's experiences, as well as through the interactions with visual and tactile objects associated with the pilgrimage, such as flasks with Zamzam water from returning pilgrims or images of Mecca and Medina which often hang on the walls of Bosnian Muslim homes. Through their writings, however, they added something new and original to the discourse, even though they did so inadvertently: their unique physical and emotional experience of the Hajj, which gained importance over time, as new audiences in the 2010s learned about their unusual travel to the Hijaz as women. The Hajj discourse is, thus, ever evolving and encompasses not only authors and their contemporaries, but also all those who interact with Hajj writings later on.

Looking at the mechanisms underlying the formation of the Hajj discourse – which consists of a large conglomerate of concepts, images, descriptions and narrations of the ritual – is a most efficient way to observe the interactions between the world surrounding the pilgrims and pilgrimage itself. At the same time, this necessitates a 'balancing act'[28] between a reduction to the socio-cultural circumstances and a decontextualised abstraction of the ritual. The Hajj discourse does not emerge in a timeless vacuum and apart from the world but shapes it also retroactively with the experience of the ritual. The Hajj discourse does not rely on constant impulses of novelty, but is built on earlier texts, visual images and practices, even when discourse radically transforms them. These textual elements – such as Qur'anic verses, hadith and prayers – mediate the transcendent to the believers; sometimes they are formulaic. Birgit Meyer calls them 'sensational forms' which are 'relatively fixed' and 'involve religious practitioners in particular practices of worship, and which play a central role in modulating them as religious moral subjects'.[29] Thus, they are organised and transmitted horizontally among practitioners, as well as vertically across different generations. Together with these forms, by 'condensation of practices, attitudes and ideas that constitute

[28] Richard J. A. McGregor, *Islam and the Devotional Object: Seeing Religion in Egypt and Syria* (Cambridge: Cambridge University Press, 2020), p. 5.

[29] Birgit Meyer, 'Introduction', in *Aesthetic Formations: Media, Religion, and the Senses*, ed. by Birgit Meyer (New York: Palgrave Macmillan, 2009), p. 13.

religious experience',[30] the Hajj discourse mediates the pilgrimage to the vast majority of Muslims who will never be able to go on the Hajj and– especially in the modern period – to non-Muslim audiences as well.

The continuity of the Hajj discourse depends on sensational forms recognizable across centuries: prayers, invocations, religious narratives and histories of the prophets all contain elements that are familiar to believers in different time periods. However, the forms also undergo changes – they are embedded in larger textual units, they are utilised in different ways or assume new meanings. Embedded in a range of genres that allowed for a variety of ways to express religious experience, these forms serve as channels for different layers of mediation. As media, they are not neutral or static, and they can be implicated in self-critical reflections on generating the authentic experience and authority within the community.[31] Through different types of textual mechanisms, these 'shared images mobilise and thrive upon shared sentiments, inducing modes, and moods, of feeling together'.[32] Hidajeta's narrative, focused as it is on the journey and the intimate experience of the holy, is peppered with the famous hadiths on the virtue of the Hajj in Bosnian translation, gently reminding the reader to ponder the significance of this duty. Through these hadiths, the travelogue acquires a didactic dimension, and its author receives additional authority to speak about the pilgrimage.

The Bosnian Hajj through the Centuries

The Hajj tradition of Bosnian Muslims has been marked by stops and flows, interruptions and continuities. As the Hajj journey generally has come to a halt during the pandemic of the early 2020s, with images of a few elect pilgrims distanced from each other in the Haram pouring in over social media, the overwhelming sentiment in the Bosnian media is one of profound sadness. The zeal to go on the Hajj has persisted throughout the centuries; the way in which this desire was cultivated, framed and expressed, however, was not timeless. This book uncovers how the contingencies of the world help us reveal how the admiration of the holy has persisted.

[30] Meyer, 'Introduction', p. 13.

[31] Meyer, 'Introduction', esp. pp. 3–6.

[32] Meyer, 'Introduction', p. 9.

The history of the Bosnian Muslims' Hajj is circumscribed by imperial settings, wars and modernity as encompassing epistemological and practical frameworks.[33] The very beginnings of the Hajj in Bosnia are inseparable from the Islamisation of the Balkan region and, as such, are part of broader Ottoman imperial history as well. After a century-long tug-of-war and a number of skirmishes, the Ottomans finally conquered the Kingdom of Bosnia in 1463 and set up the basis for establishing Ottoman institutions in the region. The Islamisation of Bosnia was a process that continued intensively over the next few centuries, and conversions to Islam also continued until the end of Ottoman rule in Bosnia.[34] Explanations for the Islamisation of Bosnia have varied throughout the twentieth century; recent studies indicate the importance of Sufi orders for proselytising as well as supporting Ottoman social institutions.[35] The circumstances surrounding the appearance of the first Hajjis in documents related to Bosnia are murky. The first names that carried the title Hajji might or might not have been Bosnian Muslim converts, but they were certainly part of the Ottoman governmental

[33] Many of the modern transformations that affected Bosnian Hajjis started in the nineteenth century and continued in some ways up to this time. Modernity is not easily definable, especially considering the Eurocentric pitfalls that the stress on certain components (such as secularism or the notion of progress) can carry. Still, the term can be utilised for explaining a range of effects that the global transformations of the long nineteenth century had on different societies around the world. James L. Gelvin stresses the importance of 'contemporary economic and state systems' that 'defined the parameters in which every functioning society had to operate', which in the context of the Middle East reflected itself in processes of integration and peripheralisation, defensive developmentalism and imperialism. James L. Gelvin, *The Modern Middle East: A History* (Oxford: Oxford University Press, 2011), p. 70, and elsewhere. Located at the border of two empires that shifted their control over the territory at the turn of the nineteenth century, Bosnia is a particularly fitting case to observe what some scholars have termed 'alternative Muslim modernities'. See Leyla Amzi-Erdogdular, 'Alternative Muslim Modernities: Bosnian Intellectuals in the Ottoman and Habsburg Empires', *Comparative Studies in Society and History* 59/4 (2017), pp. 912–43.

[34] Fahd Kasumović, 'Prijelazi na Islam u sidžilima sarajevskog šerijatskog suda iz prve polovine 19. stoljeća', in *Identitet Bosne i Hercegovine kroz historiju*, ed. by Husnija Kamberović (Sarajevo: Institut za istoriju, 2011), pp. 215–37.

[35] Ines Aščerić-Todd, *Dervishes and Islam in Bosnia: Sufi Dimensions to the Formation of Bosnian Muslim Society* (Leiden: Brill, 2015).

apparatus.[36] Within several decades, the title of Hajji started to appear in a range of contexts: toponyms, endowments and occasional remarks in official documents. The concept of the Hajj slowly entered the nascent Bosnian Muslim community.

Several centuries of Ottoman rule shaped the Hajj in multiple ways, through the organisation of the journey and the support system of lodgings and guides (*dalīl*) who helped Hajjis as part of established practice. Hajjis used several ways to reach the holy places, either embarking on a sea journey from Istanbul, or using the land route which took them through Anatolia and Sham. Joining a number of other Hajjis on the journey, Bosnians were also eager to see the famous places of *ziyāra* in Damascus or Cairo, of saints commonly known throughout the Muslim world, as well as the graves of the ulama buried in these cities of knowledge. The joys and the hazards of the journey – including Bedouin attacks or scarce provisions of food and water – were shared with other Ottoman Hajjis.

As so many Muslim communities across the world, Bosnian Muslims did not go on the Hajj in great numbers: the costs were too high, the distance too great. In the eighteenth-century chronicle of Mula Mustafa Bašeskija, a Sarajevan scribe, Hajjis constitute approximately one tenth of the thousands of names that appear over the course of fifty years.[37] Yet, the presence of the Hajj in the lives of Bosnian Muslims was marked in a variety of ways related to material culture, such as the *waqf* endowments of Hajjis, the circulation of books and other objects purchased during the journey, and a number of 'Hajj stones' erected in parts of Bosnia to signify the pilgrimage to posterity. The influence went beyond the material: the title Hajji was embedded in the surnames not only of Bosnian Muslims, but also of Christians, in a fashion prevalent in other parts of the Ottoman world as well.[38]

[36] For an overview of Bosnian Muslims' Hajj in Ottoman documents, see Aladin Husić, *Hadž iz Bosne za vrijeme osmanske vladavine* (Sarajevo: El Kalem, 2014).

[37] Mehmed Mujezinović, 'Sarajevske hadžije druge polovine XVIII vijeka', *Glasnik Islamske zajednice* 27/1–2 (1964), p. 42.

[38] Valentina Izmirlieva, 'The Title Hajji and the Ottoman Vocabulary of Pilgrimage', in *Modern Greek Studies Yearbook* 28–29 (Minneapolis: University of Minnesota, 2012/13), pp. 137–68.

Disease and war were inevitable companions of the Hajj journey and sometimes stopped the flow of pilgrims temporarily. With the global control and surveillance of the Hajj by the agents and institutions of the European colonial powers in the nineteenth century, it is possible to observe the direct effect that diseases and wars had on pilgrims[39] and how they also implicated the question of sovereignty.[40] Bosnian Hajjis, like everyone else, were affected by these changes. After the Austro-Hungarian occupation of Bosnia in 1878, the Hajj organisation fell under the new colonial authorities which tried to regulate more than health concerns, by monitoring the movements of the Bosnian Hajjis whose political, spiritual and emotional allegiances were seen as wavering.[41] The regulation of diseases such as cholera affected local and global levels of surveillance: Bosnian Hajjis had to undergo a string of quarantines, such as the one in Sawakin; at the same time, they underwent a similar procedure in local facilities such as in Bosanski Brod.[42] The regulation and control of Bosnian Hajjis turned out to be a complicated endeavour: despite the best efforts of the Austro-Hungarian authorities to register those who went on the Hajj, and especially those who passed through the Ottoman Empire, they were unable to trace all of them. This often resulted in cross-border confusion about the whereabouts and property of the many Hajjis who passed away during the journey.[43]

[39] Recent studies have paid significant attention to the imperial organisation of the Hajj and how it affected Muslim pilgrims; see Eileen Kane, *Russian Hajj: Empire and the Pilgrimage to Mecca* (Ithaca: Cornell University Press, 2015); Michael Christopher Low, *Imperial Mecca: Ottoman Arabia and the Indian Ocean Hajj* (New York: Columbia University Press, 2020).

[40] Can, *Spiritual Subjects*.

[41] Many surviving documents from the Archives of Bosnia and Herzegovina testify to that, as well as the periodicals that closely followed the organisation of the Hajj and the journey annually. See more in Hana Younis, 'Smrtni slučajevi tokom hadža u Mekku kroz primjere iz građe Vrhovnog šeriatskog suda u Sarajevu u periodu austrougarske uprave', *Anali GHB* 45/37 (2016), pp. 197–217.

[42] Zijad Šehić, 'Putovanje bosanskohercegovačkih hodočasnika u Meku u doba austrougarske uprave 1878–1918', *Saznanja, Časopis za historiju* 2/2 (2008), pp. 74–75; see also Mina Kujović, 'O prvom hadžu bosanskohercegovačkih muslimana, koji je 1890. godine organizirala Zemaljska vlada za Bosnu i Hercegovinu', *Glasnik Islamske Zajednice* 1–2 (2004), pp. 135–42.

[43] Younis, 'Smrtni slučajevi tokom hadža u Mekku', p. 214.

State control over the Hajj shaped it as a journey throughout the twentieth and twenty-first centuries as well. However, the organisation of the Hajj journey at least partly became entangled with the rise of tourism in the region, especially after World War I. From the state perspective, the Hajj became a valuable asset, especially in the first decade after World War II, when the nascent socialist state allowed a limited number of Hajjis as representatives of Yugoslav Muslims. The number of Bosnian Hajjis varied according to factors such as disease, war and available transport, but it was also dependent on the utilitarian interests of the ruling states.[44]

Wars have persistently shifted the dynamics of the Bosnian Muslims' Hajj. During the relatively well-documented Austro-Hungarian period, Hajjis were prevented from travelling for a number of years, and it is impossible to find exact information on potential pilgrims or lists of their names.[45] Wars created havoc and disruption, but they also entailed new itineraries or significant changes to the way in which the journey was conducted. During the aggression on Bosnia from 1992 to 1995, regular ways of travelling were severely disrupted. Yet, in 1994, the Kingdom of Saudi Arabia arranged a journey for a number of Bosnian Hajjis – some of them religious dignitaries and politicians, others soldiers recovering from battle.[46] More recently, the itieraries of the Bosnian Hajjis have once again shifted drastically; after a series of wars in the Middle East, Hajjis are no longer able to go on pilgrimage by bus, and the only way to reach Mecca and Medina is by airplane. Therefore, news about the solitary Bosnian Hajji who walked the entire way to Mecca in 2011/12

[44] There are abundant cases where the Hajj was made a part of foreign policy around the world. See, for example, the case of Japanese Hajjis during World War II. Mikiya Koyagi, 'The Hajj by Japanese Muslims in the Interwar Period: Japan's Pan-Asianism and Economic Interests in the Islamic World', *Journal of World History* 24/4 (2013), pp. 849–76. On the case of the Hajj journey of Moroccan pilgrims under Spanish colonialist control, see Josep Lluís Mateo Dieste, 'The Franco North African Pilgrims after WWII: The Hajj through the Eyes of a Spanish Colonial Officer (1949)', in *The Hajj and Europe in the Age of Empire*, ed. by Umar Ryad (Leiden, Boston: Brill, 2017), pp. 240–64.

[45] Šehić, 'Putovanje bosanskohercegovačkih hodočasnika u Meku', p. 79.

[46] Munir Gavrankapetanović, 'Allahu Ekber! Allahu Ekber!' *Preporod* 25/7:566 (1994), p. 20; 'Odazivamo Ti se, Bože, odazivamo!' *Preporod* 25/8:567 (1994), p. 18; 'Bosna je ćilimom zastrta,' 25/9:568 (1994), p. 20.

made headlines,[47] marking the tragedy of war and defiance of modernity at the same time.

The colonial conquest of Bosnia in 1878, as well as the rise of print and new means of transportation that went parallel to it, affected the Hajj journey of Bosnian Muslims in an unprecedented manner. Soon after the Austro-Hungarian occupation, the Hajj organisation was handed over to the Austrian company Lloyd,[48] in a way comparable to what happened in other colonised regions.[49] The beginning of the twentieth century was also marked by the Hijaz railway project, which occupied the minds and pockets of the Bosnian Muslims even when they were not able to go on the Hajj.[50] The organisation of the Hajj during the twentieth century usually included a joint endeavour between the Islamic Community as the official representative body of Yugoslav Muslims and travel agencies such as Putnik.[51] Travelling by airplane, bus, or private car replaced older ways of travel that had relied on ships and animals, making a lasting impact on the way in which the journey was experienced.

Rising nationalist tendencies affected the Hajj not only in terms of physical mobility being impeded by wars for national independence, but also in the way in which new nation-states were organised. Unlike the Hajj in the Ottoman period, which for Bosnian Muslims meant mobility inside one (albeit in terms of its experience extremely varied) sovereign territory,[52]

[47] In 2011/2012, the Bosnian pilgrim Senad Hadžić walked all the way to Mecca, passing on his way through war-torn Syria and justifying this choice of itinerary based on a dream he had had in which God told him to avoid Iraq.

[48] Šehić, 'Putovanje bosanskohercegovačkih hodočasnika u Meku', p. 71.

[49] Kane, *Russian Hajj*, pp. 86–119; Eric Tagliacozzo, *The Longest Journey: Southeast Asians and the Pilgrimage to Mecca* (Oxford: Oxford University Press, 2013), pp. 109–32.

[50] Hamza Karčić, 'Supporting the Caliph's Project: Bosnian Muslims and the Hejaz Railway', *Journal of Muslim Minority Affairs* 34 (2014), pp. 282–92.

[51] See more in Edin Lepenica, 'Organizacioni aspect obavljanja hadža u SR BiH u fondovima Gazi Husrev-begove biblioteke (1945–1992)', *Glasnik* 9–10 (2021), pp. 721–40.

[52] How Ottoman rule over the Hijaz and control over the holy places was received by non-Ottoman Muslims in an earlier period can be glimpsed from an Iranian pilgrim's account in Sanjay Subrahmanyam and Muzaffar Alam, 'Introduction: The Travel Account', in *Indo-Persian Travels in the Age of Discoveries*, 1400–1800 (Cambridge: Cambridge University Press, 2007), pp. 24–44.

the Austro-Hungarian occupation ushered in a new, modern period that marked Hajjis as an in-between body that needed to be regulated by proper paperwork. The travelogues of the twentieth century conveyed an anxiety of borders – the awareness of crossing state limits demarcated by visas and checkpoints. The first documents necessary for the transfer of Hajjis across different states were usually obtained in Belgrade, making the Hajjis detour from their path.[53] Furthermore, in the interwar period Hajjis could receive their visas in Greece or Egypt, causing them even more anxiety while also providing more freedom in terms of their itineraries.[54] After World War II and the first years of exclusively state-controlled Hajj,[55] the pilgrimage organisation was taken over by tourist agencies, especially with the rise of bus travel in the 1960s. Towards the end of the century, the Islamic Community in Bosnia and Herzegovina took over most of the logistics and planning, according to the established set of quotas for Hajjis in nation-states.[56]

In the Ottoman period, Bosnian Hajjis undertook a long journey filled with perils that often shaped how they saw the people with whom they interacted: as pleasant or fearful. While the journey as such has always included an encounter with the Other, the Hajj after the Austro-Hungarian conquest necessarily included the involvement of non-Muslims in the pilgrimage infrastructure: as doctors,[57] administrators, governmental observers,[58] or simply passengers on the same means of transport. This proximity to non-Muslim Others, as well as the passage through non-Muslim nation-states, were

[53] For example, Muhamed Krpo's travelogue shows how the Hajjis sometimes had to leave and return via Belgrade. Muhamed Krpo, *Put na hadž (putopis jednog hadžije)* (Sarajevo: Štamparija Bosanska pošta, 1938).

[54] The example of Ibrahim Hakki Čokić's travelogue, published in instalments in the journal *Hikjmet*, shows how future Hajjis could 'outmanoeuvre' the authorities by getting their Hajj visas on the way.

[55] The two travelogues of Hasan Ljubunčić, recording a state-protected Hajj journey mission, will be treated in Chapter 4.

[56] On the quotas of Hajjis in the modern world, see Robert Bianchi, *Guests of God: Pilgrimage and Politics in the Islamic World* (New York: Oxford University Press, 2004).

[57] Younis, 'Smrtni slučajevi tokom hadža u Mekku', p. 199.

[58] Many late-nineteenth-century reports give detailed information about Austro-Hungarian officials who saw off Bosnian Hajjis and accompanied the procession, as seen from the article by Hana Younis.

unprecedented and caused some tension, especially in periods after wars.[59] At the same time, as this book shows, the pilgrims' interaction with the Other within the framework of modernity significantly transformed the conceptualisation of the Hajj. The fluidity of the category of the Other and the processes of inclusion and exclusion can best be seen in the last several decades of the Hajj in Bosnia, which have been marked by airplane charter travel, which transports pilgrims directly to the Kingdom of Saudi Arabia without any layovers. Now, Hajjis from Bosnia usually interact with Muslims only, which ensues new perspectives on the inter-Muslim creation of Otherness.

It is also important to remember that, beyond the physical interactions with non-Muslims, Hajj writings were also reflective of and sensitive to opinions and criticism of the Hajj, Islam and Muslims that circulated widely in modern Yugoslav print throughout the twentieth century. In a way, the tension between the dedication to Islam and the wish to dispel critical ideas about Islamic rituals found a specific expression in modern Hajj literature. When writing about pilgrimage, Bosnian Hajjis wrote to defend it, as well.

The history of the Bosnian Hajj closely followed wider social transformations. Due to greater mobility and higher literacy rates, modernity opened doors for a number of less priviled actors, such as women, to perform the pilgrimage in person and to write about their experiences. This movement ranged from the first known female Hajjis appearing in endowment documents from the late eighteenth century, over women as fellow Hajjis in late-nineteenth- and early-twentieth-century travelogues, to women who participate in the pilgrimage in equal numbers as men and write about their experiences in different types of media.[60] Thus, the visibility of women caught up with their mobility, which has also increased progressively.[61]

[59] Bosnian – and Yugoslav Hajjis in general – were often regarded with suspicion when passing across Greek or Bulgarian borders, in years as distinct as 1937 and 1996, as it can be seen in the travelogues of Muhamed Krpo and Hasan Šestić.

[60] Dženita Karić, 'Online Bosniak Hajj Narratives', in *Muslim Pilgrimage in Europe*, ed. by Ingvild Flaskerud and Richard J. Natvig (Abingdon: Routledge, 2018), pp. 58–69.

[61] The rise of the number of female pilgrims prompted the responsible bodies in the Islamic Community to introduce additional services for women, such as Sharia consultants for women and female guides. This, of course, went hand in hand with the increase of the number of pilgrims after the Bosnian war and the development of the supporting infrastructure.

Similar to mobility, which has been directly affected by imperial frameworks, wars and modern transformations, the media – a constant companion of the Bosnian Hajj – has concurrently been sensitive to social and historical changes. Writing about the Hajj and the holy places of Mecca and Medina was often a matter of patronage and inclusion into scholarly circles in the Ottoman Empire. The ulama also copied and produced a large number of works dedicated to the Hajj as one of the religious duties incumbent on every Muslim. While much of this literature was imbued with Sufi symbols, modernity gave it a different twist, not only in terms of language and script, but also in its function as a way to convey additional meanings to the ever-growing reading and travelling populace. The media closely followed changes in literacy and the reading public and, in turn, affected them.

Much like the steamship and the railway entered the lives of Bosnian Hajjis by the end of the nineteenth century, photography, the telegraph and print became inseparable from the annual pilgrimage, as well as the postcards that often focused on depicting farewell ceremonies.[62] Together with the emergence of tourism, the Hajj also became a modern mobility, not only requiring the latest available technological and logistical support, but also increasingly necessitating an immediacy of experience between the pilgrims and the growing reading public, which was achievable by journalistic print. The emergence of organised tourism in Austro-Hungarian Bosnia, which was directed to attracting foreigners,[63] over the course of the next few decades was followed by the inclusion of some phases of the Hajj journey by the agencies that organised general travel routes, such as the Orient Express.[64]

[62] Several of those coming from Bosnia appear in Murat Kargılı, *Kutsal Yolculuk Hac/Hajj, the Holy Journey: Kartpostallarla Hac Yolu/The Hajj Route Through Postcards* (Istanbul: Kaptan Yayincilik, 2014), pp. 11–14.

[63] Zijad Šehić, 'Prilog istraživanju turizma u Bosni i Hercegovini u doba austrougarske uprave 1878–1918', in *Godišnjak Bošnjačke zajednice kulture »Preporod«* (Sarajevo: Bošnjačka zajednica kulture 'Preporod', 2011), pp. 302–22.

[64] The interwar Hajjis used the services of the travel agency Putnik, which also sold tickets for the Orient Express; see Popov D. in Živana Krejić and Snežana Milićević, 'Nastanak putničko-agencijske delatnosti u Jugoslaviji kao pokretača razvoja kulture putovanja', *Kultura* 161 (2018), p. 43.

In the twentieth century, the immediacy of Hajj writings was continuously enhanced through new media. Towards the end of the century, journalistic reporting was complemented by documentaries and, especially over the past few decades, by online media.[65] This allowed for greater participation of Hajjis in the writing process, as well as a combination of visual and written modes of representing the experience or laying out the prescription of its rites.

The In-betweenness of the Bosnian Hajj

This book deals with the genealogy of Hajj discourses in the *longue durée*, spanning several centuries to highlight a number of shifts and formations around the image, idea, or narration of the pilgrimage. While each period and each Hajj writing is unique, there are three discernible movements that characterised the history of Bosnian Muslim writing, and these can be traced diachronically as well as synchronically.

The Hajj writings reflect the constant tension between the local and the universal. This is shown in several ways: in the choice of genre and language, openness to or restriction of different audiences and the inclusivity of the vision of the Hajj for the whole of humankind. The local and the universal can coexist in the same Hajj imaginary – the borders have always been blurred. ʿAlī-dada al-Būsnawī, a sixteenth-century Ottoman Bosnian author, wrote his treatises on Mecca in the Arabic language and in genres shared with his earlier scholarly predecessors. His works were read by his Ottoman peers who shared the same intellectual framework. The vision of the holy places and the Hajj in his work is thus seemingly universalist, in tune with the common observation of the Hajj as 'the primary example' of a Muslim identity 'based on common beliefs, rituals and social practices'.[66] Yet, the universalist vision necessarily fleshed out particularities which were often bound to a certain place or time. ʿAlī-dada's universalist vision of the Hajj was still bound to the millenarian trends of the age that presupposed the Ottomans as eternal and ultimate rulers until Judgement Day. For linguistic and social reasons, his works could not be read by many of his fellow Bosnians.

[65] Karić, 'Online Bosniak Hajj Narratives'.

[66] Ira Lapidus, 'Between Universalism and Particularism: The Historical Bases of Muslim Communal, National, and Global Identities', *Global Networks* 1/1 (2001), p. 37.

However, the local and the particular in the Hajj also had the potential to be elevated to the universal. The pilgrims during the Bosnian War often likened their struggle to motives from religious narratives surrounding the Hajj (*hijra*, martyrdom), and such comparisons persisted even after the war. The universal and the particular were enmeshed in Hajj writings. The choice of media itself confirms the tension: Hajj writings were written specifically for certain audiences. ʿAlī-dada al-Būsnawī, writing in Arabic, aimed at his fellow ulama; the Bosnian Hajjis at the beginning of the twenty-first century wrote for the common reader skilled in the ways of social media and in the Bosnian language. Yet, the local vision of Hidajeta's writings could aim at a limited, even closed circle of readers *and* still carry the universalist message of the 'brotherhood and unity' of all people.

The second movement that marked the history of Bosnian Hajj writing is the rift between premodern and modern modes and ways of mediation. Modernity has proven to be a particularly daunting topic in the research of the Hajj as a ritual, with scholars in many cases avoiding the subject. While the nature of the modern is a matter of decade-long discussions,[67] the division between the premodern and the modern in the context of this book refers to the conglomerate of changes that happened in the nineteenth century and affected both the way in which the Hajj journey was undertaken and the multiple ways in which it was prescribed, described, or narrated. This, of course, does not exclude the possibility that the line of modernity can be shifted to an earlier point in time,[68] or that some of its elements were already observable in the earlier period.[69] The premodern Bosnians who wrote about the Hajj predominantly used Arabic and Ottoman Turkish, and they employed a range

[67] This includes debates about the modernity of the Ottoman Empire, especially in the context of the qualifier 'early modern'. For recent coverage of the subject, see Nükhet Varlık and Robert Zens (eds), *Chasing the Ottoman Early Modern*, special issue of *Journal of the Ottoman and Turkish Studies Association* 7/1 (2020), pp. 1–253.

[68] One example of the new shifts in the study of shifts in Muslim intellectual thought is: Ahmad S. Dallal, *Islam without Europe: Traditions of Reform in Eighteenth-Century Islamic Thought* (Chapel Hill: University of North Carolina Press, 2018).

[69] On some aspects of the rise of first-person narratives in the eighteenth century, see Dana Sajdi, *The Barber of Damascus: Nouveau Literacy in the Eighteenth-Century Ottoman Levant* (Palo Alto: Stanford University Press, 2013).

of classical genres shared with their counterparts around the Muslim world. The genres in many ways directed the intertextual frameworks and arguments available to the authors, yet this did not preclude the expression of a unique perspective on the holy places and the Hajj. Premodern writings were prone to reflect change and peculiar temporal and spatial contexts, which is especially evident in first-person narratives, such as travelogues and itineraries. Modern writings, extending from the late nineteenth to the early twenty-first centuries, were similarly written in a range of genres, but in the Bosnian language. The genres themselves – modern travelogues, newspaper reports, poems, letters, blogs – were largely enhanced by print and, later, internet culture.

However, the movement from the premodern to the modern is not a straight diachronic line. What Hajj writings attest to is the persistence of certain modes of writing about the holy, which includes not only the continued use of Arabic script or the Ottoman language deep into the twentieth century, but also the role played by fixed places of devotions, 'sensational forms' in shapes of prayers, religious narratives, or invocations. Even beyond these, a closer look at Hajj writings throughout the centuries reveals that old fascinations obtained new forms: the paintings of Mecca and Medina in *dalāʾil al-khayrāt* manuscripts turned to photography in the twentieth century; the focus on the places of *ziyāra* gave way to an emphasis on sites of Islamic history; the poetry of the first impressions of the holy shifted to confessional narratives about the experience.

The experience and understanding of the Hajj ritual leads us to the third and final movement, which is the tension between ritual 'emptiness' and the meaning-making impulse evident in the writings. The first refers to the understanding of the Hajj as solely and purely obeying God's command. The second implies a range of often divergent meanings given to the Hajj, surpassing the mere act of submission and sometimes receiving social, spiritual or political significance. The tension itself exists in relation to a number of other rituals in Islam, as it was noted by a number of scholars over the past few decades.[70] Marion Katz notes that the symbolic view of the Hajj – one

[70] The work of Marion Katz is very valuable in this regard. For her studies on wudu' and prayer, see Marion Holmes Katz, *Prayer in Islamic Thought and Practice* (Cambridge: Cambridge University Press, 2013), and *Body of Text: The Emergence of the Sunni Law of Ritual Purity* (Albany: SUNY Press, 2002).

that imbues the rites with a set of meanings – in premodern writings existed within the confines of Sufi writings, while it became more dominant in the modern period.[71] While the distinction between premodern and modern within this context is certainly relevant, the two perspectives of pure obedience to the command *and* the creation of a range of meanings are to be found in both contexts, sometimes within a single piece of Hajj writing. For one eighteenth-century Mustafa al-Mukhliṣī, the Hajj journey could mean fulfilment of the necessary ritual, a visit to the Prophet who stood at the centre of devotion and a string of *ziyāras* for additional blessings. The meanings and understandings of the Hajj differed starkly; yet in the modern period Hajjis engaged in both meaning-making processes *and* accepting and performing the Hajj rituals as a duty without further explanation.

This tension was not necessarily felt by the numerous Hajjis who wrote about their experiences. Hidajeta, our feisty pilgrim, went on the Hajj because it was a duty incumbent on all capable men and women. She also found meaning in the gathering of Muslims, the idealised *umma*, with whom she felt an immediate connection transcending the boundaries of nation or race. Finally, however, the ultimate importance of the Hajj revealed itself to her in the desert, emblematically representing the absence of any intermediary, after which she uttered no explanation.

The *Manāzil* of the Book

Observing Hajj discourses, spatial imaginaries and ritual expressions over time implies two considerations: the pilgrimage is an annual event, which makes modes of prescribing the ritual and relaying the experience ongoing and prone to constant change; at the same time, the history of the Hajj does not develop in a teleological way. For that reason, this book is divided chronologically as well as thematically, into several parts that can be read separately as well. They are categorised according to the prevalent consideration in the Hajj writings of a certain period, also reflecting the major contours of mediation. The edges between the periods were defined not only by political and social ruptures, but also by gradual changes in the media such as language or genre. The chapters also note other, lesser visible movements in mediation,

[71] Katz, 'The Ḥajj and the Study of Islamic Ritual', p. 125.

which sometimes go counter the main trend of the period. Rather than offering a neat exposé of the things that Bosnians wrote about the Hajj over the course of several centuries, this book shows that, just like the pilgrims who wrote them, Hajj writings meandered, shifted, or came to an abrupt stop, following the range of physical, spiritual and cultural itineraries. The chapters that follow are akin to *manāzil* or stations on pilgrimage, offering insight into how the writings came into being and how they paved the path for those who came later.

The first two chapters take us to the beginnings of the Hajj writings of Bosnian Muslims in the Ottoman period, tackling the premodern treatment of the holy spaces of Mecca and Medina and the pilgrimage. The first chapter discusses how in the sixteenth and seventeenth century the meaning of the Hajj and the holy places was constructed, through millenarianism, Sufi symbolism and *faḍā'il* literature, mediated through a range of genres. The holy places were built on a particular set of arguments with soteriological, cosmological and emotional value. This chapter introduces Ottoman Bosnian authors in specific traditions of writing about Mecca and Medina and suggests why these mattered at the time when they emerged. The second chapter looks at Bosnian portrayals and experiences of the Hajj as a journey through the Ottoman world in the travelogues, itineraries and exhortatory literature of seventeenth- and eighteenth-century authors and explores their visions of the world and the local.

The next three chapters focus on modern-era Hajj writings, starting with the nineteenth century. Although grouped under the umbrella of the 'modern', the three chapters present different imaginaries of the Hajj that do not neatly proceed from one another. The variety of Hajj discourses overlapped over the course of the long twentieth century; however, the chapters examine prevalent thematical modes that both mediated the Hajj for the rising and increasingly diversified audiences and used the Hajj to mediate political, social and cultural concerns. The third chapter closely examines the Hajj within the framework of modern change in travel writing, reports and essays and shows how the appearance of multiple audiences influenced the understandings of religious rituals such as the Hajj. The fourth chapter, then, focuses on interpretations of the Hajj in the post-World War II era, within the specific framework of socialist Yugoslavia, and zooms in on the feelings and expressions of dis/connection from the wider Islamic world concerning the Hajj, as the Bosnian pilgrims experienced them. The fifth chapter analyses the dynamics between the Hajj and the homeland in a range of media towards the end of the twentieth and the beginning of the twenty-first centuries, during and after the Bosnian War as a formative event of the contemporary era, and how it reflected on Hajjis' considerations of the body and emotions. The book ends with final thoughts on the major aspects of Bosnian Hajj literature, such as its versatility and persistence over time, and offers some considerations on the broader significance of the approach. Through Bosnian Hajj literature as a mediating channel, we can discover the never-ending possibilities of normative rituals to inspire meaning and add value and significance to the lives of individuals and communities.

1

THE MEANINGS OF THE SACRED

Ottoman Bosniaks had a firm and lasting attachment to places within the traditional Islamic geography. The connection was physical and directed to multiple spaces. Let us take the example of the famous seventeenth-century Sufi scholar 'Abdullah al-Būsnawī (1593–1644). If a careful observer visits his tomb in Konya – hidden within a residential area, close to a hairdresser salon, a restaurant and Ṣadr al-Dīn al-Qūnawī's[1] tomb and mosque – they can see a sign erected in 2007, briefly describing al-Būsnawī's lifepath. In green letters, the sign presents the major points of al-Būsnawī's biography: he was a scholar, a Sufi devotee and an interpreter of Ibn 'Arabī's *Fuṣūṣ al-Ḥikam* (*Bezels of Wisdom*) and Jalāl al-Dīn al-Rūmī's (1207–73) *Mathnawi*. He was born in Bosnia, spent time in Egypt, Damascus and the Hijaz, and died in Konya. His Arab students were proud of having learned from him, and he left dozens of works. According to his will, the tomb's inscription also reads that he carried the *nisbas* (names indicating belonging) of al-Būsnawī (Bosnian), al-Rūmī (Rūmī, from the lands of Rūm, a term that at this point encompassed

[1] Ṣadr al-Dīn al-Qūnawī' (1207–74), a student of Ibn 'Arabī (1165–1240) and a prominent Sufi figure in his own right.

Anatolia and the Balkans)[2] and al-Bayrāmī,[3] designating his local, cultural and spiritual leanings. ʿAbdullah al-Būsnawī was, thus, a man of many places, ranging from the Balkans to the Hijaz, just like hundreds of his compatriots whose remains today are scattered across the modern-day nation-states of the Middle East, symbolising a long-forgotten mobility.

Beyond the physical, the connection was also emotional and imaginative, especially to the holy places of Mecca and Medina. Ottoman Bosnian authors such as ʿAbdullah al-Būsnawī penned treatises describing different facets of the holy: how places were made special through God's love and mercy, how significant the presence of the Prophet Muhammad's body was in Medina, and how it contained miraculous benefits for believers and visitors. In doing so, the Ottoman Bosnians joined the ranks of their scholarly predecessors and contemporaries, and they wrote for geographically diverse audiences. As the biographical dictionaries testify, from the fifteenth to the twentieth century, many Bosnians were truly cosmopolitan through their participation in the scholarly and literary discourses of the age. As such, their writings were shaped by the prevalent Ottoman discourses on the Hajj and the holy places, and they themselves furthered the discourse and cultivated relationships to the Hijaz.

This chapter will look at the meanings given to the Hajj and the holy places of Mecca and Medina in the works of three cosmopolitan Ottoman Bosnian scholars from the sixteenth and seventeenth centuries: ʿAlī-dada al-Būsnawī, ʿAbdullah al-Būsnawī and Ḥasan Imām-zāda al-Būsnawī. Unlike the following chapter, which will zoom in on the ways in which Ottoman Bosnians went on the Hajj and observed the world, this chapter focuses on meanings given to Mecca and Medina exclusively. Thus, our journey into the world of the Bosnian Hajj opens with the central places of the Islamic imaginary, devotion to which is the common denominator of most Muslims past and present.

[2] The designation 'Rūmī' refers to an identity marker related to a 'cultural as well as a physical space', with 'Rum' including 'Asia Minor, or Anatolia [. . .] The Balkans, too, were included in Rum as cultural space after the late fourteenth century. Ottoman lands west of the Marmara Sea were called Rūm ili (Rumelia), which is another way, after all, of saying "the lands of Rum"'. Cemal Kafadar, 'Introduction: A Rome of One's Own: Reflections on Cultural Geography and Identity in the Lands of Rum', *Muqarnas* 24, *History and Ideology: Architectural Heritage of the 'Lands of Rum'* 24 (2007), pp. 9, 18.

[3] Indicating ʿAbdullah al-Būsnawī's belonging to the Malāmī-Bayrāmī Sufi order, widely popular in Anatolia and the Balkans at the time.

The scholars who wrote about holy places in this context were in many ways the Ottoman elite: their lifepaths belonged to Istanbul, Konya, or Medina, as much as (or even more so than) to Sarajevo or Mostar. By showing the range of meanings constructed in their works, I hope to present these authors not as exceptional for their time and place, but as equal participants in both the Ottoman Hajj project and the more encompassing and permanent religious discourses of the pilgrimage. The three Būsnawīs, who were imperial servants, Sufi shaykhs and teachers, aimed to convey these timeless meanings in a form bound by temporal and spatial constraints. Despite these limitations, which often remove us modern readers from the full potential of their writings, the Būsnawīs' visions of the holy places were aimed at a large cosmopolitan readership and conveyed in Arabic, the lingua franca of Islam. This chapter will focus on three treatises that provide insight into a variety of meanings given to Mecca and Medina, including the imperial view, Sufi interpretation and the vision of the Prophetic presence.

The treatises which will form the subject of this chapter belong to the wider and more encompassing Hajj discourse of the early modern Ottoman period. The Ottoman conquest of the Arab provinces in 1517, including the Hijaz, gave a new impetus to the organisation of the Hajj and related devotional activities, including the proliferation of source material dedicated to the holy places and the pilgrimage. Since the Hajj was patronised by the Ottomans, it 'became a central component of the lived religion of many of the Ottoman Empire's inhabitants, Muslim and non-Muslim'.[4] Apart from the specific mobilities that marked the Hajj of Ottoman Muslims, such as the pious visits or *ziyāra* which will be treated in the next chapter, this momentum was also evident in the rise of the new literature related to the pilgrimage and the holy places, as well as the rise of different forms of Prophet-oriented piety.[5]

[4] Nir Shafir, 'In an Ottoman Holy Land: The Hajj and the Road from Damascus, 1500–1800', *History of Religions* 1/60 (2020), p. 3.

[5] Some recent studies on the topic include Christiane Gruber, *The Praiseworthy One: The Prophet Muhammad in Islamic Texts and Images* (Bloomington: Indiana University Press, 2019); Jonathan Parkes Allen, 'Up All Night Out of Love for the Prophet: Devotion, Sanctity, and Ritual Innovation in the Ottoman Arab Lands, 1500–1620', *Journal of Islamic Studies* 30/3 (2019), pp. 303–37.

Hajj literature in its various forms, as well as works composed in praise of the holy places were not completely original: people wrote about the virtues of Mecca and Medina for centuries, sometimes juxtaposing them; the Hajj travelogue was an established genre in its own right, as the cases of Nasir Khusraw (1004–88), Ibn Jubayr (1145–1217) and Ibn Battuta (1304–1368/69) show. Likewise, the devotional objects related to the Hajj, the *mahmal* (ceremonial litter) and the *kiswa* (the Kaʿba cover), were utilised by empires and kingdoms preceding the Ottomans.[6] The Ottomans, moreover, were building on the bricolage of textual and visual elements and genres that had a longer history but were now chosen for a particular socio-historical reason and inserted into a narrative or description of the holy places. In the context of Hajj writings, these forms consisted of Qur'anic verses, hadith and various forms of prayers such as blessings upon the Prophet, as well as the genres that employed them. However, the textual creation of the holy spaces also included excerpts from Prophetic biographies, histories of the cities, chronicles and other miscellaneous material from different periods. The sacred was the subject of argumentation, and it competed against other claims to sanctity,[7] which explained the range of different techniques behind its construction. Those elements were at the same time 'timeless' because they were mostly recognized as such by the readers, and prone to change based on different interpretations according to the demands of the devotional culture of the period and the imperial framework in which they arose.

How did Ottoman Bosnians acquire these boundless treasures of knowledge about the pilgrimage and the holy places? The next section will examine the factors that led to the rise of the Ottoman Bosnian scholarly elites, which will explain the emergence of the range of genres in which they were writing about the Hajj.

[6] See more on the cultural and religious lives of these and other devotional objects in McGregor, *Islam and the Devotional Object*.

[7] For an example of the way in which competing imperial claims reflect itself in the Hajj literature of the early modern period, see Guy Burak, 'Between Istanbul and Gujarat: Descriptions of Mecca in the Sixteenth-Century Indian Ocean', *Muqarnas* 34 (2017), pp. 287–320.

Bosnian Scholars in the Ottoman Empire

With the conquest of the Arab provinces in 1517, the mechanisms of the organisation of the Hajj passed into Ottoman hands. Although happening half a century earlier, we know much less about the effect that the Ottoman conquest of Bosnia in the 1460s had on the expansion and popularisation of modes of devotion to the holy places.[8] The Islamisation of Bosnia, which extended over a couple of centuries, influenced the ways in which Bosnian Muslims were integrated into the empire's social strata. Sufi orders, guilds and educational networks all functioned in order to pull a number of Balkan Muslims to the imperial centre, and then onwards to other cities of the empire, such as Damascus, Cairo, or Medina. What is certain, however, is that by the end of the sixteenth century, or a century and a half after the Ottoman conquest and at the very peak of the process of Islamisation, Bosniak ulama, poets, translators and commentators were actively contributing to the Ottoman intellectual scene.[9] The Ottoman educational system, consisting of *maktab*s and *madrasa*s of different levels, was already well established in Bosnia and provided most of these authors with their primary education before they moved on to the imperial centres.[10] The *madrasa* system was closely connected to the *waqf* system, which meant that one of the characteristics of urban development in Bosnia (which also owes much to the *waqf* endowments) was the presence of ulama of different ranks, including low-ranking ulama that served as catalyst for the circulation of religious knowledge on a local level.

How did Bosniak scholars fit into and see themselves in the intellectual atmosphere of the early Ottoman period? Although extensive first-person narratives are not easy to find, we may get a glimpse of what it meant to be an

[8] For a study that draws attention to the necessity of studying both conquests, see Maurus Reinkowski, 'Conquests Compared: The Ottoman Expansion in the Balkans and the Mashreq in an Islamicate context', in *The Ottoman Conquest of the Balkans*, ed. by Oliver Jens Schmitt (Vienna: Verlag der Österreichischen Akademie der Wissenschaften, 2016), pp. 47–64.

[9] For a wide range of authors and their material, see Hazim Šabanović, *Književnost Muslimana BiH na orijentalnim jezicima (biobibliografija)* (Sarajevo: Svjetlost, 1973).

[10] On the Ottoman education system in Bosnia, see Ismet Kasumović, *Školstvo i obrazovanje u Bosanskom ejaletu za vrijeme osmanske uprave* (Mostar: Islamski kulturni centar, 1999).

Ottoman Bosnian scholar embedded in diachronic and synchronic networks of knowledge. One prominent example demonstrating that the sixteenth-century Bosnian ulama were eager to confirm their intellectual roots within the vast network of Islamic scholars and religious figures, sometimes even going back to the Prophet himself, is the case of the Bosnian scholar Ḥasan Kāfī al-Aqḥiṣārī – Pruščak (1544–1615). In 1600, he wrote a small biographical dictionary titled *Niẓām al-ʿulamā ila khātam al-anbiyā* (*The List of Scholars Going Back to the Seal of the Prophets*),[11] containing a short biography of his teachers.[12] Al-Aqḥiṣārī not only listed his teachers, but also placed himself in this lineage. He also included some of his students, thus positioning himself as both receiver of knowledge and teacher in his own right. Al-Aqḥiṣārī's main objective was to present Hanafi scholars throughout the centuries, including the Ottoman ulama from Istanbul, affirming the steady link between the Bosnian province and the imperial capital. However, of special interest here are the names of several scholars whom al-Aqḥiṣārī points out as having had tremendous influence on him: Kamālpasha-zāda, an Ottoman *faqīh* and *mufassir*; Mulla Aḥmad al-Anṣārī, who was also a scholar in *ʿuṣūl* and *tafsīr*; and Bālī Efendi, a Bosnian Bayrāmī shaykh who was also educated in Istanbul and had taught there for some time.[13] The last name that al-Aqḥiṣārī mentions in this chain was the name of a shaykh whom he met during his stay in Mecca, that of Shaykh al-Anwar Mīr Ghadanfar, who had been a teacher of the Mughal Sultan Akbar (1556–1605) and who resided in Mecca when al-Aqḥiṣārī was present there. Mecca, thus, appeared to be a node that connected Ottoman scholars among themselves and with those beyond imperial borders.

Apart from the scholarly links that led to Mecca, Sufi orders played an important role in facilitating the mobility of individuals to the imperial

[11] Ḥasan Kāfī al-Aqḥiṣārī (1544–1615) was a Bosnian scholar and qadi who lived in Istanbul and Prusac in Bosnia. He was known by his Ottoman contemporaries and subsequently mentioned by Evliya Çelebi.

[12] The treatise was translated into Bosnian in 1935; see Hasan Kafi-ef. Pruščak, *Nizâmul-ulemâ' ila hatemil-enbijâ*, trans. by Mehmed Handžić (Sarajevo: Islamska dionička štamparija, 1935).

[13] Bālī Efendi was also participating in the campaign against the Hamzavīs, a heterodox Sufi movement in Bosnia. For more on this topic, see Omer Mušić, 'Hadži Muhamed Sejfudin, šejh sejfija – pjesnik iz Sarajeva', *Anali GHB*, 7–8 (1982), p. 5.

centre and then onwards to other provinces, as can be seen from the biographies of the three Būsnawīs discussed in this chapter. ʿAlī-dada al-Būsnawī (d. 1598) moved from the Bosnian province to Istanbul, where he received his education and spiritual guidance; from there, he moved to Mecca. He also spent considerable time guarding the tomb of Sultan Süleyman (1494–1566) in modern-day Hungary.[14] Similarly, ʿAbdullah al-Būsnawī pursued his career path in Istanbul. Afterwards, he spent some time in Bursa and went on the Hajj in 1636, passing through Egypt. He also lived in Damascus, close to Ibn ʿArabī's grave, before he died in Konya.[15] The lifepath of the third author, Ḥasan Imām-zāda al-Būsnawī (fl. 1660), is not quite as clear, but according to the information that can be extracted from his writings, his family was located somewhere around Imotski (current-day Croatia), and he moved to Medina. He was a teacher in this city, but he retained a close connection to scholarly circles in Bosnia by sending them his work. His works are also found in Cairo.

One final question emerges before we immerse ourselves in the Būsnawīs' world of arcane meanings of the Hajj and the holy places: where was Bosnia in the vision of its scholarly Ottoman elites? It stubbornly appears in the marginalia of the three Būsnawīs' autographs and manuscript copies, denoting serpentine pathways of ownership, family lineages and local scholarly circles, in the word *waṭan* (homeland) scribbled longingly, and in the persistence of the *nisba* al-Būsnawī, the signifier of their origins, which the authors and their biographers never left out. Yet, while the authors were aware of their origins and wrote for the local public as well, they participated in the more encompassing imperial intellectual world of the sixteenth and seventeenth centuries.

It is precisely in the context of Ottoman imperial claims where we encounter one of the oldest Ottoman Bosnian Hajj treatises. ʿAlī-dada al-Būsnawī, the protagonist of our next section, wrote a treatise dedicated to the Maqām Ibrāhīm (Abraham's Station) in Mecca, positioning it both in the atemporal framework of permanent value and as an object of Ottoman imperial care.

[14] See Hazim Šabanović, *Književnost Muslimana BiH*, p. 96; ʿAlī-dada appears in biographical dictionaries of many Ottoman chroniclers, too.

[15] Džemal Čehajić, 'Šejh Abdulah Bošnjak 'Abdi' bin Muhamed al-Bosnevi (um. 1054/1644)', *Zbornik radova Islamskog teološkog fakulteta u Sarajevu* 1 (1982), p. 75.

In this way, the holy places were given meanings beyond the imperial, yet remained easily recognizable to Ottoman contemporaries.

The Universal Values of the Holy Places

Towards the end of the sixteenth century, ʿAlī-dada al-Būsnawī was a venerable shaykh who was guarding the tomb of Sultan Süleyman in Szigetvar for a couple of decades, giving lectures on mysticism and arcane knowledge. As *türbe şeyhi* (shaykh of the tomb), as he was called, he was probably expecting to spend his final years teaching in his Khalwatī *tekke* on the volatile Ottoman-Habsburg border. An invitation from Sultan Murad III (1546–95), however, offered ʿAlī-dada a return to the geography of his younger years. He was instructed to go to Mecca and supervise the renovation of the Maqām Ibrāhīm in close proximity to the Kaʿba, the place from where the Prophet Ibrāhīm had built the structure containing the imprint of his feet.

In many ways, ʿAlī-dada's own life was marked by the swift transformations in the Ottoman Empire, and he himself was a willing participant. Born in Mostar somewhere at the beginning of the sixteenth century, only a few decades separated him from the Ottoman conquest of Bosnia in 1463, although the Ottomans had been visibly present in the region much earlier.[16] His educational path took him to Istanbul, where he entered the Khalwatī Sufi order under Shaykh Musliḥ al-dīn ibn Nūr al-Dīn and received the *ijāza* (license) from him, thus confirming that he was allowed to spread Khalwatī teachings across the empire. ʿAlī-dada spent time in Mecca where he studied Ibn ʿArabī's works. The expansionist plans of the Ottomans moved ʿAlī-dada to Szigetvar in modern Hungary, where he became a guardian of the tomb of Sultan Sulayman in 1575, built at the initiative of Mehmed-pasha Sokolović (d. 1579), the Grand Vizier who also hailed from Bosnia. Old age, however, brought him no respite from service in the Ottoman cause: ʿAlī-dada was sent to Mecca to supervise the restoration of the Maqām Ibrāhīm before he returned to Szigetvar and died there.[17] The multiple geographies of his life

[16] On Sufi mechanisms of Ottoman conquest of Bosnia, see Aščerić-Todd, *Dervishes and Islam in Bosnia*.

[17] More details on ʿAlī-dada are available in Ibrahim Peçevî, *Tarih-i Peçevi* (Istanbul: Matbaʿa-i ʿĀmire, 1866), pp. 219–20, and Ahmed Mehmedović, *Leksikon bošnjačke uleme* (Sarajevo:

bestowed on him the various *nisbas* of al-Mostarī, al-Sigetvārī, al-Būsnawī, al-Ḥārīmī, al-Nūrī and al-Khalwatī,[18] reflecting his origins, as well as his allegiance to the empire and the Sufi order of the Khalwatīs.

ʿAlī-dada was also a prolific author. In the late nineteenth century, his two encyclopaedic works were printed: *Muḥāḍarat al-awāʾil wa-musāmarat al-awākhir* (*Lectures on the 'Firsts' and the 'Lasts'*)[19] and *Khawātim al-Ḥikam* (*The Seals of Wisdoms*).[20] Apart from these two works, his other writings include *Risālat al-intiṣār li-l-qidwa al-akhyār* (*The Treatise on the Victory of the Elect*), *Tamkīn al-Maqām fī al-Masjid al-Ḥarām* (*The Restorations of the Station in al-Masjid al-Ḥarām*; also existent in a variant titled *Faḍl al-Maqām wa-l-Masjid al-Ḥarām*, *The Virtue of the Maqām and the Masjid al-Ḥarām*) and *Risāla fī bayān rijāl al-ghayb* (*The Treatise on the Transcendental People*).[21] Based on the notes in some of his writings, we also know that he penned a treatise titled *Asrār al-ḥajj wa-ḥaqāʾiq al-āyāt al-Makiyya* (*The Secrets of the Hajj and the Meaning of the Meccan Verses*),[22] which is unfortunately lost.

ʿAlī-dada heeded the sultan's call and went to Mecca to oversee the restoration. We can glimpse some of his experiences from his treatise *Tamkīn al-Maqām fī al-Masjid al-Ḥarām*, dedicated to an argumentation of the virtue and primacy of this specific place. Why is Mecca holy? The question seemed to press upon ʿAlī-dada as he wrote this treatise. Its sanctity needed to be argued – a common approach of premodern Islamic discourse, not only on Mecca and Medina, but also on various other places around the

Gazi Husrev-begova biblioteka u Sarajevu, 2018), pp. 32–33. The most comprehensive overview of ʿAlī-dada's life and work is in Ismet Kasumović, *Ali-Dede Bošnjak i njegova filozofsko-sufijska misao* (Sarajevo: El-Kalem, 1994).

18 Kātib Çelebi/Hajji Khalīfa, *Kashf al-ẓunūn ʿan ʾasāmī al-kutub wa-l-funūn* (Bayrūt: Dār ʿiḥyā al-turāth al-ʿarabī, 1941), p. 686.

19 ʿAlī-dada al-Sikitwārī al-Būsnawī, *Muḥāḍarat al-awāʾil wa-musāmarat al-awākhir* (Misr: al-ʿĀmira al-Sharafīya, 1893).

20 ʿAlī-dada al-Mawlawī, *Kitāb Khawātim al-ḥikam al-musammā bi-Ḥall al-rumūz wa-kashf al-kunūz* (Al-Qāhira: al-Maṭbaʿa al-Sharafīya, 1896).

21 For more on ʿAlī-dada's works, see Ismet Kasumović, 'Rukopisi djela Ali Dede Harimije Bošnjaka na arapskom jeziku', *Prilozi za orijentalnu filologiju* 38 (1988), pp. 153–75.

22 Kasumović, 'Rukopisi djela Ali Dede Harimije Bošnjaka na arapskom jeziku', p. 172.

world, from al-Quds to Balkh.[23] Writing about the holy in its multiple forms required a number of techniques, such as the affirmation and elaboration of its virtues found in the revered sources, the exposition of related rituals and the sense of temporal order that fitted all things into their beginnings. This elucidation was shaped in several mediation channels – that is, through the genres and forms of the Arabic literary tradition such as the *faḍāʾil* and the *awāʾil* which moulded the material, often containing verses from the Qurʾan and the hadith. This way of constructing the sacred space was common throughout Islamic textual history. However, what sets ʿAlī-dada apart is that, through a number of argumentative techniques, he was also making a case for the Ottoman claim over Mecca and Medina, at a particularly crucial time when the empire's geographical expansion collided with millenarian expectations across the Mediterranean and beyond. These techniques, which will be explored further below, implied contrasting the Ottomans with other pursuants of the claim (such as the Safavids), thus placing them in a historical line of protectors of the holy places and creating a cosmological vision of the Ottomans at the end of time.

In his treatise on the restoration of Maqām Ibrāhīm, ʿAlī-dada started by delineating the specific sacred place, which is the Station of Abraham. This focus on a particular place within a wider sacred space can be understood as a way of mapping the very specific virtue (*faḍl* or *faḍīla*) within an unquestionable broader sanctity.[24] This type of spatial practice was often performed through the genre of *faḍāʾil*, which encompassed diverse texts in praise of places, people or religious duties such as the Hajj.[25] The *faḍāʾil* also used hadith as an argumentative tool, often without chains of transmitters and thus

[23] Arezou Azad, *Sacred Landscape in Medieval Afghanistan: Revisiting the Faḍaʾil-i Balkh* (Oxford: Oxford University Press, 2013).

[24] Over the past two decades, there has been a rise in studies on mapping the sacred in Islamic context. Some of the examples include Josef Meri, *The Cult of Saints among Muslims and Jews in Medieval Syria* (Oxford: Oxford University Press, 2002); Zayde Antrim, *Routes and Realms: The Power of Place in the Early Islamic World* (Oxford: Oxford University Press, 2012); Harry Munt, *The Holy City of Medina: Sacred Space in Early Islamic Arabia* (Cambridge: Cambridge University Press, 2014); Simon O'Meara, *The Kaʿba Orientations: Readings in Islam's Ancient House* (Edinburgh: Edinburgh University Press, 2020).

[25] R. Sellheim, 'Faḍīla', *The Encyclopaedia of Islam* (Leiden: Brill, 1991).

beyond the pale of authenticity as established by the canonical collections of Prophetic narrations.

The focus on the virtue of a particular place also speaks to the importance of ascertaining the boundaries of the sacred,[26] so that the emphasis of ʿAlī-dada's work is not on Mecca as an undefined category, but on the very concrete place of the Maqām which is distinguished by its own narrative. Prophet Ibrāhīm's Station, thus, firstly assumes its virtue by the connection to its sacred origins, as argued in the Qur'an and the hadith. These texts explained the ontological reasons for the existence of the Maqām, its pre-Islamic origins and the very connection of the Prophet Ibrāhīm to this locale.[27] In the process of establishing the virtue of the place, its essential multi-facetedness is recognized. Maqām Ibrāhīm is simultaneously a place for prayer, a place of revelation for knowledge on rites and a station during the visit to the Prophet.[28]

This sacred space, however, was not passive.[29] Using a range of sources, ʿAlī-dada brings in a number of traditions testifying to its sentience. The Maqām gains ability to sense through sight, speech and reactions to touch. Thus, the Maqām is a witness to those who are faithful.[30] As objects liable to the touch and sight of others, places such as the Maqām serve as places of worship (*ṣalāt*), drawing both humans and jinn into the process of heeding God's call.[31] As such, the visit to the Maqām (and other holy spatial objects) enhances the way in which believers reach forgiveness of sins or intercession.

[26] On the boundaries of the sacred and its paradoxes within an Islamic Sufi framework, see Michel Chodkiewicz, 'Le Paradoxe de la Ka'ba', *Revue de l'histoire des religions* 222/4 (2005), pp. 435–61.

[27] Esad Efendi 3814, fols 5b–7a.

[28] Esad Efendi 3814, fol. 7b.

[29] Jonathan Z. Smith poses the question of place as an 'active product of intellection rather than its passive receptacle'; see Jonathan Z. Smith, *To Take Place: Toward Theory in Ritual* (Chicago, London: The University of Chicago Press, 1992), p. 26. As we shall see throughout the chapter, the holy places functioned as humans, or at least as sentient beings, with the ability not only to sense, but also to intercede or witness the presence of believers in their vicinity. They actively oriented believers' lives.

[30] Esad Efendi 3814, fol. 7b.

[31] Esad Efendi 3814, fol. 8b.

While places such as the Maqām in their corporeality presented a means of reaching the divine or fulfilling a soteriological plan, they also contained mysteries (*asrār*) that opened a new set of meanings ascribed to them. Thus, apart from being effective through their sheer existence, the sites also evoked a set of meanings implying a reality behind it.[32] This tension between outward effectiveness and inward meaning was expressed by terms of *ẓāhir* versus *ḥaqīqa*. In this regard, ʿAlī-dada relayed the interpretation that the Maqām outwardly was the place where the Prophet Ibrāhīm proclaimed the Hajj; in truth (*ḥaqīqa*) the Maqām referred to the exalted spiritual stations that he achieved, such as contentment with God's will, submission to God's decree and certainty.[33] These qualities, thus, have an ethical dimension which, even though they relate to the Prophet Ibrāhīm, were also oriented towards the common believers.

Through this particular arrangement of different traditions and, more importantly, through the addition of other modes of attaining knowledge, such as his own dreams, ʿAlī-dada was pointing to the multiple ways in which the sacred could be approached and from which one could derive benefit. Thus, one night after working on the site, ʿAlī-dada saw the Prophet Ibrāhīm while he was in a state between sleep and awakening, and the vision included the appearance of the sites in the form of young people.[34] The whole event, reminiscent of Ibn ʿArabī's vision of the youth in Mecca,[35] served to bolster the sanctity of the Maqām.

While the sacredness of the Maqām Ibrāhīm was firstly argued in its own right, through an argumentation for its effectiveness and hidden meanings, ʿAlī-dada's treatise was also a contribution to sixteenth-century millennialist

[32] Seeing that the place is both effective and meaningful puts an additional layer to what Marion Katz wrote about understandings of the ritual in the legal sources of the pre-modern Islam. Katz, 'The Ḥajj', p. 99. It is possible to claim that the rituals in the premodern Islamic non-legal discourses could do both: refer to themselves and to the presupposed reality behind them.

[33] Esad Efendi 3814, fol. 11b.

[34] Esad Efendi 3814, fols 14b–15a.

[35] Ibn ʿArabī was not the only Sufi author who described out-of-ordinary experiences in the vicinity of the Kaʿba. See O'Meara, *The Kaʿba Orientations*, esp. ch. 4.

thought, which witnessed the emergence of a number of narratives linking eschatological religious perspectives to ideological interpretations of the ruling power. In his treatise, just like many of his contemporaries, ʿAlī-dada developed his argument in favour of the Ottoman dynasty, 'through a unified epistemology in which intuition, rational science, and conveyed scriptural knowledge were reconciled'.[36] The next section will show how the discourse on the holy places was intertwined with the promotion of the Ottoman dynasty.

The Eternal Protectors of the Holy Places

The elaborate praise of the Ottoman dynasty, situated at the confluence of extraordinary time and sacred place, was embedded within the wider religious history that promised to the Ottomans a place of this-worldly permanence. The Ottomans, according to ʿAlī-dada, were to rule forever: 'May God make their rule eternal until the end of time and may He prolong their rule concluding with the allegiance to the Mahdi at the end of times'.[37]

Although it was a commonplace for early modern authors to dedicate their work to the ruling sultans by using a standard set of praise and titles, it is nevertheless important to investigate the terms employed here, since they reflect, at least partially, the current preoccupation with imperial representation. The beginning of the treatise sets the ruling sultan (Murad III) as the renewer (*mujaddid*) of the century,[38] a claim that was devised beforehand by the careful enumeration of the precise year and period in which he ruled.[39] His titles, therefore, included the following:

> The Imam, the Exalted Succor, Noble Caliph, the Servant of the two Holy Places, the Conqueror of the two grand Iraqs, the one to whom God has opened the doors known as '*Demir kapu*' and who crushed the roots of

[36] Huseyin Yilmaz, *Caliphate Redefined: The Mystical Turn in Ottoman Political Thought* (Princeton: Princeton University Press 2018), p. 272.

[37] Esad Efendi 3814, fol. 24a.

[38] On the tradition supporting the notion of the *mujaddid*, see Ella Landau-Tasseron, 'The "Cyclical Reform": A Study of the Mujaddid Tradition', *Studia Islamica* 70 (1989), pp. 79–117.

[39] Esad Efendi 3814, fol. 5a.

> Shiʿism in the lands of Iraq [. . .] so he is the first who is known as the *khaqān al-khawāqīn* of the descendants of the fighters, may God be pleased with all of them.[40]

ʿAlī-dada was trying to show the Ottomans as unique and exceptional in their time. One of the ways to accomplish such an aim was to compare the Ottoman rulers to their Abbasid precedents, through the example of service to the holy places:

> There is no doubt that the noble service to Mecca is bound to miracles (*karāmāt*) and [enhances] conquests for kings, and because of that some of the grand Abbasid caliphs and others were striving to serve the Sacred Sanctuary, such as al-Manṣūr al-ʿAbbāsī and al-Mahdī and al-Rashīd and others.[41]

The way in which ʿAlī-dada shaped the image of the expanding empire based on the Abbasid model reveals the wish to incorporate the Ottoman Empire into the long line of other Muslim dynasties. Moreover, ʿAlī-dada wanted to place it at the very end of time. The Ottoman exceptionalism that emerges from these lines is reflected in ʿAlī-dada's insistence that the ruling sultan was a renewer of faith (*mujaddid*), as well as in his emphasis on the Ottomans vanquishing their enemies and, prominently, his description of dynastic figures who gave a certain amount of support to Mecca through their connection to members of the early Muslim community. Thus, Sultan Murad III himself was associated with the second caliph ʿUmar al-Fārūq (d. 644) who also had repaired the Maqām Ibrāhīm.[42]

However, occasional references to the other empires or rulers can be found in *Tamkīn al-Maqām*, related to their role in the preservation or protection of Mecca. Comparing the Ottoman sultans' performance as protectors of the pilgrimage with that of their Mamluk predecessors was a frequent motif. This may reflect the fact that the Ottoman sultans tried to adhere to practices

[40] Esad Efendi 3814, fol. 5a.

[41] Esad Efendi 3814, fol. 5b.

[42] Esad Efendi 3814, fol. 5b.

linked to the Mamluk sultans Qā'it Bay (1468–96) and Qānṣūh al-Ghūrī (1501–16).[43] In this context, 'Alī-dada mentions Qā'itbay's madrasa, a result of his architectural contributions to the city's development.[44]

The eulogy for the Ottoman family holds a significant textual space in the narrative. In his praise, 'Alī-dada is making specific claims not only about the sultans, but also about their wives and daughters. He does this by using the genre of *awā'il* ('the firsts') which, as its name suggests, categorises and lists events or objects according to their historical appearance. Since the *awā'il* genre is preoccupied with the question of 'firsts' and therefore 'can pertain to every conceivable subject in the context of Arabo-Islamic civilisation, ranging from theological and legal themes to historical, political, and cultural topics',[45] it became a useful tool for creating a distinctive identity for whichever community employing it. It was often paired with the genre of the last things (*awā'khir*), which was suited to present the role of the Ottomans as the protectors of the holy places until the end of times:

> The last one who made the streams flow in the Sacred Precincts and made from them ponds and fountains for ablution [. . .] and made pious endowments is the pious wife of Rüstem-pasha, a second Rābi'a (al-'Adawiyya). She improved those fountains and spent on them enormous amounts of money. [. . .] The citizens of Mecca live in blessing of her goodness, may God bless her with the good in the two abodes and may He bestow upon her glory among the daughters of kings and good wives. Balqīs of the time, who is unique among the wives of the kings and notables, also endowed in the name of God. She excelled because of her pious endowments in Mecca the Radiant. Her unique *zawiya* is at Ṣafā and her kitchen where the meals are prepared for the poor is on the way of al-Mu'allā. One thousand or more people live off her grace and goodness. This is a unique virtue, through which she surpassed the kings of the time, and there is no doubt that she is by the Grace of God the queen of all wives of kings, and she is the mother of Ottoman caliphs, may God prolong their rule until the Day of Judgement.[46]

[43] Suraiya Faroqhi, *Pilgrims and Sultans: The Hajj Under the Ottomans* 1517–1683 (London: I. B. Tauris, 1994), p. 33.

[44] Esad Efendi 3814, fol. 14b.

[45] Monique Bernards, 'Awā'il', *Encyclopaedia of Islam*, third edition (Leiden: Brill, 2007); this entry gives an exhaustive overview of the history of *awā'il* works.

[46] Esad Efendi 3814, fols 23b–24a.

What the previous paragraph describes is, firstly, the laudable deeds of Mihrimah (1522–78), Sultan Süleyman's daughter and the wife of Rüstem-pasha, who was responsible for improving the water system after it failed following a long period of neglect. What is implied here is that the Ottoman Empire with all their dynasty members is the final and ultimate empire to rule until the end of time. Interwoven into the narrative is also a praise of Hürrem Sultan (d. 1558): apart from improving the waterways, Sultan Süleyman's wife also established a *tekke* and soup kitchen for the poor. The gender hierarchy is kept intact in this excerpt: Mihrimah and Hürrem can excel, but only over other wives of kings and notables and in complimentary comparison to legendary women of religious lore.

While Sultan Süleyman's wife and daughter stand at the end of a long line of benefactresses of the holy places, in some cases, however, the Ottomans were the first to initiate the tradition, according to ʿAlī-dada. Thus, in the section on the imperial purse (*ṣurre*), ʿAlī-dada mentions how the tradition was started by Mehmed Han (Mehmed II) who was sending it.[47] Other parts of the *awāʾil* confirm the same idea; thus, Sultan Murad III is mentioned in association with the building of the water fountain,[48] and the chronogram that follows affirms his special status: 'He excelled above the King and the Khusro (*Fāqa ʿala qayṣar wa-kisro*)'.[49] The title itself, once again, implies the numerous campaigns undertaken by Murad III against the Habsburgs and the Safavids. Both of these adversaries presented not only a military, but also an ideological enemy. The Habsburgs shared the same claim to universal monarchy, while the Safavids propagated the claim to define true Islam and rule over the Muslim community.[50] The latter, in some ways, presented an additional challenge for the Ottoman authors who had to deal with alternative claims to Islamic authenticity.

The narrative in praise of the Ottomans is the most visible when they are listed alongside other dynasties in Islamic history. Thus, in his *awāʾil*

[47] Esad Efendi 3814, fol. 24a.

[48] Esad Efendi 3814, fol. 24a.

[49] Esad Efendi 3814, fol. 24b.

[50] Kaya Şahin, *Empire and Power in the Reign of Süleyman: Narrating the Sixteenth-Century Ottoman World* (Cambridge: Cambridge University Press, 2013), p. 4.

entry on the *kiswa* (the cloth that covers the Kaʿba), ʿAlī-dada enumerated the previous dynasties: the Abbasids, the Fatimids, the Egyptian Turks (the Mamluks), ending with the Ottomans.[51] Not only was the Ottoman dynasty placed at the end of the temporal cycle, but Sultan Süleyman himself was mentioned as someone who would come at its culmination. He was a martyr, a claim that implied that he had died expanding the territories and defending the empire. The enumeration of the dynasties and empires before the Ottomans speaks to how the imperial narrative intended to incorporate itself into a genealogy leading back to the Prophet himself. This search for affirmation in the shape of a genealogy also shows the struggle to find a 'convincing genealogy', which was necessary for Ottoman self-legitimisation.[52] The Ottoman dynasty was described as standing at the very end of time, although its very end might not come very soon.[53]

This insistence on the intermediary role of the Ottomans as protectors of the holy places can be interpreted in accordance with what Juan Campo has alluded to as ways that 'both conceal and reflect the workings of hegemonic forces'.[54] In this way, the Hajj is interpreted as a representational and relational tool for the expression of power. This power is enhanced not only through the image of the protector of rituals and places, but also through additional ceremonies (such as the *ṣurre* procession). While serving as a treatise dedicated to enhancing the eschatological value of a particular site, the imperial narrative in its pervasiveness serves to prove how the holy place was embedded within relations other than purely spiritual.

The variety of his writings reveals ʿAlī-dada's committment to classical textual genres, shaped by pre-Ottoman traditions of learning, while at the same time opening up these forms of mediation to his own time. The following section will take a closer look at the further formation and promotion of

[51] Esad Efendi 3814, fol. 24b.

[52] Hakan Karateke and Maurus Reinkowski, 'Introduction', in *Legitimizing the Order: The Ottoman Rhetoric of State Power*, ed. by Hakan Karateke and Maurus Reinkowski (Leiden, Boston: Brill, 2005), p. 6.

[53] Esad Efendi 3814, fol. 24a.

[54] Juan E. Campo, 'Visualizing the Ḥajj', p. 287.

the sacred space and its virtue through the Ottoman Bosnian employment of earlier Sufi writings that disrupted the anthropocentric paradigm in worship.

Mediating Worlds through the Black Stone

ʿAlī-dada's writings show us the variety of ways in which the holy space could mediate between the believers and the transcendent, including the power that it bestowed upon deserving Muslim dynasties. The holy space had agency: it could even be conceived as a sensing and witnessing body, with human attributes.[55] However, while assuming the functions of a human body (such as mediation, intercession and witnessing), the holy space could also destabilise the position of humans in the cosmological scheme of beings and worship. This section will investigate the subversive role of the holy place, specifically the Black Stone (*al-Ḥajar al-Aswad*), a meteoric rock in the eastern corner of the Kaʿba, in a treatise by ʿAbdullah al-Būsnawī, as framed by a longer Sufi tradition of mystical visions.

The author of the treatise on the Black Stone with whose life story we started this chapter, ʿAbdullah al-Būsnawī, is widely known as *Shāriḥ al-Fuṣūṣ* (*The Interpreter of the Fuṣūṣ*) indicating his intellectual and spiritual connection to Ibn ʿArabī and his work *Fuṣūṣ al-Ḥikam* (*The Bezels of Wisdom*). In the previous section, we saw how ʿAlī-dada's allegiance to the Khalwatī order was not separate from his service to Ottoman power. Other Sufi orders, which held different positions in the power hierarchy of the Ottoman state, forged their own intellectual networks or contributed to those evolving in different cities of the empire. One such order was the Bayrāmī-Malāmī, to which ʿAbdullah al-Būsnawī belonged; after a turbulent relationship with the Ottoman state in the sixteenth century, this order tried to rebuild its position. In the seventeenth century, the order had a trans-imperial network spanning from Istanbul to Mecca, spreading and defending the ideas of Ibn ʿArabī which were often deemed controversial in the early modern Ottoman milieu.

The text of ʿAbdullah al-Būsnawī's treatise *Kitāb al-yad al-ajwad fī istilām al-ḥajar al-aswad* (*The Book of the Right Hand in Greeting the Black Stone*) was not intended for a wider audience because of its highly specialised language. The short treatise starts with a Sufi introduction to the tenets of the

[55] O'Meara, *The Kaʿba Orientations*, p. 58.

pilgrimage. As the author states at the beginning, the treatise is dedicated to some of the pious brothers and to all the believers in general.[56] Apart from Qur'anic verses, 'Abdullah al-Būsnawī used parallelisms such as comparing the Kaʿba to the *'Arsh* (the Throne of God) and the pilgrims who circumambulate the Kaʿba to angels (*malā'ika*).[57] The beginning of the treatise is similar to a *faḍā'il*, in terms of the frequent comparisons that aim to secure a unique place for the Masjid al-Ḥarām and the Black Stone, specifically. One of the concepts permeating this work is the pledge of allegiance (*mubāyaʿa*).[58] The Black Stone is, thus, presented as 'God's oath (*yamīn Allah*)', containing a special characteristic (*ikhtiṣāṣ*) because of its deputyship (*khilāfa*) and agreement (*bayʿa*). Therefore, if a believer touches the Black Stone, he has pledged allegiance to the Truth (*al-Ḥaqq*).[59] The stone itself, as al-Būsnawī writes, is the same as all the other stones, but it was chosen because of its intermediary role in the process of allegiance.[60] The Black Stone is anthropomorphised and presented as the shaykh of the place; it grants the right of approach.[61] The final virtue of the Black Stone is its ability to testify on the Day of Judgement, implying a role of intercession given to this object. Thus, the Black Stone also fits within a soteriological plan, since it will carry the responsibility of testimony during Judgement Day.[62] In that role, the stone would have the human abilities of sight and speech, which means that the stone would shift from mineral into human state.

In both ʿAlī-dada's and 'Abdullah al-Būsnawī's treatises, the holy sites of the Maqām and the Black Stone have sentience, especially when related to their intercession for humans. However, 'Abdullah al-Būsnawī's treatise takes it one step further and not only interrogates the relationship between the sites and the believers, but also inverts the hierarchy of beings. Through heavy reliance on Ibn ʿArabī's *Al-Futuḥāt al-Makiyya*, 'Abdullah al-Būsnawī proposes the idea of 'minerality' as elevated state for a human being. This proposition implies

[56] Carullah 2129, fol. 1b.

[57] Carullah 2129, fol. 1b.

[58] See especially Carullah 2129, fols 2a, 6a.

[59] Carullah 2129, fol. 2a.

[60] Carullah 2129, fol. 6b.

[61] Carullah 2129, fols 6b–7a.

[62] Carullah 2129, fol. 7a.

that the state of inactivity is the state of subdued or annihilated senses. In this inversion of the standard cosmological scheme, the mineral state becomes the preferred state because of its innate worship of God, unencumbered by the weight of the senses. The narrative is, consequently, oriented towards the non-human, non-animal and non-vegetative, and it exalts the mineral state which is a characteristic of the Black Stone. ʿAbdullah al-Būsnawī uses the example of the stone thrown into the air. At some point, because of its nature, the stone starts falling downwards because of the fear of God (*khashyat Allah*). Interweaving the Qur'anic verse 'Those truly fear Allah, among His Servants, who have knowledge' (Fatir, 28),[63] ʿAbdullah al-Būsnawī is also putting the Black Stone in the position of a possessor of knowledge. The stones are, also, the verifyers (*muḥaqqiqūn*).

While the Black Stone is praised for its annihilation of the senses, it remains embedded in comparisons with the human body. Thus, ʿAbdullah al-Būsnawī draws parallels between the object of the Kaʿba (and the Black Stone) and the human body (and particularly the heart, *qalb*). Just as the first house (*bayt*) was built for people in Mecca, likewise the heart of the believer is the first thing which manifested itself to the Truth and appeared in it. It is the ruler of the body and its king.[64] If the heart goes astray, it is followed by the body. It needs to be cleansed, just as God ordered in the Qur'an (al-Baqara, 125). The heart is the ruler of the body (*al-jism*). Furthermore, the Black Stone is said to be an image (*al-ṣūra*) of the poor slave who needs the doors of his Lord.[65]

The work is intended as an instruction for pilgrims on how to approach the Black Stone and can be read in two ways: as directed to the average pilgrim who wants to benefit from the blessings of the stone and thus be cleansed of sin, and to the initiated who aim for higher goals. The parallelism permeates the rest of the narrative as well and is expressed in the division of different sections into practical language (*lisān al-taṭbīq*) and language of interpretation (*lisān al-ta'wīl*).[66] While the treatise explains the

63 Translation by Yusuf Ali.

64 Carullah 2129, fol. 6b.

65 Carullah 2129, fol. 4a.

66 Carullah 2129, fols 5b–6a.

regular pilgrimage requirements connected to the Kaʿba (such as *ṭawāf*), the practical part does not simply imply the practical application of the ritual's legal rules. It rather focuses on the ways through which a seeker can reach the spiritual aim. The narrative is, thus, never simply a ritual manual: this intricate text has to be read as an instruction to a seeker (*sālik*). For example, the reference to the definition of the Hajj as the repetition of intention at a defined time is juxtaposed with the heart which aims for the Divine Names in a special state (*ḥāl*).[67]

ʿAbdullah al-Būsnawī offers a string of traditions which affirm the touching and kissing of the Black Stone, as well as the prostration (*sajda*) in front of it.[68] In the development of his argument, ʿAbdullah al-Būsnawī is relying on the agreement of the 'predecessors' (*salaf*): 'know that the *salaf* agreed that kissing the Black Stone is a peculiarity of the customs of circumambulation, and they disagreed about kissing the Yamani corner'.[69]

The personification of the Kaʿba and the Black Stone, as Hava Lazarus-Yafeh notes, first became prominent in the hadith literature and was further developed in subsequent Sufi literature.[70] ʿAbdullah al-Būsnawī elaborates the image and describes the stone as 'earthly' (*arḍī*), juxtaposing it to the image of the human face as the most noble outward form. The qualities of earth are, still, contrasted positively with that of the human: human lowliness becomes worse than that of the earth because the human being was ordered to worship God, but instead worships the created (*al-makhlūq*).[71] The earth is a manifestation of God's name, just as the Perfect Human (*al-insān al-kāmil*) is a manifestation of many of God's names.[72] The complicated anthropomorphism of the Kaʿba and the Black Stone are also connected to the concept

[67] Carullah 2129, fol. 6a.

[68] Kissing the Black Stone and the traditions surrounding it have been a point of debate among researchers of the ritual, who saw in it the argument for or against treating the Hajj in the context of an interpretative framework of sacramentalism. See the above-mentioned article by Marion Katz for a more complete bibliography.

[69] Carullah 2129, fol. 2a.

[70] Hava Lazarus-Yafeh, 'The Religious Dialectics of the Hadjdj', in *Some Religious Aspects of Islam: A Collection of Articles* (Leiden: Brill, 1981), p. 29.

[71] Carullah 2129, fol. 2b.

[72] Carullah 2129, fol. 2b.

of purity (*ṭahāra*) which on a ritual level is a requirement for pilgrims, but on a spiritual level a requirement for approaching God.[73] The Kaʿba, and by implication the Black Stone as well, is at the centre of the treatise, superceding even the Prophet.[74]

While the attention to Maqām Ibrāhīm and the Black Stone retained their centrality in the connection to the Hajj, Medina, as the site of the Prophet's life and death, was also persistently present in the discourse on holy places in the early modern period. In the previous treatises of ʿAlī-dada and 'Abdullah al-Būsnawī, devotion to the Prophet was not given primacy, even when his name was mentioned to bolster the argument for Mecca. As we turn to the third author of this chapter and his treatise on the virtue of Medina, we will see how the Prophet's figure assumes new importance, through the insistence on vigorous argumentation, as well as the cultivation of particular emotional styles of reverence and love.

The City and the Prophet

As seen in the writings of ʿAlī-dada and ʿAbdullah al-Būsnawī, the space of Mecca contained primacy due to its virtue, based on soteriological, chiliastic and cosmological functions. Based on an analysis of the treatise of Ḥasan Imām-zāda al-Būsnawī, this section will focus on the construction of the virtue of Medina, the city where believers visited the Prophet, and the place of *mujāwara* (residing) in the vicinity of the Prophet's Tomb and Mosque. Parallel to the construction of the virtue of Mecca, Medina also derived its primacy from soteriological and cosmological arguments; however, as the following pages will show, its ultimate virtue rested in the cultivation of emotions among the believers, emotions that led them to the Prophet. Nurturing emotions towards the Prophet was mediated through a range of textual sources, most notably the hadith.

Medina has been a site of continued reverence throughout the centuries, and many pilgrims noted unique feelings of attachment to the city. Its virtue

[73] The notion of purity in the context of the sacredness of holy place in Mecca is discussed in Brannon Wheeler, *Mecca and Eden: Ritual, Relics, and Territory in Islam* (Chicago: The University of Chicago Press, 2006), pp. 47–70.

[74] Carullah 2129, fol. 2a.

was in many ways compared to Mecca's and placed next to Jerusalem's.[75] Similarly to Mecca and Jerusalem (and many cities across the Muslim world),[76] a significant textual tradition arose to construct the virtue of Medina, most notably in the form of the *faḍāʾil* (treatises on the virtues of cities, provinces and regions), as well as of histories of the city. However, as Harry Munt notes, the sanctity of Medina has been somewhat neglected by contemporary scholarship, with precedence given to Mecca and Jerusalem.[77] Considerably less is known about Medina in the Ottoman context, even though recent studies have pointed to its overwhelming importance for scholarly circles in the early modern period.[78]

The virtue of Medina as a holy place was derived from a number of arguments, including the early Islamic history that focused on the *hijra* (migration) of the Prophet and his companions from Mecca to Medina, as well as, significantly, the presence of the Prophet's body buried in the vicinity of his mosque. Fascination with the Prophet's body persisted in both Muslim and non-Muslim texts, which led to continued debates on the sentience of the Prophet (and other prophets in general) in the grave.[79]

While the sanctity of Medina was derived from a multitude of arguments, this section will pay attention to those used in one early modern Ottoman treatise on its *faḍāʾil*. The work was written by Ḥasan Imām-zāda al-Būsnawī (fl. 1661), a scholar who resided in Medina and who wrote other works in praise of the Prophet, including a *miʿrāj* treatise and a treatise inspiring love towards the Prophet. His opus points to the centrality of the Prophet

[75] On a long tradition of grouping Mecca, Medina and Jerusalem together, see M. J. Kister, '"You Shall Only Set for Three Mosques": A Study of an Early Tradition', *Le Muséon* 82 (1969), pp. 173–96.

[76] Works that praised the virtues of other cities were also prominent throughout Islamic history, including the *faḍāʾil* not only of the Sham region, but also of cities as far as Balkh. See Azad, *Sacred Landscape in Medieval Afghanistan*. The *faḍāʾil* works could be written on a range of topics beyond the spatial. See more in R. Sellheim, 'Faḍīla'.

[77] Munt, *The Holy City of Medina*, p. 3.

[78] Sohaib Baig, 'Indian Hanafis in an Ocean of Hadith: Islamic Legal Authority between South Asia and the Arabian Peninsula, 16th–20th Centuries' (PhD diss., University of California, Los Angeles, 2020).

[79] For an extensive overview of these debates in the late Mamluk period, see Fritz Meier, 'Eine Auferstehung Mohammeds bei Suyuti', *Der Islam* 62 (1985), pp. 20–58.

in early modern devotion. The rest of this chapter will discuss the mechanisms through which Medina's sanctity was argued based on soteriological and cosmological claims, similar to the previous two sections on holy places in Mecca; it will illuminate how Medina was compared to other places in the hierarchy of sanctity and how an additional element was brought into the picture: the cultivation of emotions.

The *Dalīl al-saʾirīn ilā ziyārat Ḥabīb Rabb al-ʿālamīn* (*A Guide for Those Who Want to Visit the Beloved of the Lord of the Worlds*) is a *faḍāʾil* work in praise of Medina, which has several copies extant across the Balkans, Turkey and Egypt, indicating that it may have been Imām-zāda al-Būsnawī's 'best-seller'.[80] Imām-zāda was in all probability also the author of two more treatises that contained elements of *faḍāʾil*, one titled *Tashwīq al-labīb ila maḥabbat al-Ḥabīb* (*Inciting a Sensible Person to Desire Loving the Beloved*) which is found together with a copy of the *Dalīl al-saʾirīn*,[81] and a treatise titled *al-Ilhām al-ilāhiyya fi miʿrāj khayr al-bariyya* (*Divine Inspiration in the Nightly Celestial Journey of the Best of the Creatures*).[82] Although information on its authorship is scant and indicated only by the copyist's note at the beginning of each respective manuscript (in which we find out that Ḥasan al-Būsnawī became al-Madanī, a citizen of Medina, and that he was famous as Imām-zāda), the subject-matter of all three works indicates a sustained preoccupation of the author. All three treatises give the Prophet Muhammad a central position in devotion, from three distinct angles. *Dalīl al-sāʾirīn*, the treatise discussed here, is a work in praise of Medina, for numerous reasons related to events from the Prophet's life, as well as his place in the overall hierarchy of Islamic piety. As the Prophet becomes central in the devotional structure of the *faḍāʾil*, the space that pertains to the Prophet, Medina, is contrasted with other places, including Mecca, as the place which the Prophet chose as his abode.

80 While it is harder to ascertain what truly constituted a 'bestseller', the number of extant copies and the probability that it was read by different audiences might suggest this. Compare this with the case of Ibn ʿAbd al-Hadi, a 'middling' scholar, in Konrad Hirschler, *A Monument to Medieval Syrian Book Culture: The Library of Ibn Abd al-Hādī* (Edinburgh: Edinburgh University Press, 2019).

81 Gazi Husrev-bey's Library, R-8584.

82 Available in the Special Collections at the Princeton University Library, Rare Books and Special Collections, Islamic Manuscripts, Garrett no. 2302Y.

The fact that Imām-zāda is the author of three different works dedicated to the Prophet frames our understanding of some aspects of seventeenth-century piety and as such contributes to the growing research on Prophet-oriented or 'Prophet-centered'[83] forms of piety. The centrality of Medina was constructed through a series of arguments related to the Prophet, mostly based on Qur'anic or hadith quotations and enhanced by a range of prayers and instructions for the pilgrims on how to cultivate their behaviour in the Prophetic presence. In this way, while the *faḍā'il* of Medina sought to focus on the city as an object of praise, it necessarily engaged with arguments that favour the Prophet. Considerations of the space were thus tied in with the cultivation of proper behaviour and emotional deportment in the Prophet's presence. That is why the following analysis treats the intertwinement of arguments in favour of Medina and the Prophet, as well as how they merged into a promotion of *ziyāra*, the visit to the Prophet.

Loving the Prophet

The eight chapters of the treatise *Dalīl al-sa'irīn* delineated different sites in Medina and their virtues: from the details of the visit to the Prophet's grave, followed by the explanation of the virtues of the Righteous Caliphs Abū Bakr and 'Umar who were buried in the same space as the Prophet and the description of the graveyard al-Baqī', al-Qubā Mosque and Uḥud. The unifying thread for all these sites was their proximity to the Prophet, and the treatise recommended ways to obtain such proximity to the common visitor as well. This could be achieved through the elaborate cultivation of love towards the Prophet. The motive of love in the treatise was multi-directional. God's love towards the Prophet (emphasised in the title of the treatise itself) underpinned other layers, directions and objects of love which appeared in the work. The Prophet himself was at the centre of devotion, as exemplified by the beginning of the treatise:

> He is the intention of all existence and the lord of what gives birth and is born. He is the point around which circle the spheres of creation, and He is

[83] Gruber, *The Praiseworthy One*, p. 20.

> the light that fills the earth and the heavens. He is the first in the order and the last in the seal.[84]

This centring of the Prophet which uses the symbol of light is part of the larger and older Sufi tradition of the 'Muhammedan Light' harking back to some of the early reports.[85] The formulated idea is ascribed to the ninth-century Sufi mystic Sahl al-Tustarī,[86] heavily quoted by Imām-zāda in this and his other treatises and taken up by a long line of devotees. The Muhammedan Light became prominent in early modern Ottoman piety through textual and visual imagery and 'extends the prophetic corpus beyond literal forms of physical imagination and visualisation'.[87] That this treatise begins with the luminous image of the Prophet who is also spatially, temporally and cosmically centred implies that, even though the *faḍā'il* extols Medina, this happens solely on account of the Prophet.

The relationship between Medina and the Prophet is framed through the emphasis on love. This love, however, is embedded in a derivative framework that posits love towards Medina through God's love towards the Prophet, reflected in the dominant tradition interwoven throughout the treatise:

> There is no place on this earth that I would rather have my grave in, other than Medina. And Medina is dearer to the Prophet (Peace be upon Him), and to His Lord (Almighty) because the Love of the Prophet follows from the Love of His Lord. And if it is dearest to Allah and His Prophet, how can it not possess virtue?[88]

The juxtaposition of love and virtue further develops into a rationalising discourse: why should believers love Medina, and why is it so exalted? Through the listing of different textual authorities including, but not limited to, hadith

[84] MS 0719, fol. 2a.

[85] Marion Katz, *The Birth of the Prophet Muhammad: Devotional Piety in Sunni Islam* (Oxfordshire: Routledge, 2007), p. 13.

[86] See more in Annemarie Schimmel, *Mystical Dimensions of Islam* (Chapel Hill: University of North Carolina, 1975), p. 215.

[87] Gruber, *The Praiseworthy One*, p. 260.

[88] MS 0719, fols 3b-4a.

scholars, Imām-zāda states that there is a consensus on the 'preference of the place which contains the Prophet's body even over the Ka'ba'.[89] The variations on the motif of the Prophet's burial place interweave in the text, and this points to the narration's place in the context of a wider fascination with prophetic bodies' fate, a fascination that was particularly intense in the late Mamluk period.[90] Moreover, with the emphasis on Medina as the place where the Prophet Muhammad was buried, other people buried there (in al-Baqīʿ, for example) were also noted. However, Imām-zāda brings out a range of discussions that emphasise uncertainty: if all the places of prophetic bodies possess virtue, where does that place the body of the Prophet Muhammad? Using a range of narrations and relying on al-Tirmidhī's (824–92) *Shamāʾil* and Ibn al-Jawzī's (d. 1201) *al-Wafā*, the author stresses that the superiority of the Prophet's burial place is, again, derived from God's decision to take the Prophet's soul in Medina.[91] Derivative aspects of love are further demonstrated by the obligation of love towards the people of Medina, and more specifically the Prophet's Family (*ahl al-bayt*), the instructions of which are interspersed throughout the treatise.[92]

As the place where the Prophet was buried assumed primary significance and preference, narrations about other events from the Prophet's life and broader Islamic sacred history (such as the Prophet's migration from Mecca to Medina, or *hijra*) also influenced the construction of Medina's virtue. These elements all function in order to cultivate love towards the Prophet. The treatise instructs the seeker and the pilgrim on how to increase love (*maḥabba*) by clearly defined and verbalised acts of devotion.[93] In that context, the Cairene copy of Imām-zāda's *faḍāʾil* is especially interesting, because it is paired with his treatise on *tashwīq* – an encouragement of love directed more closely to devotees through a number of delineated prayers.[94]

[89] MS 0719, fol. 3b.

[90] See more on this debate in Meier, 'Eine Auferstehung'.

[91] Laleli 1363, fol. 3b.

[92] MS 0719, fol. 29a; the obligation of love towards the Prophet's family is presented as a religious obligation (*farāʾiḍ al-dīn*). MS 0719, fol. 30b.

[93] MS 0719, fol. 16b.

[94] Imām-zāda himself starts the treatise by noting how some of his contemporaries do not know that love towards the Prophet Muhammad is a commanded religious duty and that they are

If observed together, the writings lay down a framework for *ziyāra*, as well as the promotion of *mujāwara*, or residence in Medina.

While love draws devotees to Medina, and while Medina is chosen because of the interlocking relationships of love, the willing departure from the city – other than for approved reasons such as spreading knowledge, conquest of the lands of unbelievers and fighting enemies – is blameworthy, especially if accompanied by the denial of its virtue or the virtue of its inhabitants.[95]

Living and Dying in Medina

While love towards the Prophet formed the central way to achieve proximity to him, there was something for visitors in return as well. In other words, visitors to Medina could expect a prophetic intercession (*shafā ʿa*) that addressed their soteriological concerns. This promise was based on the hadith stating that 'whoever visits my grave, I will be their intecessor', repeated many times throughout the treatise. This linked the visit to the Prophet's grave to the broader concept of intercession.

The hadith was followed by instructions directed to the believers. The ideal believer was encouraged to be patient regarding the harsh and difficult climate of Medina, in compensation for the Prophet being their intercessor (*shafī ʿ*) or witness (*shāhid*).[96] In a side note of his autograph copy, Imām-zāda offered a definition of intercession taken from Mulla ʿAlī al-Qārī's (d. 1605) interpretation of the hadith on intercession for those who suffer from the excessive climate and environment and consequently die in Medina. According to that definition, intercession (as delineated in this hadith) is granted only to those who die in Medina, as response to a wider polemic about the virtues of the *mujāwara* in Mecca and Medina.[97] All of this is to persuade the believer that they should wish to die in Medina, because it is a religious obligation.[98] The importance of having one's earthly remains in Medina is

not working on knowing this duty (R-8584, fol. 2a). Love is not a one-dimensional notion in Imām-zāda's work. It is divided into natural (*ṭab ʿī*) and rational (*ʿaqlī*), in which rational love is appreciated more because of the effort which has to be put into it (R-8584, fol. 2b).

95 MS 0719, fol. 4b.

96 MS 0719, fol. 7b.

97 MS 0719, fol. 8a.

98 MS 0719, fol. 8b.

elaborated upon in a section on narrations about the possibility that the head of the Prophet's grandson Ḥusayn is in this city (and not in Cairo).[99] This particular detail is indicative of the intersection between geographical relevance and the symbolic value of earthly remains and graves, which directs the narrative towards historically unreliable conclusions. Observed within a larger context of upholding the orthodoxy of geography, this could be interpreted as involving 're-evaluation and sometimes rewriting of the past'.[100]

In a way similar to the precedence of Medina centring on the Prophet's grave, intercession is also related to a believer's death in its vicinity. However, even the event of death had different categories of virtue; death in the righteous war (*jihād*) is highly esteemed, which is why Imām-zāda discusses a possible combination of two types of death: death in Medina while being engaged in *jihād*.[101] While prophetic intercession could not be spatially limited, one of the narrations ordered the precedence of those in Medina for obtaining intercession first, after which came the inhabitants of Mecca and Taif.[102]

Intercession also extended to those who visit the Prophet's grave, according to the narration saying that one who goes on pilgrimage and visits the grave after the Prophet's death is like one who visited him in his lifetime;[103] this narration is amplified by others emphasising the Prophet's sentience (ability to hear, recognize and respond) even in the grave.[104] Such ordering of narrations implies interest in the question of *baraka*, or the possibilities offered by the interacting prophetic body to believers.[105] The sentience of

[99] MS 0719, fols 59a–59b.

[100] Ahmed El Shamsy, 'The Social Construction of Orthodoxy', in *The Cambridge Companion to Classical Islamic Theology*, ed. by Tim Winter (Cambridge: Cambridge University Press, 2008), p. 109.

[101] MS 0719, fol. 8a.

[102] This hadith was introduced without reference to an authoritative work; see fols 9a–9b.

[103] MS 0719, fol. 11a.

[104] MS 0719, fol. 11b.

[105] 'Muhammad's grave enables access to baraka, whether baraka should be understood here as a force emanating from the remains of Muhammad's materiality or divinely awarded credits earned for approved devotional acts'. Michael Muhammad Knight, *Muhammad's Body: Baraka Networks and the Prophetic Assemblage* (Chapel Hill: The University of North Carolina Press, 2020), p. 143.

other people buried in the graves of Medina is emphasised as well, especially on certain days, such as Fridays.[106]

Finally, the treatise also suggested other ways in which visitors should be drawn to Medina, based upon an array of hadith narrations related to all the beneficial characteristics of the city that might help believers in different aspects of their lives. Thus, the treatise is peppered with hadith related to the curing aspects of its dust,[107] its safety, even in the last days of time, because the one-eyed creature named Dajjāl will not enter the city, and its resistance against plague (*ṭāʿūn*). By quoting al-Samhūdī (d. 1505) who suggested that some scholars tried the dust of Medina to heal fever and confirmed that the news about its healing powers were correct,[108] Imām-zāda fortified his argument on the common benefits of residing in Medina.

While the preference for Medina could be justified based on reasons connected to the Prophet's life and death, as well as the *hijra*, Imām-zāda had to envision a way to locate Medina in relation to other places of spiritual and soteriological value for Muslims. In accentuating the virtue of Medina, Imām-zāda had to present its superiority by comparing prayer in the mosque of this city to the validity of prayers in other sacred cities. The comparative element in the *faḍāʾil* overlaps with its insistence on hierarchy: Mecca is almost always posed above Medina in terms of the benefits and blessings to be earned, which is why al-Masjid al-Ḥarām is positioned above the Prophet's Mosque.[109] Still, the power of prayer is used in another direction as well: Imām-zāda mentions prayers to encourage greater love towards Medina rather than Mecca.[110] At the same time, however, the author is careful about instructions related to the physical approach to the Prophet's grave and kissing it because that would interfere with customs connected to approaching the qibla.[111] Yet, Medina and the Prophet's Mosque were consistently

[106] MS 0719, fol. 55b.

[107] MS 0719, fol. 5b.

[108] MS 0719, fol. 6a.

[109] MS 0719, fol. 12a.

[110] MS 0719, fol. 9b.

[111] MS 0719, fol. 35b. While offering different types of narrations elsewhere, the author is keen on careful distinguishing between licit and illicit actions of devotion on that site and invokes the authority of the ulama on the issue.

positioned above Masjid al-Aqsā,[112] which completed the canonical triad of mosques.[113]

Conclusion

Over the course of a mere two centuries following the Ottoman conquest of Bosnia, scholars such as ʿAlī-dada al-Būsnawī, ʿAbdullah al-Būsnawī and Ḥasan Imām-zāda participated in the creation, upholding and maintenance of the Ottoman Empire's early modern spatial culture focused on Mecca and Medina. Sets of different mechanisms were sometimes instigated by Ottoman political necessities, as we could see from the example of ʿAlī-dada's chiliastic vision of the holy places. At the same time, upholding the holy places went beyond top-down pressure: places were venerated, not because it was an imperial order, but because their virtue and merit was based on a set of soteriological and cosmological arguments enhancing salvation in the other world and benefit in this one. This was done through the emphasis on virtue pertaining not only to these cities, but also to the loci inside, such as Maqām Ibrāhīm and the Black Stone. The virtue – often expressed by, but not limited to, the word *faḍl* or *faḍīla* – was bestowed to the place by God or the Prophet. The places, still, had human characteristics, even when they subverted the human-centric hierarchy, as we could see in ʿAbdullah al-Būsnawī's treatise.

This spatial discourse was indeed created to encourage and inspire people to go on pilgrimage to Mecca and *ziyāra* and *mujāwara* in Medina. In this way, these treatises also contributed to the devotional culture of the period, as diverse as it was and marked by imperial, Sufi or scholarly discourses. Their mediative role was layered: between the believers and the transcendent, royal families and holy places, and between early modern Ottomans and their intellectual and spiritual predecessors.

What ʿAlī-dada al-Būsnawī, ʿAbdullah al-Būsnawī and Ḥasan Imām-zāda shared is the active role in constructing sanctity through different but compatible textual means and genres. They used the form of *faḍāʾil* as part of their

[112] MS 0719, fol. 13a.

[113] On debates about the hadith referring to these three mosques and other devotional places see M. J. Kister, 'You Shall Only Set out for Three Mosques'.

treatises as the primary genre dealing with the virtue of a place. More specifically, the Qur'anic verses, the hadith, as well as excerpts from chronicles and prophetic biographies formed the major textual tool for promoting the virtue of a place and constructing the *faḍā'il*.

In more ways than one, premodern Ottoman Bosnian authors participated in the period's shared culture and they contributed to it as well. Their treatises established a discourse for the time to come. What happened when believers heeded the call to visit the holy places? The next chapter looks at a different mode of Hajj writing that marked the seventeenth and eighteenth centuries, which will take us from relatively static sacred spaces to the dynamic transitoriness of the journeys undertaken by Ottoman Bosnians.

2

THE ROADS TO MECCA

As elite Ottoman Bosnians belonged to multiple places, the pilgrimage equally belonged to their native society. Even though going on the Hajj was an unreachable goal for most Ottoman Bosnians, the pilgrimage was deeply embedded in society in a variety of ways. Its presence in the imagination as well as the emotional and spiritual attachment to it were continuously nurtured, not only through the social prestige that returning Hajjis accrued through the coveted title of Hajji, but also, and even more persistently, in the way in which textual and visual material mediated believers' aspiration to the sacred. Depictions of Mecca and Medina in manuscripts called *dalā'il al-khayrāt* circulated in great numbers, bringing an almost palpable presence of the sacred places into Bosnian homes and cultivating believers' devotion to the Prophet in domestic settings.[1] Other material objects from the Hijaz helped to nurture not only the emotional, but also the sensorial connection: perfumes, oils and eye make-up were some of the most desirable items that Hajjis brought from the pilgrimage.[2] Some material objects linked believers

[1] On the role that the *dalā'il* works played in domestic devotions in the early modern Ottoman period, see Jonathan Parkes Allen, 'Sanctifying Domestic Space and Domesticating Sacred Space: Reading Ziyāra and Taṣliya in Light of the Domestic in the Early Modern Ottoman World', *Religions* 11/2 (2020), p. 59.

[2] Rašid Hajdarović, 'Medžmua Mula Mustafe Firakije', *Prilozi za orijentalnu filologiju* 22–23 (1972), p. 308.

to both the holy places and the other world – for example, the shroud (*ihram*, the cloth also worn by pilgrims), as well as the outer cover (*ćuburtija*)[3] were directly connected to the performance of the pilgrimage and the cycle of life.

Apart from figuring in material culture, the pilgrimage was made visible to local Bosnians in the annual succession of farewell and greeting ceremonies for Hajjis. The flow of Hajjis from Bosnia was not steady throughout the Ottoman period, and the numbers varied according to factors beyond the control of individual believers: wars, plague and Bedouin raids on pilgrim caravans all affected the physical mobility of the Hajjis and shaped the expectations of Bosnian Muslims. The rich and the learned were more likely to go to the Hijaz, but, as we will see, those less privileged also managed to travel great distances and emerge from the depths of anonymity thanks to that feat.

One of the main sources for retracing the paths of Ottoman Bosnians is the *mecmua* (collection of texts, scrapbook) of Mula Mustafa Bašeskija (1731–1809). Over the course of several decades, Bašeskija listened to the rhythm of the city, noting not only the mundane, but also the unusual and out of the ordinary: *pehlivan*s that levitated in the air, artificial horses with eyes in the shape of the letter ن, fireworks that amazed the spectators. The Hajj, too, was woven into the inner workings of city life. Among many Hajj-related events in Bašeskija's *mecmua*, one stands out as it combines the interest in the unusual and gives us insight into the Hajj of the less privileged. In 1777, a group of rowdy men was sitting in one of the Sarajevan coffee houses, listening to music and enjoying themselves. Coffee houses were notorious as places of potential subversion; yet, probably for most visitors they were spaces of socialisation and sometimes transgressed the dividing line between home and public.[4] Perhaps it was that kind of ambiguity and transgression of rules that made one of the young men euphorically announce that they should all sell their property, decide to go on the Hajj, help each other and leave matters to God! The others were puzzled: going on the Hajj was not a common endeavour, even in

[3] Muhamed A. Mujić, 'Jezičke i sadržinske osobenosti vakuf-nama iz Mostara (druga polovina XVI stoljeća)', *Prilozi za orijentalnu filologiju* 25 (1975), p. 217.

[4] Alan Mikhail, 'The Heart's Desire: Gender, Urban Space and the Ottoman Coffee House', in *Ottoman Tulips, Ottoman Coffee: Leisure and Lifestyle in the Eighteenth Century*, ed. by Dana Sajdi (London, New York: I. B. Tauris, 2007), pp. 133–70.

Sarajevo. There were years when only one Hajji would set off on the journey, and the vast majority of those who managed to reach the holy lands of Mecca and Medina had financial or at least significant social capital. It was not that the feat was impossible for others – some managed to go to the Hijaz as *badals* multiple times. Yet, the Hajj was no ordinary journey, and it involved taking enormous risks concerning life and property: in the late nineteenth century, decades after Mula Mustafa Bašeskija had died, the Hajj journey could end up in losses of almost half of the pilgrims as result of epidemic diseases.[5]

The men in the coffee house were swept away by the idea to go on the Hajj at a moment's notice. They solemnly declared: '*Hoćemo li? Hoćemo!* (Shall we go on Hajj? Yes, we shall!)'. The news quickly spread around Sarajevo. The *ikrār* prayer, which announces the intention of a future Hajji to go on pilgrimage, was recited for each one of them, and they left the city. However, the man who had initiated the idea, a person by the name of Kasapović (Kassāboglı), escaped the city in ignominy, because he had been in debt.[6] The entire event, even though it minted some pilgrims, was met with puzzlement: the Hajj was not supposed to be associated with lies and deceit, and people in debt were not supposed to think of such ideas. Despite Kasapović fleeing the city in dishonour, the rest of the Hajj party made their way to the Hijaz. While they fade away into the unknown pages of history, by looking at contemporary sources on the Hajj, we can partly reconstruct how they travelled as Bosnian pilgrims, what they possibly experienced and what significance they ascribed not only to the places, but also to the journey itself.

Unlike the previous chapter, which focused on the meanings that Bosnian elite scholars attributed to the holy places of Mecca and Medina and the pilgrimage itself, this chapter shows how the Hajj was experienced by Ottoman Bosnians, by examining their itineraries and travelogues. The two perspectives offered by these two chapters are compatible: the plethora of meanings constructed by scholarly texts that were mostly, but not exclusively, of Sufi provenance, created a ready *habitus* of symbols and imagery for common

[5] Younis, 'Smrtni slučajevi tokom hadža u Mekku'.

[6] *XVIII. Yüzyıl Günlük Hayatına Dair Saraybosnalı Molla Mustafa'nın Mecmuası*, ed. by Kerima Filan (Sarajevo: Connectum, 2011), p. 130. For an in-depth thematic study of Bašeskija's mecmua, see Kerima Filan, *Sarajevo u Bašeskijino doba: Jezik kao stvarnost* (Sarajevo: Connectum, 2014).

practitioners to fall back on. Diverse pilgrims used these frameworks, which helped cultivate their devotions and emotional reactions. At the same time, the Hajj journey brought pilgrims in close bodily contact with the world itself, out of which they created new meanings. Yet, the search for meanings should not obscure the fact that, for many pilgrims, the very act itself of journeying and performing the rituals was enough – it was the act of obedience that moved people to traverse long distances from Bosnia to the Hijaz.

The pilgrims' journey started long before physically setting onto the road. To paraphrase Richard McGregor's insistence that the Hajj is (also) locally grounded,[7] it began on the streets of Sarajevo as much as in Mecca and Medina. It began with the embeddedness of the Hajj in the local Bosnian setting, through visual and material objects, as well as through its presence in religious discourse and oral culture. The textual discourse on the Hajj was not solely created by scholars through legalistic, spiritual or hadith literature of the kind discussed in the last chapter. The Hajj was, perhaps increasingly so over time, becoming a matter of interest to non-ulama members of Bosnian society as well. Traders, merchants and anonymous persons with a bit of Ottoman Turkish penned their guidebooks to the Hajj throughout the eighteenth century, describing the journey and suggesting what a future pilgrim might expect. The ulama – which did not constitute a compact social group, as it is usually thought – actively contributed to the discourse through travelogues and poetry, among other genres.[8] The *mecmua*s, scrapbooks with various texts that were sometimes passed on over generations, often contained prayers for the Hajj and instructions for pilgrims on a range of issues and in two languages: Arabic and Ottoman Turkish.

[7] McGregor, *Islam and the Devotional Object*, p. 20.

[8] The sharp differentiation between the ulama and other social groups in premodern societies often leads to artificial differentiations of normative and lived, with the assumption that the former – the ulama – acted in opposition to the practices of the vast majority of premodern Muslims. As it is possible to observe through the examination of Hajj literature, the ulama was not creating solely prescriptive material. Also, the existence of normative material, such as guidebooks, reveals much about the practices of people who were not religious scholars yet contributed to the development of the Hajj *habitus*.

The cultivation of knowledge about the pilgrimage also coexisted with different types of devotions: the above-mentioned *dalāʾil al-khayrāt* works combined devotion to the Hijaz and the Prophet; during their journey, Hajjis visited the tombs of famous shaykhs on the way, thus performing pious visits or *ziyāra*. The ability to combine multiple modes of devotion should not be seen as being in contradiction with the Hajj itself: collecting blessings and meeting pious and learned people was part and parcel of the premodern journey, and these did not displace the importance of Mecca and Medina. Nor did attention to the journey's mundane elements – such as food, water and shelter – decrease the value of the holy journey: the body is, after all, the major tool of religious practice.[9]

Before turning to the Hajj journeys of Ottoman Bosnians, the next section will investigate types of material that circulated and shaped their expectations, making the pilgrimage present in palpable form, even in the lives of those who were not mobile.

The Habitus of the Hajj

The Hajj often began in the mosques, libraries and *tekke*s of Bosnian cities and towns, as people read, wrote, copied, uttered and looked at images, texts and words depicting the holy places. One did not even have to be literate to learn about the Hajj: pictures of Mecca and Medina were sometimes painted on the walls of mosques, such as the Mišćina Džamija in Sarajevo, which was decorated by the local artist Mustafa Faginović towards the end of the nineteenth century.[10] Faginović translated his long-time engagement with another genre – the *dalāʾil al-khayrāt* – onto the walls of the mosque, a work that remains until today (Fig. 2.1 and Fig. 2.2).[11]

[9] 'Believers carry the holy and the sacred all the time within them in a particular corporeal format. It is both outside and inside their bodies' (Verrips 2008, in Birgit Meyer, 'Media and the Senses in the Making of Religious Experience: An Introduction', *Material Religion* 2/4 (2008), p. 130.

[10] Mehmed Mujezinović, *Islamska epigrafika Bosne i Hercegovine* 1 (Sarajevo: Sarajevo Publishing, 1998), pp. 273–74.

[11] Enes Halimić, *Iz mape Faginovića* (Sarajevo: Bošnjački Institut – Fondacija Adila Zulfikarpašića, 2010), p. 12.

Figure 2.1 A detail on the walls of Mišćina džamija depicting Medina. Photo by Merjema Karić.

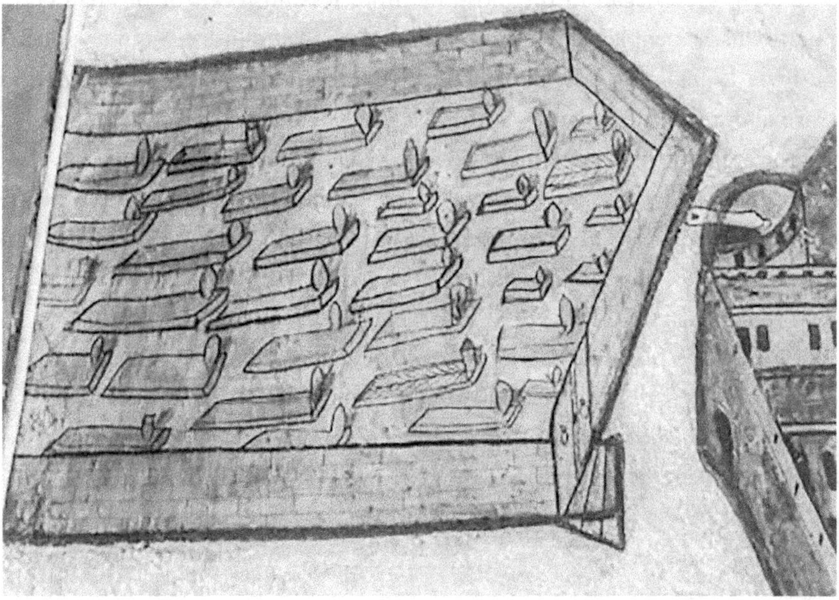

Figure 2.2 A detail on the walls of Mišćina džamija depicting al-Baqīʿ graveyard. Photo by Merjema Karić.

The *Dalāʾil al-khayrāt*, a collection of prayers originating in the fifteenth-century Maghrib, was immensely popular throughout the Ottoman domains, and its widespread popularity also led to the creation of numerous commentaries directed at its learned population.[12] The distinctive characteristic of the *dalāʾil al-khayrāt* were the images of Mecca and Medina; the first locale brought the viewers into the presence of the Hajj, an experience far out of reach for most, and the second drew them into the presence of the Prophet, to whom much of the premodern Ottoman devotion was directed. Copies of the *dalāʾil* were present in family libraries, as well as in *tekke*s and madrasas. A nineteenth-century copy of the *dalāʾil al-khayrāt* from Sarajevo shows the line of female ownership far into the twentieth century.[13] As seen in the example of Mustafa Faginović, some Bosnians illustrated *dalāʾil al-khayrāt* copies, probably for local devotees; one example is the calligrapher Ibrāhīm ibn Muhammad (Ibrahim Šehović) who drew Medina in a copy that reached the Bosnian chronicler Muhamed Enveri Kadić (1855–1931).[14]

The Hajj encompassed a string of connected devotional practices, oriented towards the Prophet, but also towards saints and scholars along the pilgrimage route. As the Hajjis themselves participated in the creation of knowledge about these devotions, they referred to the books they had read along the way. The books that pilgrims brought home indicated a strong interest in devotional practices along the way: in 1758, while passing through Damascus, Hajji Halil-efendi Gračaničevi bought a *mecmua* containing ʿAbd al-Ghānī al-Nāblūsī's (1641–1731) treatises, including one on Ibn ʿArabī's grave located in the same city.[15]

[12] Guy Burak, 'Collating *The Signs of Benevolent Deeds*: Muḥammad Mahdī al-Fāsī's Commentary on Muḥammad al-Jazūlī's *Dalāʾil al-Khayrāt* and Its Ottoman Readers', *Philological Encounters* 4/1–2 (2019), pp. 135–57.

[13] *Katalog arapskih, turskih, perzijskih i bosanskih rukopisa*, edited by Lejla Gazić (Sarajevo: Orijentalni institut Sarajevo, 2009), p. 39.

[14] See his copy of the codex containing different devotional material in GHB R2569; Mehmedović, *Leksikon bošnjačke uleme*, pp. 470–71.

[15] As shown by Nir Shafir, the somewhat controversial reception of the Ottoman state initiative to promote Ibn ʿArabī's tomb found at least one prominent Arab supporter in al-Nāblūsī. Shafir, 'In an Ottoman Holy Land'.

The enormous undertaking of the Hajj has always produced a conglomerate of texts that aim to aid, support and promote the pilgrimage. It is not surprising, then, that most of the preserved manuscripts related to the pilgrimage belong to *manāsik* literature, written in Arabic or Ottoman Turkish, which discusses the ritual from its legal side and explains the rites according to the Hanafi perspective. Thus, Ottoman Bosnians read the *manāsik* works that circulated in other parts of the empire, too: *Manāsik al-ḥajj* by Sinanuddīn Yūsuf b. Ya'qūb ar-Rūmī al-Ḥanafī existed in multiple copies, some of them copied by Bosnian scribes such as Muḥammad al-Travnikī, 'Alī Rušdī b. Muḥammad al-Būsnawī in Sarajevo in 1814, Hajji Ḥasan b. Ya'qūb from Zagora in 1593, 'Abdullah Naẓarī b. Aḥmad Burek Ghazghānī, in Sarajevo in 1794, his son Aḥmad al-Mukhtārī b. 'Abdullah al-Naẓarī Burek in 1828 and Ibrāhīm b. Muḥammad Hadžiosmanović in 1848. Another *manāsik* copy from the eighteenth century is *Bayān fī manāsik al-ḥajj* (prepared in Tešanj in 1783).[16] Ottoman Bosnians also wrote the *manāsik* for the local population: Abdulwahāb al-Būsnawī (d. 1791 in Egypt), a teacher and imam in Mecca, wrote *Manāsik al-ḥajj* and sent a copy to Bosnia.[17] *Adā' manāsik al-ḥujjāj* written by Ibrāhīm al-Būsnawī in 1792 was another such work.

As the previous chapter showed, the Hajj had to be promoted. As one of the five crucial duties of Islam, the Hajj stood as a blueprint for obeying God's orders, but at the same time reflected concerns regarding ethical living; it also prompted a feeling of belonging to a larger community. One example will show how the pilgrimage was presented to Bosnian audiences. In *Muḥarrik al-qulūb* (*The Mover of the Hearts*), a mid-seventeenth-century exhortative work treating a range of topics, Aḥmad Mu'adhdhin-zāda al-Mostārī dedicated a part of the treatise to the Hajj. In less than twenty pages within the fourteenth, fifteenth and sixteenth chapters of the larger collection of sermons, the author combined the Abrahamic origins of the rituals, narratives on the uniqueness of the Prophet's community (*ummat Muḥammad*), cautionary warnings about what happens when one ignores the

[16] Several of the listed works were destroyed during an attack of the Army of Republika Srpska on the Oriental Institute in Sarajevo in May 1992. The information on the Bosnian copyists and authors of the *manāsik* works in this paragraph was taken from the unpublished bibliography of Hajj manuscripts and published works collected by Osman Lavić.

[17] Mehmedović, *Leksikon bošnjačke uleme*, p. 7.

pilgrimage and miraculous stories as well as the virtues of Mecca and Medina in order to incite people to perform Hajj. The pilgrimage was presented as a crucial duty which, if neglected without good reason, could lead one to die in a state similar to that of a Jewish or Christian person,[18] an idea that has been used as caution by Muslim scholars for many centuries. Yet, despite the pilgrimage being an essential duty that could determine one's ultimate fate, the Hajj itself was bound to a framework of moral obligations that preceded it: people had responsibilities to their families and society, which came before the performance of the pilgrimage. More than a sign of blind obedience to the divine, the Hajj was implicated in the network of other relations to oneself and others. The pilgrimage also depended on the right intention of the believer. Muʾadhdhin-zāda thus delineated ways in which the purpose of the Hajj could be appropriated by worldly goals: trade, the opinion of other people, or amusement. While the form of the pilgrimage might be fulfilled, it was the ethical core that must never be ignored, and it was defined in relation to other people through the debts and obligations which come to the fore.

So how was the ethical core of the pilgrimage revealed? The author suggested moving beyond the form and looking at the essence itself. This understanding of the Hajj was in line with the Sufi underpinnings of the work: the Hajj of the body (*ḥajj al-abdān*) happened only once per year and was considered to be the pilgrimage of the rich (*ḥajj al-aghniyā*). The Hajj of the heart (*ḥajj al-qulūb*) happens every hour (*fī kull al-sāʿa*), and it pertains to the gnostics (*al-ʿurafā*).[19] The value of the heart is higher than that of the Kaʿba even: Muʾadhdhin-zāda emphasised that the people look at the Kaʿba, but God looks at the heart.[20] By stressing the spiritual dimensions of the pilgrimage, Muʾadhdhin-zāda was actually offering alternative ways for those unable to go on pilgrimage themselves.[21]

[18] R-3731/5, fol. 2a.

[19] R-3731/5, fol. 2a.

[20] R-3731/5, fol. 2a.

[21] As such, the form-less Hajj described here is comparable to other Hajj discourses in which the inability to perform the pilgrimage led to its sublimation as a tenet of the belief rather than 'a critical aspect of [. . .] religious practice'. Kristian Petersen, 'Routes of the Hajj Pilgrimage: Belief, Practice, and Performance', in *Interpreting Islam in China: Pilgrimage, Scripture, and Language in the Han Kitab* (Oxford: Oxford University Press, 2017), p. 101. The distance from the holy places and the inability to perform the Hajj often led to an increase in substitution rituals; see Petersen, *Interpreting Islam in China*, pp. 106–9.

Ultimately, the Hajj as a journey was marked by its arduousness, as well as the distance that had to be traversed. This also implied the vastness of the Muslim community and their geographical expansion. So how did Ottoman Bosnians perceive their relative remoteness in relation to the Hijaz? An anecdote in the *Muḥarrik al-qulūb* reveals how Ottoman Bosnians positioned themselves not only in relation to the holy places, but also towards their fellow Muslims. To demonstrate the sacrifice that the pilgrimage necessitates, Muʾadhdhin-zāda narrated a famous story about the encounter between the scholar Abū al-Qāsim b. Yāsīn from Khorasan and an elderly man who came from a faraway unnamed land. As they circumambulated the Kaʿba, the old man asked the scholar about Khorasan, his homeland. Upon hearing that it only took two or three months to reach Mecca, he responded in astonishment, asking why people living in Khorasan do not perform the pilgrimage every year, and added the following verse:

> Visit your beloved no matter the distance,
> Even should veils and screens come between you.[22]

It is not difficult to understand why this particular narration would be embedded in a work meant to popularise the Hajj. If we replace Khorasan with Bosnia, we might receive roughly the same answer – performing the pilgrimage was not absolutely impossible, even every year. The excerpt is also indicative of the Islamic geographies that were not only known, but also constituted an inseparable part of the larger affective imaginary of the religion.

Finally, the authors and compilers of Hajj literature produced and consumed in Bosnia were aware of their geographical remoteness from the perceived core lands of Islam. They were aware of the physical and financial difficulties that prevented most of the Bosnian population from going on the most desired journey. That is why they thought of substituting acts that could benefit the believer in the same way as the Hajj. It is tempting to think that writing was deemed one such act.

[22] R-3731/5, fol. 10a.

And this is where we will start: through an exploration of the world that the Ottoman Bosnian Hajjis experienced and described on their way to Mecca and Medina. As Bosnian Hajjis navigated routes, places and their own fragile bodies, they also left several accounts through which we can reconstruct how they mediated the pilgrimage to their contemporaries. Written in Ottoman Turkish, these travelogues, logbooks and notes scribbled in *mecmuas* reveal the ongoing devotion to the holy places, as well as the importance of the *manāzil* on the way there and back. While pious commitment was cultivated by the elaborate habitus of texts and images, the pilgrims discovered the world through their senses as well. The tangible world was revealing itself to the Hajjis, and they were not discovering it alone.

Setting Off on the Voyage

If we return to the story about the Hajj group from the Sarajevan coffee shop about which Bašeskija told us, Kasapović's ignominy partially lay in him deserting his friends. The Hajj was a long and arduous journey; choosing the right company could literally save one's life in times of thirst and hunger. Hajjis also bonded over shared experiences and forged close friendships. And while we do not know much about Ottoman friendships,[23] a close connection to literate friends was probably one of the motifs for writing about one's pilgrimage experiences. It was often the case that the authors referred to their friends in Bosnia who were eagerly waiting for news about their journey, or they even dedicated to them sections of the travelogue, much like poems.[24]

[23] A relatively recent study points to some of the aspects of male friendships in the early modern Ottoman period, through the prism of dreams. Asli Niyazioglu, *Dreams and Lives in Ottoman Istanbul: A Seventeenth-Century Biographer's Perspective* (London, New York: Routledge, 2016).

[24] Jusuf Livnjak, one of the authors discussed in this chapter, ends the pilgrimage narrative with a poem for his friend Zamîrî efendi. The fact that he mentions the poem as a gift (*yâdigâr*) to his friend indicates the increased importance of male friendships in autobiographic literature. For more on friendships in autobiographical literature, see Cemal Kafadar, 'Self and Others: The Diary of a Dervish in Seventeenth Century Istanbul and First-Person Narratives in Ottoman Literature', *Studia Islamica* 69 (1989), pp. 121–50.

However, one thing was certain: many of the Bosnian authors of travelogues and itineraries were writing for a local audience, sometimes narrowly confined to one's own family circle.[25] The travelogue of Jusuf Livnjak (d. after 1647), written in 1616 and possibly the earliest extant Bosnian Hajj narrative, shows this rather clearly. Although the beginning of the travelogue – the Prophetic blessings and the usual introduction – was written in Arabic, the author soon switched to Ottoman Turkish which was used throughout the narrative. He stated his intention to describe places of rest, sites of general interest that could be seen on the way, and places of visits to God's friends (*awliyā*). The choice of language was not surprising: despite a rising tide of writing in the local Bosnian language and in Arabic script, many Bosnians used Ottoman Turkish as the primary means of written communication. The language was present in the public and acquired through education and religious instruction; it was ubiquitous in judicial and administrative matters, as well as trade. One also had the opportunity to learn Ottoman Turkish in *tekke*s or libraries.[26] Thus, it would not be inconceivable to imagine Livnjak writing a Hajj travelogue for his friends in Bosnia. The influence of the local language was still visible in some terms he used; for example, he used a Bosnian word for June, *Lipanj*. The local resting stops for pilgrims mattered, as did the places further along the journey, and Livnjak was quite specific when naming Bosnian places, emphasising at some point even his own village ('Županja Potok').

While popular stories played a relevant part in his travelogue, Livnjak was not overly cautious when narrating religious traditions related to the places that he saw on the Hajj. Places triggered the recountings of religious narratives, especially those connected to early Islamic history. In this sense, Livnjak's narrative served multiple functions: it was a guidebook for future pilgrims, a compilation of short narratives about Islamic or Ottoman history, a description of events and environments, as well as a self-narrative in which the author showed his passive and active participation in the experience of places together with his companions.

[25] One Ottoman Bosnian Hajji, Mustafa Novalī from the eighteenth century, even wrote a note about leaving the travelogue in possession of his family, stating that it must not be sold; R-10310, fol. 4a.

[26] Kerima Filan, 'Turski jezik u osmansko doba', *Anali GHB* 43/35 (2014), pp. 151–78.

Hajjis often travelled with family members and people they knew. Livnjak, who was a local *mujezin* in Duvno, was engaged in trade as well,[27] which made him a rather well-connected person who was welcomed on his journey through Bosnia. Jusuf Livnjak often mentioned by name his companions, including his brothers, and included them in his narrations but did not delve into more elaborate depictions, unless something extraordinary, such as a death, occurred.[28] While crossing Bosnia, Hajjis stopped in familiar places, visiting friends who bid farewell to them in the small villages through which they passed, showing their embeddedness in 'the labyrinthine network of companionship spun by a group of individuals neither of whom the diarist cares to singly depict or analyze'.[29] Yet, Hajjis most certainly enjoyed company and used the opportunity to frolic: in an eighteenth-century itinerary of a certain Boro-efendi from Foča, the pilgrims stopped somewhere on the road and tried to weigh themselves against a tree. Boro-efendi diligently marked the weight of each pilgrim and said that they stopped when a branch broke under the weight of a particularly corpulent member of the group.[30]

On the Journey

We can only speculate how Bosnian Hajjis felt about themselves as a distinct group within the vast sea of other pilgrims. While they usually started their journey in Bosnia – some, like Mustafa Mukhliṣī, on whom more later, began the journey from the place where they were serving as officials – they would pass through some of the larger cities on the Balkans, noticing monuments such as a bridge in Kosovo and a mosque in Plovdiv built by Sultan Murad. For some of them, such as Jusuf Livnjak, the arrival in Edirne was enthralling, because the Hajjis manage to see Sultan Selim's Mosque and climb the

[27] Mehmedović, *Leksikon bošnjačke uleme*, p. 305.

[28] The analysis of the travelogue was based on the copy existing in the chronicle of Enver Kadić (R-7303). The travelogue was translated into Bosnian in 1981: Hadži Jusuf Livnjak, *Odazivam Ti se, Bože . . . – Putopis sa hadža 1615. godine*, trans., intro. and comment. by Mehmed Mujezinović (Sarajevo: Starješinstvo Islamske zajednice u SR Bosni i Hercegovini, Hrvatskoj i Sloveniji, 1981).

[29] Kafadar, 'Self and Others', p. 148.

[30] Boro Efendi, *Manāzil min Foça ʿan Makka Mukarrama*, GHB, R-10309, 2, fols 3a–3b.

stairs of its minarets. Farther along, the Hajjis would encounter Istanbul, whose centrality in their imagination was undoubted – or at least it was conventionally posited as such, as in the short remark given by the author: 'One cannot describe with the tongue or with the pen the beauties of the city of Istanbul'.[31]

Bosnian Hajjis usually passed through Istanbul and then either took the land route together with other Ottoman pilgrims, or they embarked on a ship across the Eastern Mediterranean which would take them to Alexandria and then Cairo. As for Jusuf Livnjak, after reaching Istanbul, his Hajj group crossed the Mediterranean to Alexandria and continued onwards to Cairo. While in Cairo, the author mentioned visiting different sites, such as the castle of the Copts.[32] In Cairo, he visited a certain Altı Parmak efendi, of whom he gives no further information, apart from saying that he saw him a couple of times. Altı Parmak efendi had been born in Skopje, and there is reason to believe that Jusuf Livnjak visited him because they came from the same geographical region.[33] That Livnjak had a certain predilection for places that showed a link to the Balkans is shown sporadically in the travelogue, as in a remark about tombs in the Meccan graveyard Muʿalla.[34] Livnjak specifically divided those whose gravestones mentioned the name 'Rūmī' (indicating that they had belonged to the Balkans or Anatolia). His listing of the seven Rūmī scholars in Mecca might be a sign that Livnjak only wanted to emphasise their geographical origins, without knowing anything about their scholarly or spiritual merit.

In Cairo, the Hajjis joined the pilgrim caravan for another sea journey across the Red Sea towards the Hijaz. Sometimes, Hajjis would also go on a sea journey via Dubrovnik and Venice and then onwards to Cairo.[35] Through these itineraries, Hajjis had a chance to encounter and perhaps interact with non-Muslims. Jusuf Livnjak mentions seeing the 'unbelievers' vessels.[36] The journey was long and arduous, and they had to rely on their own little group,

[31] R-7303, p. 182.

[32] R-7303, p. 188.

[33] R-7303, p. 189.

[34] R-7303, pp. 202–3.

[35] Husić, *Hadž iz Bosne za vrijeme osmanske vladavine*, p. 73.

[36] R-7303, p. 179.

as well as on the extensive Ottoman administration of the Hajj. The knowledge of Ottoman Turkish, which in Bosnia was widespread also outside of scholarly circles,[37] certainly helped them along the way. Knowing Arabic would have been even more useful, and some Bosnians could get by with colloquial expressions: the eighteenth-century qadi Mustafa Mukhliṣī noted the use of '*mā fish* (there is none)', probably as result of some exasperated exchanges with the locals on the market.[38]

Judging by the later travelogues from the print era, Bosnian Hajjis also visited other Bosnians who resided in the great cities of the empire. Hajjis would often encounter a random Bosnian *mujāwir* (resident of Mecca and Medina) while on pilgrimage.[39] The ties of mutual recognition in an unfamiliar world worked also across confessional lines: in one eighteenth-century case, Bosnian Christian pilgrims told of their encounter with a Bosnian Muslim soldier in Jerusalem, who excitedly took them out for coffee.[40]

Friendships were important, but so were the communities with which the pilgrims associated themselves. Even before the nineteenth century and the rise of Muslim intellectuals who promoted the idea of a unified Muslim World, Hajjis felt that they belonged to a greater body of believers marked by specific practices. At the beginning of his travelogue, Jusuf Livnjak stated the purposes of his journey, which were hierarchically ordered to indicate a particular type of Prophet-oriented belonging:

> Thanks be to God who made me closer to the Prophet's Mosque and with his generosity allowed me to reach Ahmad's qibla and brought me to visit the graves of God's friends who are perfect and perfected. They are friends of God and the Prophet's deputies. Blessings be upon the Prophet – the one for whom God said, 'if it were not for you (I would not create the heavens),' and

[37] Filan, 'Turski jezik u osmansko doba', p. 170.

[38] Bağdatlı Vehbi 1024, fol. 18b.

[39] R-7303, p. 204.

[40] *Sveta zemlja u srpskoj književnosti od XIII do kraja XVIII veka*, ed. and trans. by Tomislav Jovanović (Belgrade: Čigoja Štampa, 2007), pp. 26–27; see also Wendy Bracewell, 'The Limits of Europe in East European Travel Writing', in *Under Eastern Eyes: A Comparative Introduction to East European Travel Writing on Europe*, ed. by Wendy Bracewell and Alex Drace-Francis (Budapest, New York: CEU Press, 2008), p. 68.

> his descendants who are the fruits of kings and his followers who are distinguished by the usage of *miswāk*.[41]

The passage above indicates the centrality of the Prophet to the way in which Jusuf Livnjak, his fellow Bosnian travelers and possibly many other Ottoman Hajjis conceived of their spiritual belonging. From the sixteenth century onwards, Ottoman devotional practices focused on the Prophet, 'at the fertile intersection of love and power'.[42] The previous chapter showed some of the mechanisms that situated Medina, as a place that the Prophet had loved, at the centre of scholarly attention, which relied on a range of textual sources including the hadith. Here, however, we can see the trickling down of that discourse into the imagination of the Hajj itself, through references to the famous *ḥadīth qudsī* – 'If it were not for you, Muhammad, I would not have created the heavens' – and the practice of using the toothbrush (*miswāk*), a practice that indicated following the Prophetic example.

The excerpt also points to something else. The Hajj was imagined as a multi-layered journey that also included visits to God's friends and kissing the hands of *awliyā* and pious people.[43] On their Hajj journeys, Bosnian pilgrims often spent considerable time – even several months – in Damascus and Cairo, to recuperate and prepare for the onward journey,[44] and because these were holy places due to the many tombs of the prophets, *awliyā* and ulama, which Hajjis eagerly wanted to visit. To many a modern observer, the fact that *ziyāra* and the Hajj coexisted and were attended by many Ottoman pilgrims presents a conundrum that has to be observed in terms of contestation. Yet, as we will see, for Bosnian and many other Ottoman pilgrims, *ziyāra* was not a force competing with the Hajj: the two held complimentary, yet different roles during a pilgrim's journey, each different in terms of the form, intent and significance ascribed to them.

[41] R-7303, p. 175.

[42] Gruber, *The Praiseworthy One*, p. 255.

[43] R-7303, p. 175.

[44] Husić, *Hadž iz Bosne za vrijeme osmanske vladavine*, p. 68.

Pious Visitations

Hajjis visited renowned places of *ziyāra* on the way to the Hijaz and back, and their exact itinerary depended on the route taken. It seems that *ziyāra* was an integral part of the pilgrimage in the Ottoman period; some, such as the famous Sufi thinker Abdulghānī al-Nāblūsī (1641–1731), even embarked on the Hajj journey almost a year in advance so as to be able to visit all the places of visitation.[45] Recent studies suggest that the Ottoman administration actively encouraged *ziyāra* practices and even invented new ones, such as the visitation to the tomb of Ibn ʿArabī in Damascus.[46] Somewhat akin to medieval Christian pilgrims' collection of souvenirs from different holy places, Hajjis also strove to visit as many holy people as possible, living or dead.

What did places of *ziyāra* mean to their visitors? In her work on medieval pious visitations, Daniela Talmon-Heller suggests that *ziyāra* was, among other things, a joyful experience.[47] These places did not require a defined behaviour, and they were prone to a certain randomness: one could choose where to go and in what order. People would read the Qur'an and pray, meet other people and share food. Women were also present, albeit sometimes criticised for their purportedly frolicking behaviour.[48] Yet, the air was certainly permeated by holiness: people went to graves and tombs because their inhabitants in life had proven themselves through their steadfastness, ascetism, miraculous deeds and perceived closeness to God. In that sense, this coexistence of the holy and the mundane was natural for visitors, including learned ones, since 'in their minds – as mirrored in the biographical and theological works they have produced – knowledge of religious lore (*ʿilm*), successful intercession with God and with secular powers (*shafāʿa*), and spiritual

[45] Elizabeth Sirriyeh, *Sufi Visionary of Ottoman Damascus: ʿAbd al-Ghanī al-Nābulusī 1641–1731* (London and New York: Routledge), p. 97.

[46] Shafir, 'In an Ottoman Holy Land'.

[47] Daniella Talmon-Heller, *Islamic Piety in Medieval Syria: Mosques, Cemeteries and Sermons under the Zangids and Ayyūbids (1146–1260)* (Leiden, Boston: Brill, 2007), p. 181.

[48] Hoda Lutfi, 'Manners and Customs of Fourteenth-Century Cairene Women: Female Anarchy versus Male Shar'i Order in Muslim Prescriptive Treatises', in *Women in Middle Eastern History: Shifting Boundaries in Sex and Gender*, ed. by Nikki R. Keddie and Beth Baron (New Haven, London: Yale University Press, 1991), pp. 114–16.

metaphysical powers (*baraka*) were interconnected, intertwined, and even organically tied to each other'.[49]

Hajjis did not come unprepared. As seen from Livnjak's travelogue, the pilgrims visited living ulama and Sufi shaykhs, as well as the tombs of the dead. As the narrative progresses, it becomes clear that Livnjak's travelogue at the same time serves as a specific *ziyāra* guide, like the genre that had existed in the Islamic world since the ninth century.[50] Different religious and historical narratives were interwoven in his notes about the significance of a particular holy person. This is particularly the case in Livnjak's treatment of Ottoman and, more generally, Islamic history, especially regarding the early Muslim conquests.[51] In many ways, the previously acquired textual knowledge shaped the way in which places were observed. For example, as the Hajjis passed through Gallipoli, Livnjak noticed how two of the regional saints, the brothers Meḥmed and Aḥmed Bīcān Yazıcıoğlu, were buried there. When describing this, Livnjak listed their works titled *Muḥammediye* and *Anwār al-ʿāshiqīn*. Apart from their role as authors of influential works, Livnjak pointed out that they were also performers of wonders, known to the 'people of Unity' (*ahl al-tawḥīd*).[52] The places of *ziyāra* were also liable to temporal organisation, which dictated the days on which it would be more rewarding to visit the graves.[53]

Considering that the largest part of Livnjak's travelogue was dedicated to *ziyāra* and that he put considerable effort into giving an informed description of the locations, we are compelled to unearth what the practice meant for him. Livnjak mentioned people and tombs renowned both locally and

[49] Daniella Talmon-Heller, ''Ilm, Shafāʿah, and Barakah: The Resources of Ayyubid and Early Mamluk Ulama', *Mamlūk Studies Review* 13/2 (2009), p. 18.

[50] See more in Christopher S. Taylor, *In the Vicinity of the Righteous: Ziyāra and the Veneration of Muslim Saints in Late Medieval Egypt* (Leiden: Brill, 1999), pp. 5–7.

[51] R-7303, p. 182.

[52] R-7303, p. 179; on these two brothers and the enormous influence that their works had in shaping early modern Ottoman piety, see Carlos Grenier, *The Spiritual Vernacular of the Early Ottoman Frontier: The Yazıcıoğlu Family* (Edinburgh: Edinburgh University Press, 2021).

[53] Apart from marking dates, Livnjak is also concerned with explaining different ceremonies related to saints. For example, he mentions that captains (*keştibân*) would not start a journey without visiting the grave of a certain Veli-dede; R-7303, p. 180.

more widely in the Ottoman Empire. As in the case of Imām-zāda's *faḍā'il*, one of the primary reasons for visiting these sites was their role in the process of intercession. Among the prominent sites that Livnjak mentions is the mosque of Sayyida Nafīsa, a descendant of the Prophet's family, whose intercession for enslaved non-Muslims he stresses.[54] Miraculous deeds happened due to the intercession of other *awliyā* as well, such as Aḥmad al-Badawī.[55] To increase this saint's significance, Livnjak mentioned a number of central cities to which his fame had spread: Cairo, Quds, Sham, Ka'ba (Mecca), Medina and others.[56] The *mawlid* in Tanta had attracted people from different social strata for centuries. Jusuf Livnjak's interest in Aḥmad al-Badawī and the wish to convey information about him to his Bosnian readers are testaments to the notion that premodern Ottoman religiosity was more receptive to different spiritual influences, which later was curtailed by the modernist disdain for the 'popular', in contrast to the scriptural.[57]

Intercession was closely related to another motive – that is, blessing. In that respect, *baraka* (blessing) could be juxtaposed to the Christian concept of *praesentia*, where blessing was mobile together with the physical remains of the saint. The Muslim view of sanctity of the grave prevented *baraka* from being dispersed across different spaces.[58] What Livnjak and his fellow Hajjis seem to have sought was immobile blessing, related to a place more than to a holy person's body. These places were not just of local importance, and Hajjis from all over the world sought to visit them.

There was also a certain kind of overlap between visits paid to the *awliyā* and to prophets. The local *awliyā* graves were mentioned together with the graves of prophets.[59] In both categories, figures from popular and Qur'anic

[54] R-7303, p. 185.

[55] R-7303, p. 185.

[56] R-7303, p. 184.

[57] For more on the *mulid* in Tanta, see Catherine Mayeur-Jaouen, *The Mulid of Al-Sayyid Al-Badawi of Tanta: Egypt's Legendary Sufi Festival* (Cairo: American University in Cairo Press, 2019).

[58] Taylor, *In the Vicinity*, pp. 54–55.

[59] R-7303, p. 180; Prophet Daniyal's grave is mentioned twice, in relation to Rodos and Alexandria (R-7303, p. 181). It seems that the author was not sure which one was the true location.

lore appeared, as well as stories about their supernatural capabilities, the most obvious example being Livnjak's remark on Dhū al-Qarnayn,[60] a mysterious figure often identified as Alexander the Great. Jusuf Livnjak describes his sealed treasure as out of reach for anyone.

An important category of *awliyā* whose graves were visited by Livnjak and other Ottoman pilgrims were the ulama. Livnjak's wish to map and localise the existence of a network of authorities who were no longer alive led him to suggest the connection between some scholars and mystics, even when they were not buried in Qarāfa. Thus, for example, he elaborated on the connection between Farīd al-Dīn ʿAttār (d. 1220 in Nishapur) and Cairo.[61] Even more strikingly, he suggested that Ibn ʿArabī was buried in Qarāfa[62] when, in fact, he was buried in Damascus. This mistake on Livnjak's part is considerable, because Ibn ʿArabī's grave was rebuilt a century before Livnjak wrote his travelogue.[63] Ibn ʿArabī was further mentioned in the context of *tawḥīd* remembrances and other gatherings, as well as for having followers in Yemen, Mecca, Medina and other parts of the Muslim world.[64]

Although Livnjak's goal was to present places of *ziyāra* primarily for their soteriological value, he occasionally tried to confirm the claims he had heard about the shape or height of a certain tomb by physically experiencing it through touch or sight.[65] The experiential was valued more than the textual – it confirmed

[60] R-7303, p. 182.

[61] R-7303, p. 184.

[62] R-7303, p. 186.

[63] It seems that there was a certain ambiguity regarding the exact burial place of other saints, too. The most popular figure of all female saints, Rābiʿa al-ʿAdawiyya, appears in Livnjak's travelogue during his stay in a place called Rābi' Eshme/Rābigh. As the Bosnian editor of the translation noted, the grave of Rābiʿa is not there; Livnjak, *Odazivam Ti se, Bože*, p. 47. Nevertheless, it is important to remember how the reference to Rābiʿa al-ʿAdawiyya appeared also in ʿAlī-dada al-Būsnawī's *awāʾil* as part of the description of the women from Sultan Süleyman's household, which might be explained by the symbolic weight carried by the name of this female mystic and the image of the saint as a spiritual ideal.

[64] R-7303, p. 186.

[65] Similar interest in measurements can be seen from other travelogues, such as the anonymous traveler from Travnik who described the Hagia Sophia and Sultan Süleyman's mosque. R-4342, fol. 1b.

the presence of the pilgrim and the veracity of the claim.[66] The religious historical narrative was thus permeated by remarks about the pilgrim's experience on his way to Mecca and Medina. The dead and the living were not separated; the memory of the former was sustained by the latter, while the dead had the possibility to offer blessings for those who paid their respects to them. For Livnjak, the stories and narratives about the early Muslim community were intertwined with the extraordinary experiences that some Hajjis had when encountering the places where some of the first battles of Islam occured. At one point during the journey, while approaching Medina, Livnjak says that his group of Hajjis and their camels heard eery sounds of drums and the neighing of horses, which scared them, made them halt and spend the night there.[67]

Places of Highest Importance

While seeking intercession and blessing was a primary motive for visiting tombs during the journey, Livnjak also sought out general places where prayer was accepted. This can be found in the focus of Livnjak's descriptions of Mecca and Medina, which list in detail not only the places of crucial religious significance (such as the Kaʿba), but also places of *ziyāra* to the figures of early Islamic community. While he naturally perfomed the rites, he did not describe them in any elaborate detail, rather preferring to focus on describing the inscriptions on Meccan buildings. Still, he composed a poem for the holy precincts in several parts, where he delineated the main sites important for a visitor to Mecca: the Kaʿba, minarets, domes and madrasas, Maqām Ibrāhīm and the Zamzam well. The poem started with praise to the Lord and the Prophet, after which the author mentioned his four companions who had been chosen because they mentioned God plenty.[68] The poem further on described the importance of the five pillars of Islam, with a special focus on the Hajj. Ignoring the Hajj, as Livnjak says, is dangerous

[66] One is reminded of Nasir Khusraw's famous depiction of the well in Jerusalem where one could allegedly hear the screams of those in hell. In his laconic way, Nasir Khusraw simply stated that he heard nothing. Nasir-i-Khusrau, *Diary of a Journey Through Syria and Palestine*, trans. and ann. by Guy Le Strange (London: Palestine Pilgrims' Text Society, 1893), p. 26.

[67] R-7303, p. 207.

[68] R-7303, p. 194.

and exposes one to the risk of dying like a Christian or a Jew.[69] Yet, in order to show how Mecca's environment is universally beneficial, Livnjak tells his readers how non-Muslims also visit this city secretively to drink Zamzam water and how the latter helps everyone but hypocrites.[70]

The *ziyāra* places of Mecca are distinguished by their symbolic hierarchy: the text lists the house of the Prophet, the houses of ʿAlī and Khadīja, and the birthplace of Fatima. The narrative is interwoven with longer historical narratives, including ones that focus on the Abrahamic past centred around Prophet Ibrāhīm and his son. Still, the author's attention always switches back to the description of the *ziyāras*.[71] In this regard, the historical framework in the narrative serves as a prelude to the key point, which is arguing for the value of the place and a presentation of the ways in which prayer is accepted there. Thus, for Livnjak, the place's holiness needed to be textually reconfirmed.

Places of *ziyāra* in Mecca and Medina were sites where one went to for a specific reason (for example, to find a lost camel), but even more so sites where pilgrims learned about the early Islamic community. Everything, starting from the Prophet's house to the hand mill of his daughter Fatima, merited the pilgrims' attention. Pilgrims were interested in places where various miraculous and mundane events related to the Prophet had occurred: the site where the Prophet split the moon, as well as where he sold his personal items to help pay for the burial of the poor. Apart from visits to objects and sites related to the Prophet, Livnjak and his companions visited graveyards in both cities, seeking out not only the tombs of the famous Companions, but also of scholars and Sufi shaykhs. Death levelled all differences: Hajjis paid respects to female members of the Prophet's family, making some of the tombs very popular. In Medina, Livnjak visited the grave of the Prophet's wife ʿAisha and described her role not only as the Mother of the Believers (*Umm al-muʾminīn*), but also as a woman-mufti.

Most modern Bosnian pilgrims would probably find themselves strangers to many of the places and practices mentioned here. The twentieth century,

[69] R-7303, p. 195.
[70] R-7303, p. 199.
[71] R-7303, p. 201.

as we will see in the following chapters, irrevocably broke some of the spiritual and spatial links that existed in the Ottoman period; this is perhaps true for pilgrims from other regions as well. With the rise of nation-state borders, the shared languages of *ziyāra* and their bountiful narratives were also pushed into the background. But for Ottoman Bosnians, the worlds of the Hajj were more than pathways of obedience to God's command. Pilgrimage involved moving in spaces of varied sanctity, which allowed them to collect blessings from saints and to ask for favours. The Hajj journey also enabled pilgrims to accrue benefit from paying visits to scholars. Yet, all of this happened in a demanding space, a space that required exertion and effort and helped the Bosnian Hajjis to position themselves in relation to the world.

Places and Senses

Hajjis were firmly embedded in the world around them. Many recent studies deal with objects characteristically associated with Hajj-related ceremonies, such as such as the *maḥmal* (palanquin) or *kiswa* used during imperial processions,[72] as well as the consumption of materials such as *zamzam* water.[73] While research on devotional objects in Islam has increased in volume, it is primarily those objects recognized as 'Islamic' that are at the centre of attention. In a range of innovative approaches, they are observed as contested, in flux of meaning, prone to appropriation and challenging the normative discourse. What seems to be missing is the turn to the mundane and unassuming objects, materials and human encounters that constitute the devotional and religious experience, and that 'have observable effects and affects as they resonate beyond their physical limits in producing and manifesting feelings, concepts, changes, and affirmations'.[74]

These objects, materials and spaces of mundanity – such as food and water for humans and animals, shelter from Bedouin attacks and sights and sounds of the pilgrimage journey – all contributed to the overall religious experience.

[72] McGregor, *Islam and the Devotional Object.*

[73] Anna M. Gade, 'Twelve Zamzam Water: Environmentality and Decolonizing Material Islam', in *Islam through Objects*, ed. by Anna Bigelow (London: Bloomsbury Academic, 2021), pp. 189–204.

[74] Ana Bigelow, 'Introduction: Thinking with Islamic Things', in *Islam through Objects*, pp. 8–9.

While, as we could see in the previous chapter, Hajjis developed and assigned a range of meanings to the pilgrimage and while many of those spread among premodern believers from all walks of life, the Hajj, as a journey and as a ritual, was not imagined solely as an abstraction. It was very much a matter of pilgrims' bodies, a palpable and often difficult experience that engaged all the senses by way of lack or excess. As this section will show, Hajjis undertook the journey while carrying with them the memories of the places that they had left behind. In other words, as pilgrims came closer to Mecca, Bosnia appeared more frequently on their mind as a site of comparison and longing.

Before we turn to see how Bosnian Ottoman pilgrims experienced the Hajj, something has to be said about the habituation: did bodily and sensorial experiences shape the world of the Hajj – that is, the literal places of Mecca and Medina, as well as places along the journey? Or were sensorial experiences also predicated by previous conceptions and imaginations of people and spaces? The answer probably implies both: the Hajj was primarily experienced through the senses, but the senses were not neutral, and in order to process the events and circumstances of the journey, the pilgrims had to rely on what was already familiar to them.

To shed light on these questions, we will look at the eighteenth-century travelogue by Mustafa Mukhliṣī, a qadi who served in numerous places on the Balkans and went on the Hajj in 1748, when he was serving in Ağriboz in modern-day Greece. Mustafa Mukhliṣī was a relatively well-known author in the eighteenth century: apart from his Hajj travelogue in verse, he also wrote a poem in praise of Hekimoğlu Ali-pasha after his victory over the Austrians in 1737, in Turkish, Arabic and Persian, and he also penned poems mostly of romantic and satirical nature. The date of his death is unknown.[75] His works remained in some circulation across the empire: the travelogue *Dalīl al-manāhil wa-murshid al-marāḥil* (*A Guide to the Springs and an Adviser on the Stations of a Journey*) was relatively popular in Bosnia, as seen from several remaining copies of his work in the Bosnian archives. A copy of his work is also found in Istanbul, and an edition of the work was published in Isparta

[75] Omer Mušić, 'Hadži Mustafa Bošnjak-Muhlisi', *Prilozi za orijentalnu filologiju* 28–29 (1973), p. 89.

in 2007.[76] In comparison to Livnjak's travelogue, which was mostly in prose, Mukhliṣī's travelogue was in verse, possibly intended for a more educated readership than was the case with other Hajj travel writers from this period.[77]

Mustafa Mukhliṣī's itinerary was somewhat different from Jusuf Livnjak's. Mukhliṣī started his journey in Istanbul and took a 'fast ship' to Cairo, passing by islands such as Rodos. Mukhliṣī returned by land and passed through Damascus. Like Livnjak, Mukhliṣī saw visits to religious sites in various locations, such as Cairo and Damascus, as one of the key motives for pilgrimage. However, in Mukhliṣī's account the prevailing focus was on the circumstances of the journey which included observing people on the Hajj route and commenting candidly on the harsh environment that affected their mobility.

Much like Livnjak's narrative, so does Mukhliṣī's also begin in prose in Arabic, as he describes the reasons behind writing his travelogue.[78] The first reason he mentions is to inspire people to perform the Hajj rituals if they are able to, as well as to encourage them to obtain the state of everlasting forgiveness and felicity for visiting the Prophet. The travelogue, according to Mukhliṣī, also offers an explanation and description of the blessed places and the wonders that lead to the reflection of Divine Power, as well as a warning to those who are about to set off on this glorious journey, so that they would be aware that the resting places require caution because of the trickery of unruly Bedouins and immoral robbers. Finally, the travelogue aims to serve as instruction on what Hajjis should be aware of regarding food and drink because, according to Mukhliṣī, to ignore these matters is to throw one's soul into forbidden dangers. The last rationale was followed by a quotation from the Qur'an (al-Baqara, 195): '. . . and make not your own hands contribute to your destruction'.[79]

[76] Menderes Coşkun, *Bosnalı Muhlis'in Manzum Seyahatnamesi: Delîlü'l-Menâhil ve Mürşidü'l-Merâhil* (Isparta: Fakülte Kitabevi, 2007).

[77] Another author who wrote about Mukhliṣī is Muḥammad al-Arnāʿūṭ, 'Ṣūrat Makka al-Mukarrama fī riḥlāt al-ḥajj lil-bashāniqa: numūdhaj al-shāʿir Muṣṭafā al-Busnī', in *Dirāsāt fī al-ṣilāt al-ʿarabiyya al-balqāniyya khilāl al-tārīkh al-wasīṭ wa-l-ḥadīth* (Bayrūt: Jadawel, 2012), pp. 173–83.

[78] Bağdatlı Vehbi 1024, fol. 1a

[79] Translation by Yusuf Ali.

In accordance with this stated framework, Mukhliṣī started his travelogue with an explanation of the wisdom behind God's command to perform the Hajj:

ḫudâ'dur mûcid-i ecsâm u a'râż
Mu'allel hiç değül fi'li bi'l-aġrâż.[80]

God is the Creator of bodies and accidents
His actions with aims are not distorted.

Heme ef'âli mebnî ḥikmet üzre
Her iḥsânı ḳula bir hikmet üzre

All His good deeds are based on wisdom,
All His goodness to the slave is based on wisdom.

God's wisdom encompasses all the creation, and it is by His decree that they become physically manifested:

Vuḥûş u ṭayr u hem ferzend-i Âdem
Vücûda geldi bir lafẓıyla 'âlem.

Wild beasts and birds and all descendants of Adem,
With one word of His, the world came into being.

The lofty beginning went hand-in-hand with the stated mundane purpose of the pilgrimage account: to help future pilgrims and others, for the common good.[81] Mukhliṣī describes how his poem will be an inseparable guide (*delîl*) for Hajjis during the journey. Apart from using the word *delîl*, the author employed the term *mürşid*, which corresponds to the title of the travelogue. This word – its primary meaning is 'guide' – is also used in the context of Sufi guidance, which adds a further layer to the framework of the narrative.

[80] Transliteration according to Menderes Coşkun's edited version of the travelogue.
[81] Bağdatlı Vehbi 1024, fol. 1b.

As soon as the formalities of the introduction were over, Mukhlişī could focus on the physical progress of the journey, starting with the description of Rūm:

İdüp ṭayy-ı meraḥil Rûm iliden,
Bilür vaṣfını ṣorsan her deliden.

Were you to travel through Rumelia, and on your way
Asked anyone, they would all know about its qualities.

What was present in Livnjak's narrative as occasional reference to Rūm is now present in Mukhlişī's travelogue to a much fuller extent. Descriptions of Rūm and, more importantly, its comparison and contrast to other parts of the empire are dominant throughout the first part of the travelogue. The impulse to draw local connections, however, goes further and seems to create an additional spatial division in the narrative. Mukhlişī, apart from mentioning Rūm, also mentions Bosnia as a separate entity, which is especially evident in the following verses:

Diyâr-ı Bosna'nuñ âb u havâsı
ḳarâbetle olur Rûm âşinâsı
Velî Rûm'un bilâd ile ḳurâsı
ġanîdür Bosna'dan mîr ü gedâsı

The water and air of the lands of Bosnia
Is closely similar to those of Rūm,
But in the land and villages of Rūm,
Both the leaders and the paupers are wealthier than those in Bosnia.

While Mukhlişī did not actually start his journey from Bosnia, since he served as judge in Ağriboz, it is possible that the author actually meant the area that he saw on the way from this city to Istanbul. In some ways, his references to Bosnia in this context are still significant, because they point to the importance of belonging and the connection to Bosnia cultivated even by those who had built their careers outside of it. In many ways, the image of Bosnia assumes centrality even when Mukhlişī is in Mecca:

Bilâd-ı Bosna'dan 'aşk-ı ḥaḳîḳî
Olup bu Muḫliṣ'a ni'me'r-refîḳı

The true love from the lands of Bosnia
has been a good friend to this Mukhliṣī.

While not with the same intensity, places where blessings could be found were still important to Mukhliṣī. The recounting of the Hajjis' arrival in Gallipoli, as in Livnjak's travelogue, stressed the importance of the Yazıcıoğlu brothers' graves[82] and confirmed that, even a century later, visits to these graves still took place. Some of the places through which the Hajjis passed were probably chosen for logistical reasons; yet, visiting them also meant collecting blessing, hence the previously acquired spatial knowledge prepared the pilgrims for the sights. Readers were also expected to be familiar with Qur'anic spatial references, such as 'the city of Irem', or 'Alexander's dam', used abundantly throughout the travelogue. Akin to a modern-day guide, the descriptions were peppered with tidbits of history and common lore, with a special focus on the Ottoman history of places, mostly related to conquests, and sometimes even referring to pre-Ottoman Bosnian history.[83] These narratives sometimes frame how the place is seen and are utilised for instructing the readers. Thus, when describing a place called Tih Banī Isrā'īl, a place where the Jews had allegedly wandered in the desert for forty years, Mukhliṣī explains:

Çü bir ḳavm ola Mevlâ'sına 'âṣi
olur elbet o ḳavmüñ şûm cezâsı

Because if a people are disloyal to their Master
Their punishment becomes [being] cursed.

The descriptions of places tend to get even shorter and more cryptic at some point:

[82] Bağdatlı Vehbi 1024, fol. 2b.

[83] At one point, Mukhliṣī refers to Ahmed-pasha, who was a member of the Bosnian royal family during the Ottoman conquest. Bağdatlı Vehbi 1024, fol. 34b.

Bulâğ u Mıṣr'a geldük seyr ü ârâm ü temâşâsı
güzel amma değül lâzım dimek elfâ-ẓı lev-lâsı

We came to Bulak and Cairo, we rested and observed
it is beautiful but does not invite the phrase 'lev-lā'.

It seems that Mukhliṣî was trying to refer to the famous *hadīth qudsī* called '*lawlâka*' ('if it were not for you, oh Muhammad, I would not have created the universe'); in a peculiar intertextual twist, he tried to show his lack of enthusiasm upon seeing Cairo, because to Mukhliṣī it seems that nobody should utter this phrase of excitement regarding the city. This candour also turns into full-scale prejudice, probably fueled by the experiences with the Bedouins which the Hajjis had on their journey:

Bilâd-ı Mıṣr u şehr-i Mıṣr'a söz yok cümledür âbî
eğer olmazsa esvâḳında rîg ü rûy-ı A'râbî

There is no word to be said to Egypt and Cairo in whole,
if it were not for the dust and faces of the Bedouins on the markets.

The stereotyping of people such as Bedouins or Circassians,[84] once again, points to the difference between Livnjak's and Mukhliṣī's depictions of people and places. Mukhliṣī's negative stereotyping could be due to the fact that there was increased insecurity for Hajj caravans after the Habsburg-Ottoman war of 1683–99, which led to a periodical loss of control over the pilgrimage route.[85] Mukhliṣī could thus have reacted out of simple fear, as reflected in the progress of his narrative: when not constituting obstacles along the way, the Bedouins are presented in a positive light. For example, when visiting a place called Hudayra, Mukhliṣī mentions that the Bedouins are courteous in demeanour and conduct (*edeb üzre ḳu'ûd ve hem selâmı*).

The images of places were tied to the people encountered along the way, which also reflects the symbiotic relationship between the pilgrims and the

[84] See, for example, description of Circassians in BağdatlıVehbi 1024, fol. 3b.
[85] Faroqhi, *Pilgrims and Sultans*, p. 53.

local population. Mukhliṣī's observations usually revolve around the existence of suitable conditions in the area (water, food), animals (those which are helpful, *ṣâlih*) and the behaviour of people (evil, mean, helpful, or *munâfiqûn*, that is, hypocrites). Even the descriptions of regions such as Sham are critical of the locals, projecting the common anxiety caused by the Bedouins' frequent attacks on Hajjis.[86] Yet, their generosity or hostility were not the only markers. The awareness of ethnic and linguistic differences is evident throughout the narrative, but it excludes any political connotation in the modern sense. Thus, while describing Antakya, Mukhliṣī notes that there are no Arabs in this city and adds that people are good there.[87] The author also notes the existence of other ethnic and linguistic groups, such as Kurds, presumably distinct from the rest of the Turkish population in Anatolia.

Pilgrims were not only at the mercy of the locals, but also endangered by the harsh conditions of nature. Staving off death sharpened their senses beyond vision: water was the most valuable resource, with Hajjis discerning between sweet, bitter and suitable only for animals. Water was not available everywhere: Hajjis sometimes collected rain, or they drank it from dubitable wells and got sick. Apart from looking for nourishing food such as meat, milk, wheat, bread and fat for themselves, pilgrims also searched for grass for their horses. The animals were also vulnerable to mishaps on the rugged terrain, which could endanger the journey. Sometimes, pilgrims could obtain popular items, such as halwa, biscuits, dates, pomegranates, watermelons and 'pleasant smelling lemons'.[88] Since Hajjis were responsible for their own upkeep, we can only imagine how the less wealthy among them fared.

As pilgrims passed through the rough terrains of the Ottoman Hajj pathways, it seems that images of Bosnia consistently lurked in the background. Sometimes Mukhliṣī compares the rough terrain through which he and his fellow pilgrims were passing with the Bosnian mountains:

[86] Thus, for example, the author describes how a number of Hajjis were killed and ascribes that to actions of the people of Sham. Bağdatlı Vehbi 1024, fols 25a–25b.

[87] Bağdatlı Vehbi 1024, fol. 27b.

[88] Bağdatlı Vehbi 1024, fol. 8a.

Memerr-gâh-ı cibâl-i Bosna ṣa'bî
değül bu rütbede 'unvân ta'abı.

Mountainous passages of Bosnia are difficult
But they are not known to be this cumbersome.

Yet, the journey had enjoyable sides, too. In a manner similar to Evliya Çelebi, Mukhliṣī liked to comment on the appearance of the locals, especially those who were kind to the Hajjis, using the common poetic imagery of fair girls and handsome youths.[89] For example, the people of Istanköy were described as 'those who were given beautiful shape by the Giver'.[90] Women also appear in certain contrasting images such as, for example, the description of Adana,[91] where the author juxtaposed pretty women with ruby lips with unruly Kurds and Turkmen. That Mukhliṣī was not always generous with his compliments is attested by the description of women and men from Eskişehir, whom he calls plain in appearance.[92] Although premodern Hajj literature did not often discuss women (unless in religious stories or concerning the regulation of pilgrimage practices, as seen in the previous chapter), the image of women as weaker beings does appear in the context of the Kurdish attacks on the Hajjis:

Memerr-gâhında olur merd çün zen
Heme eṭrâfda Kürdân-ı reh-zen.

In the passage men became like women,
With Kurdish brigands all around.

How was the pilgrimage journey different from being in the holy places? Like Livnjak, Mukhliṣī changed his narrative when he reached Mecca, signifying a textual break when entering the new, hierarchically superior space. Mukhliṣī praised the city and emphasised its special status of seniority and respect. The spatial hierarchy was transmitted onto the city itself, with the Ka'ba being

89 Bağdatlı Vehbi 1024, fols 23b–24a.
90 Bağdatlı Vehbi 1024, fol. 2b.
91 Bağdatlı Vehbi 1024, fol. 29a.
92 Bağdatlı Vehbi 1024, fol. 33b.

elevated as the most important part of Mecca for its role in intercession and forgiveness.[93] Further on, the Prophet was deemed the ultimate intercessor, thus making Medina a place of soteriological value because of that virtue. The poem that Mukhliṣī composed for the Prophet paralleled the one in praise of the Kaʿba, and the focus of the journey turned to the hope of intercession, instead of observations about the material circumstances of the journey.[94] In contrast to the journey to Mecca and Medina, the return journey was rarely described in detail.

Away from the glories of sultanic service, Sufi heights and scholarly circles, these Hajj narratives show us religiosity on the move. The mundanity and arduousness of the journey was an integral part of the search for blessings along the way. In a peculiar way, the premodern Hajj journey was far from the touristic pursuit of modern-day travelers: while curiosity was an inseparable element of the experience, it was channeled towards understanding the miraculous aspects of God's creation. This understanding was expressed in the word '*aca'ib*', meaning astonishing and wondrous, often repeated on the pages of Mukhliṣī's travelogue.

Conclusion

The last chapter showed how Bosnians created a Hajj discourse for scholars dispersed across the empire and sometimes in the service of the empire. Not neglecting the range of meanings ascribed to the ritual, this chapter turned to the Hajj as it was experienced during the journey. The Hajj of the Ottoman period was a gigantic project that fostered a number of adjacent devotional practices: owing to their geographical position, Bosnian Hajjis could move from their province to multiple centres, managing their bodies in places of wonder and mundanity.

The travelogues of Jusuf Livnjak and Mustafa Mukhliṣī indicate that Hajjis wrote about their experiences for the public at home. Some of these writings remained in family possession, carefully treasured for decades, only to be lost in the mayhem of the twentieth century. The tradition of writing about the Hajj for local and sometimes very narrow audiences would

[93] Bağdatlı Vehbi 1024, fol. 11b–12b.

[94] Bağdatlı Vehbi 1024, fol. 13b–14b.

remain constant in the centuries to come, as will be seen in the following chapters.

The geographical position of Bosnia meant that Hajjis used several routes – the land route and the sea route, sometimes combined, to see several cities that held importance in the Islamic imaginary and played different roles that were not mutually exclusive. These places were both sites of travellers' interests and places where they could receive blessing (*baraka*) because of the graves of the saints and holy figures. For the pilgrims, the Hajj was thus a wholesome project, made once in a lifetime and probably the longest journey that they would undertake in their entire life.

The journey also presented an educational opportunity. Apart from the blessings that Hajjis could accrue by visiting the dead and the living, travelers could direct their readership to material objects and buildings and further add to the Hajj's presence in the lives and lived environment of Ottoman Bosnians. The Hajj enabled 'ways in which a sense of place or space transcended the local, reaching toward the wider region and beyond its horizons'[95]; however, it also strengthened the relationship between the local Bosnian population and the vast Muslim world beyond. This relationship was not a given. The unwieldy universe of devotional literature and works supporting the Hajj in its various aspects testify to the ongoing need to pull the Hajj and its related spaces closer to the Bosnian readership.

The exhortatory literature also indicates underlying anxieties about the motivation of Hajjis who might allow worldly concerns to interfere with their religious duty. In a manner that doubtlessly appealed to many a premodern Hajji, *Muḥarrik al-qulūb*, the treatise in favour of the pilgrimage mentioned at the beginning of this chapter, repeatedly warned against these dubious impulses that make one embark on a journey. According to the author, Aḥmad Muʾadhdhin-zāda al-Mostārī, people, and especially the wealthy, should not go on the Hajj for the sake of fun of sheer wonder and frolicking (*nuzha*, *sayr*, or *tafarruj*). The Hajj was not for flimsy-minded and whimsical individuals, like Kasapović from Bašeskija's chronicle. The next chapter will illustrate how this warning assumed new relevance in the modern age.

[95] Ronit Ricci, *Islam Translated: Literature, Conversion, and the Arabic Cosmopolis of South and Southeast Asia* (Chicago: University of Chicago Press, 2011), p. 265.

3

CHANGE

Are there slaves on Arabian markets? Is it true that prostitution is rampant in Jeddah's dens of vice and debauchery? What is the meaning of Islamic rites? What do Hajjis *really* do in Mecca and Medina? These questions seemed to be ubiquitous among the fierce Yugoslav public of the interwar period, together with debates on Muslim women's clothing and education, the plausibility of translating the Qur'an into local languages, or seemingly more mundane discussions on the permissibility of the gramophone. In the decades following the Austro-Hungarian occupation of Bosnia and Herzegovina in 1878, the annexation in 1908 and the period of the Kingdom of Yugoslavia (1918–41), different facets of Islamic belief and practice were opened to scrutiny, not only in the local Bosnian press, but also in Serbian and Croatian publications. This caused anxieties and tensions over who had the right to interpret and (re)present Islam. The Hajj was a frequent topic of these debates which drew in Muslim and non-Muslim participants engaged in defining and describing Islam and its role in the society.

This chapter will address the encounter of ritual and print within the framework of change, by examining the presence of the Hajj on the 'market of news', the importance of Islamic geography in the light of new local and global dynamics, and the transformation of the Hajj ritual's meaning in the late nineteenth and first half of the twentieth century. To do so, it will shift back and forth between different decades to highlight these specific issues.

Unlike the previous chapters, where the focus was on premodern Ottoman Bosnians, sometimes in conversation with their Muslim scholarly predecessors or contemporaries, this chapter will feature Bosnian Muslims in argument with each other, their non-Muslim critics, Orientalists, ideological enemies or, simply, broader competing concepts of various backgrounds that imposed themselves on the way in which the Hajj was perceived. The media, understood here as both genres and venues of publication, created new possibilities for different participants in the public sphere, but at the same time flattened the discourse under the influence of homogenising and reifying modernist discourses on Islam. Paradoxically, the more the Hajj became a real possibility in terms of both mobility and writing, the more it became a contested issue in terms of its meaning and significance.

Interwar Debates on the Hajj

In the mid-1930s, the growing reading audiences could follow a fierce debate raging across several travelogues and reportages, some of which were published in instalments, allowing the readers to intrude with questions of their own. The person who sparked the debate was Ismet Varatanović (d. after 1948), a journalist and Hajji, who briefly emerged from the depths of interwar anonymity with his critical writings on the Hijaz published in the Sarajevan newspaper *Jugoslovenska pošta* and the Serbian daily *Vreme*. The content of his writings, as well as the venues where he published his travelogue, sparked a debate that points to the fault lines surrounding the Hajj in the modern age: the decline of its value to mere tourism, the exoticisation of Hajj travel and the emphasis on the binary of decline and progress that has been used ever since to give meaning to the Hajj not only as a religious duty, but also as an event with social repercussions.

Ismet Varatanović wrote about his Hajj experience in 1933. He described his disillusionment with the state of things in the Hijaz and the existence of slavery, corporeal punishment and prostitution there; tied to poverty, this presented a grim view of the post-Ottoman Kingdom of Saudi Arabia and the state of the pilgrimage and the pilgrims themselves. Descriptions of decay and neglect could be a normal part of any travelogue, but in the Hajj narrative they resonated differently. Apart from the generally unspoken *adab* rule that whatever inconvenience happened during the pilgrimage should not be talked about, Varatanović's sin was that he divulged whatever did or did not happen in the Hijaz (his critics had their suspicions) to a wide and dangerous readership. There were multiple problems with Varatanović's Hajj publication: it confirmed stereotypes of an unchanging and decadent Muslim East inclined to sexual depravity and slave ownership, and it also offered the Hajj as one morsel in the banquet of other news, turning it into a touristic endeavour with no intrinsic value superior to other types of travel.

Varatanović's critics were Muhamed Krpo (1897–1965) and Ibrahim Hakki Čokić (1871–1948), members of the Bosnian interwar ulama and public figures themselves; they replied to Varatanović with their own respective travelogues. Raised and educated under Austro-Hungarian rule, Krpo and Čokić moved in the world of changing forms of literacy. They were fluent in German, apart from Turkish and Arabic, and Čokić even became a professor of Arabic after passing his exam in Vienna in 1904.[1] Both of them, however, also lived through the post-imperial turbulences of the Kingdom of Yugoslavia (Kingdom of Serbs, Croats and Slovenes from 1918–29), with its progressive state limitation on the autonomy of Muslim religious representative bodies. This state of crisis was especially prominent during the '6 January Dictatorship' imposed by King Alexander I (1888–1934) in 1929, which aimed to practically put the Islamic religious community under the direct control of the Ministry of Justice in Belgrade and thus strip the Bosnian ulama of any power they might exert from Sarajevo.[2] As the ulama critical of the regime was removed from their posts and, like *Raīs al-ʿulamā* Džemaludin Čaušević (1870–1938), sent into retirement, Belgrade emerged as a place that attracted pro-Serb Muslim politicians and public figures. Apart from this centripetal pull of Belgrade, the ulama and intellectuals of the interwar period – and, indeed, any Bosnian Muslim living in the post-imperial world – had to reckon with Serb and Croat nationalist forces that exerted themselves not only through state pressure, but also through educational and cultural institutions.[3]

[1] Mehmedović, *Leksikon bošnjačke uleme*, p. 96.

[2] See more in Denis Bećirović 'O položaju Islamske vjerske zajednice u Kraljevini Jugoslaviji (1929–1941)', *Historijska traganja* 2 (2008), pp. 191–208.

[3] The position of Bosnian Muslims in Serb and Croat nationalist projects was succinctly described by Edin Hajdarpašić through the concept of (br)other as 'a figure that is neither

This is the regional historical background against which we must observe the emergence of the debate on Hajj in the 1930s. Rather than defensively reacting to events unfolding around them, Bosnian Muslim ulama and intellectuals actively contributed to ongoing debates about the changing material realities and often placed these 'modern things on trial'[4] by using their own journalistic media. Ibrahim Čokić established the journal *Hikjmet* (*Wisdom*), which was supported by his brothers as well, where he argued with his intellectual and religious adversaries. Muhamed Krpo, however, appears more randomly in different journals of the time, as both author of shorter notices and participant in various activities organised by the Islamic religious community. In many ways, Krpo, and to a lesser extent also Čokić, were the 'ordinary people'[5] who at the same time 'subvert these categories' (of 'ordinary people, subalterns, and elites').[6] Not particularly well-known outside their circles in Bosnia, they still eagerly participated in and commented on the transformations in the world that was sometimes far beyond them (Fig. 3.1).

So how did Krpo and Čokić react to Varatanović's characterisation of the Hajj and its practitioners? In an almost postmodernist vein, Krpo argued that there are different ways in which one can observe a certain place (and every place could carry a potential to be grimy or criminal).[7] Yet, the difference

enemy nor ally, neither "ours" nor "theirs", neither "brother" nor "Other"'. This figure of (br)other reflected 'struggles around Muslims' status as potential co-nationals in the process of nation-making. Edin Hajdarpašić, *Whose Bosnia? Nationalism and Political Imagination in the Balkans, 1840–1914* (Ithaca, London: Cornell University Press, 2015), p. 16; for an ambiguous set of responses to these projects among the early-twentieth-century Bosnian ulama and intellectuals, see Harun Buljina, 'Empire, Nation, and the Islamic World: Bosnian Muslim Reformists between the Habsburg and Ottoman Empires, 1901–1914' (PhD Diss., Columbia University, 2019), esp. ch. 3.

[4] Leor Halevi's book on the new material culture of the late nineteenth and early twentieth centuries and the religious debates it sparked points out the flexible approach that Muslim scholars took to 'make sense of dynamic changes in their universe', making them agents and not just mere recipients of Western products and technologies. Leor Halevi, *Modern Things on Trial: Islam's Global and Material Reformation in the Age of Rida* (New York: Columbia University Press, 2019), p. 15.

[5] Can, *Spiritual Subjects*, p. 31.

[6] Can, *Spiritual Subjects*, p. 37.

[7] Krpo, *Put na Hadž*, p. 112.

Figure 3.1 Muhamed efendija Krpo. Source: *Put na hadž (putopis jednog hadžije)*. Sarajevo: Štamparija Bosanska pošta, 1938.

lay in the eyes of the visitor, since the person who goes to Mecca is no mere tourist or stern critic, but a pilgrim with a sacred duty, who has no time for frivolous loitering or worse – such as visiting the alleged brothels. Placing the onus on the visitor reflects the modernist primacy given to the Hajji as opposed to the pilgrimage itself.[8] It also reflects the functionalist approach to travel writing: it was supposed to carry a duty beyond the mere descriptive, and it was expected to preserve the sanctity of the holy places intact. This task was arguably made harder by the new media that accompanied the Hajj in the twentieth century: Krpo noted the pernicious effect that photography had on the creation of the image of holy places, yet stated that he used it, too.[9] But perhaps the harshest critique of Varatanović's depiction happened by way of defending Saudi control and rule over the Hijaz: in Krpo's eyes, Ismet Varatanović was behaving like a 'spoiled English or American tourist, who is disgusted by the "barbaric" cutting of the right hand of a thief'[10] and

[8] Metcalf, 'The Pilgrimage Remembered', p. 87.

[9] Krpo, *Put na Hadž*, pp. 113–14.

[10] Krpo, *Put na Hadž*, p. 118.

who forgets this Qur'anic truth that contains God's order. Similarly, Krpo defended the death punishment, correcting Varatanović by saying that 'the punishment is performed by the surgeon, and not by the "executioner", and they do not use boiling oil for disinfection'.[11]

Čokić was equally irritated by Varatanović's description of corporal punishments in the Hijaz, but he turned the critique against Varatanović's presumed ideal – Europe – instead. So, what if there is public disciplining of drunkards in Jeddah? Wahhabis rule according to the Sharia, and 'the context is purely Islamic there'.[12]And who cares if small quantities of alcohol are smuggled into Mecca? Europe smuggles bombs![13] In this 'reversal of the gaze',[14] Čokić turned to the critique of European culture and society, prompting his interlocutor to take off the Orientalist lenses and look at the realities of contemporary life in major cities and ports in Europe (Marseilles, London, Paris) where corporal punishment, poverty and selfishness exceeded those ever known in the Hijaz.[15]

Varatanović's account in the eyes of his opponents necessarily lead to the profanisation of the Hajj due to the place of its publication (Belgrade), the manner in which the author wrote about Muslims in the Hijaz and the way in which the Hajj itself became a touristic endeavour similar to any other travel. The response of his interlocutors reveals that they were grappling with the exposure of Islamic rites and geographies to the prying eyes of outsiders, as well as an effort to reclaim the meaning and purpose in the rapidly changing world. The Hajj was becoming a contested issue for different participants in the public sphere; as such, Bosnian Muslim debates were not local and isolated, but part of a larger trend that concerned Muslim intellectuals around the world.

[11] Krpo, *Put na Hadž*, p. 118.

[12] Ibrahim H. Čokić, 'G. H. Ismeta Varatanovića prikazivanje puta u Meku', *Hikjmet* 51 (1933), pp. 93–94

[13] Čokić, 'G. H. Ismeta Varatanovića prikazivanje puta u Meku', p. 95.

[14] Reversing the gaze was by no means unique to Bosnian Muslim authors. A recent edited volume sheds light on the Muslim reactions to Orientalist imaginings and framings; see Susannah Heschel and Umar Ryad (eds), *The Muslim Reception of European Orientalism: Reversing the Gaze* (Abingdon: Routledge, 2019).

[15] Čokić, 'G. H. Ismeta Varatanovića prikazivanje puta u Meku', pp. 122–25.

Transforming the Hajj

Globally, the rise of print went hand-in-hand with tremendous changes in mobility and literacy, ushering in what is sometimes dubbed as 'the age of steam and print',[16] the period which was 'for Muslims [. . .] also an age of discovery and differentiation, creativity and crisis'.[17] However, technological advancements that enhanced travel, and especially the Hajj, were vigorously used by the nineteenth- and twentieth-century imperial powers and later nation-states,[18] and thus affected not only Muslims, but also non-Muslims who themselves had to grapple with the perception of Muslim Otherness and diversity. The Hajj, an enormous and complex endeavour that enhances the visibility of Muslim bodies and objects across different geographies, regained a new importance outside of the domain of the ritual. This included the presence of Hajj symbols, imagery and references in printed media; the significance of Islamic geographies recast in the light of modernity; and the debates, controversies and apologia surrounding the pilgrimage and its practitioners. Islamic rituals themselves did not remain intact in the period, which witnessed many Muslim societies under colonial rule: for a range of reasons, they were examined by Muslims and non-Muslims alike, spurring the intense meaning-making processes that remained constant throughout the twentieth century.

During this period, hitherto unprecedented numbers of people participated in shaping the Hajj discourse. As we will see in Chapters 4 and 5, this 'democratisation' of writing has expanded further in the twentieth and twenty-first centuries, bringing into the Hajj domain neglected actors, such as women.[19] The vast expanse of literature shows us the variety of meanings

[16] James L. Gelvin and Nile Green, 'Introduction', in *Global Muslims in the Age of Steam and Print*, edited by James L. Gelvin and Nile Green (Berkeley: University of California Press, 2013), 1–22.

[17] Gelvin and Green, 'Introduction', p. 2.

[18] The last decade has witnessed intense interest in the relationship between the Hajj and imperial control. Some of the studies on the subject include Can, *Spiritual Subjects*; Low, *Imperial Mecca*; John Slight, *The British Empire and the Hajj: 1865–1956* (Cambridge, MA: Harvard University Press, 2015); Kane, *Russian Hajj*; Tagliacozzo, *The Longest Journey*.

[19] Tagliacozzo, *The Longest Journey*, p. 261 (and the rest of Chapter 11).

that the pilgrimage has taken on and the increasing number of connections that it has forged across pilgrims' lives. Yet, as the Hajj became consistently present on the pages of Bosnian newspapers and journals in the local language, its universalising vision slowly gave way to more immediate concerns of the home and the homeland. From Arabic and Ottoman Turkish, the cosmopolitan and koiné languages of the Ottoman Empire and beyond, the Hajj has been increasingly described and prescribed in Bosnian for the local audience(s). This deprived Bosnian Muslims of the possibility to communicate with coreligionists across new nation-state boundaries yet opened the space for debates on the Hajj ritual and journey within local and regional contexts.

As we will see in this chapter, the Hajj was at the crux of debates on authority, interpretation and modernity. It was rethought, reconceptualised and reimagined in a process that seems to have had multiple parallels among different Muslim thinkers. In her article on the Egyptian travel writer Muhammad Labīb al-Batanūnī (d. 1938), Ammeke Kateman shows how the Hajj and its elements were represented and fashioned for his Muslim and non-Muslim contemporaries.[20] As such, this development was part of the modern production of knowledge on Islam, which was not the exclusive right of Orientalists.[21] The ways in which Muslim participants in these debates recognized the role of Orientalists tells us something about the 'recognition' of Orientalism before Edward Said's intervention.[22]

At the same time, a similar development was taking place regarding the mediating role of the Hajj. The plethora of meanings given to the Hajj in the premodern period was related to the Sufi framework characterised by inner (*bāṭin*) and outward (*ẓāhir*) perspectives, a framework that was pervasive in the larger devotional context as well. The Bosnian Hajjis from the previous

[20] Kateman, 'Fashioning the Materiality of the Pilgrimage'.

[21] See Heschel and Ryad (eds), *The Muslim Reception of European Orientalism*, esp. the introduction.

[22] 'From the beginning of the region's colonization by European powers, anticolonial activists have noticed the centrality of knowledge, as a form of representation, to the subjugation of the Arab people'. Such realisations occurred to non-Arab scholars as well. Hussein Omar, 'Unexamined Life: The Too Many Faces of Edward Said', *The Baffler* 58 (2021), https://thebaffler.com/salvos/unexamined-life-omar (accessed on 30 July 2021).

chapters saw the pilgrimage in this light, too – through the prism of cosmological, soteriological and spiritual arguments. It is possible that pilgrims also saw the rites without seeking a rationale behind them, as Marion Katz suggests regarding the premodern normative discourse, with symbolism taking its stage outside of the Sufi context only in the modern period.[23] This, of course, does not deny the enormous meaning-making potential of the Hajj, which has persisted over time and gained sometimes radically new shapes in the modern period, without old frameworks being completely discarded. The authors still imbued the pilgrimage with a range of meanings, yet these tended to be focused on the functionalist and utilitarian role of the Hajj in the world. The Hajj, in other words, had to be explained in a rational way to an increasingly incredulous public.

All these transformations were intricately bound to new media as well as new genres of writing: the journalistic media provided a suitable venue for the travelogue form, which could be published over a limited time-period, yet annually engaging a large number of readers. Journalistic media, enhanced by and in connection to other technological developments such as the telegraph, allowed authors to keep updating their readers on the progress of their journey, while the readers themselves could ask questions. Thus, several years before he embarked on his Hajj journey, Krpo advertised his wish to go on the Hajj in the newspapers, marketing his knowledge of languages as an asset for potential believers who might want him as their *bedel*.[24] Inhibitions had no place in these intense interactions between Hajji-authors and their readership: Čokić was happy to clarify the issue of a strange wind in the Hijaz that causes diarrhea and thus answered the curious but understandably anonymous reader.[25] After they had been published, travelogues often embarked on a path of their own: Krpo's book was reviewed in *Novi Behar*, where the author was criticised for his flamboyant style that resembles a 'bon-vivant (*teferičlija*)' for his descriptions of Umm Kulthum's music, thus denigrating the perceived role of a somber and pious Hajji (Fig. 3.2).[26]

[23] Katz, 'The Ḥajj and the Study of Islamic Ritual', p. 125.

[24] 'Vodić na hadždž', *Islamski Svijet* 24 (1933), p. 6.

[25] 'Odgovori uredništva', *Hikjmet* 10 (1935).

[26] 'Nove knjige', *Novi Behar* 11/17–19 (1938), pp. 291–92.

Pisac ove knjige H. H. M. Krpo u sjeni piramida

Figure 3.2 Muhamed Krpo on a camel in the shadows of pyramids. Source: *Put na hadž*.

The modern experience of the pilgrimage was also shaped by the travelogue form. Apart from its adjustment to the journalistic form, which rendered the Hajj one among many other news items, travelogues also offered an opportunity to construct the personality of a Hajji (sometimes understood as self-promotion),[27] to explore the self,[28] to communicate with the readers, or to participate in the relevant debates of the time.[29] In that sense, Jacques Le Goff's statement that 'times of marked social change are ideal for observing the relationship between material and imaginary realities'[30] can be applied to the transformation of the Hajj imaginations in both dimensions: changes in the Hajj as a journey and in the Hajj as a ritual. The following section will show how the Hajj was imagined and shaped by different actors. At the same time, writings on the Hajj reflected a range of interrelated issues, from religion to politics. In both functions, Hajj writings affected the public sphere.

27 Brunner, 'The Pilgrim's Tale', pp. 270–91.

28 Tagliacozzo, *The Longest Journey*, pp. 259–69.

29 Kateman, 'Fashioning the Materiality of the Pilgrimage'.

30 Jacques Le Goff, in Gabrielle M. Spiegel, *The Past as Text: The Theory and Practice of Medieval Historiography* (Baltimore: Johns Hopkins University Press, 1997), p. 5.

The Hajj on the Marketplace of News

The Hajj was a frequent topic on the pages of Bosnian and regional journals, all the way from the last years of the Ottoman rule to the Austro-Hungarian period and thereafter. The colonial control of the Hajj was reflected in the news coverage of this annual event. Through notices on Hajjis and the doctors who accompanied them, as well as through the focus on local customs, farewell ceremonies and new transportation means that took pilgrims to the Hijaz, we can see how the pilgrimage was duly monitored and reported on.[31] The possibility of travel to the two holy places, which was still overwhelmingly, but not exclusively a privilege of the upper class, attracted extensive attention in the budding Bosnian journalism. News on the departure of Hajjis occupied a significant part of journalistic notices every year, and the mixture of the factual and the romanticised comprised the content of these journalistic accounts.

Despite the existence of literature on the Hajj in Ottoman Turkish, which was still published during the Austro-Hungarian period,[32] the amount of

[31] Austro-Hungarian authorities in many ways acted similarly to other contemporary colonial powers in their control of the journey, which included organising Hajjis in one group under the leadership of the *raīs al-hujjāj*, as well as sanitary and travel regulations. See more in Zijad Šehić, 'Putovanje bosanskohercegovačkih hodočasnika u Meku'. On the Austro-Hungarian regulation of the Hajj journey and the registration of deceased Hajjis' property, see Younis, 'Smrtni slučajevi tokom hadža u Mekku'; Valeria Heuberger, 'Die Pilgerfahrt nach Mekka von Muslimen aus Bosnien-Herzegowina unter österreichisch-ungarischer Herrschaft (1878–1914)', in *Bosnien-Herzegowina und Österreich-Ungarn, 1878–1918*, ed. by Clemens Ruthner and Tamara Scheer (Tübingen: Narr Francke Attempto, 2018), pp. 193–210.

[32] One of the first articles on the Hajj in the Austro-Hungarian period is an article on Mecca and Medina published in the *Salname* ('Yearbook') for the year 1892. The *salname* form is a rich source of material for investigating the intellectual history of the period and points to the limits of the geographical and historical interest of the common educated reading public. The article in question was published in Ottoman Turkish under the title 'A Few Words about the Region of Hijaz (*İklîm-i Hicâz Hakkında Birkaç Söz*)'. Apart from descriptions of the physical geography, the article contains a section on the names of Mecca, the four *maqāms*, the borders of the harem, the important days for the pilgrims, the Kaʿba's cover (*qiswa*), the procession of *maḥmal* and certain other instructions for the pilgrim. Anonymous, 'İklîm-i Hicâz Hakkında Birkaç Söz', *Bosna ve Hersek Vilayeti Salnamesi* (Sarajevo: Vilajetska uprava Bosanskog vilajeta, 1892), pp. 110–18.

published material in Bosnian speaks about the intention of the Hajj authors to reach the widest possible audiences, as well as to send a message that exceeded the purely informative. These writings took the form of shorter and longer essays and were published either exclusively on the topic of the Hajj, or as part of series dealing with other rituals and duties in Islam (such as fasting, *zakat* and prayer). The Hajj was generally defined as a duty incumbent on all capable men and women, but with a specific emphasis on those who were able to afford it. This aspect would matter in the overall development of the idea of the Hajj as a duty, which brings together wealthy and powerful Muslims for a common, mutually uplifting cause. As with other duties in Islam, so the Hajj was also defined as having a distinct duality of form and essence.[33] The Hajj itself could become a marker and form of outward piety for proving belief.[34]

Yet, as the Hajj entered the seemingly equalising market of news, it increasingly became a topic of interest for different actors and reading audiences. This does not mean that a developed Hajj imaginary shared between different actors had not existed beforehand: as Arthur Asseraf shows in his research on communication in colonial Algeria, 'new forms of media piled onto existing ones, generating ever more intense and complex news—news that was electric both technologically and socially'.[35] The new did not just appear out of nowhere – it coexisted with old conceptions and 'inventories of language, of experience, of arguments, of emotions and more'.[36] Decades before *Vreme* started publishing Varatanović's Hajj travelogue, Serbian and Croatian writers took an interest in the Muslim pilgrimage, often using denigrating tropes. In much of European premodern writing, the Hajj was regarded as a sign of Muslim fanaticism, exacerbated by the near impossibility for non-Muslims

[33] Fehim Spaho, 'Panislamska ideja', *Behar* 7/3 (1906), p. 26.

[34] H. Mehmed Handžić, 'Važnost vanjskih znakova sa šeriatskog gledišta', *El Hidaje* 3/6–7 (1939), p. 81.

[35] Arthur Asseraf, *Electric News in Colonial Algeria* (Oxford: Oxford University Press, 2019), p. 9.

[36] Stefan-Ludwig Hoffmann and Sean Franzel, 'Introduction: Translating Koselleck', in Reinhart Koselleck, *Sediments of Time: On Possible Histories*, trans. and ed. by Sean Franzel and Stefan-Ludwig Hoffmann (Palo Alto: Stanford University Press, 2018), p. xv.

to visit Mecca and Medina. This led to a proliferation of different stories and myths regarding the places and motivations of Hajjis,[37] which later often reflected a strong anti-Ottoman bias. For example, while describing his journey to Istanbul in 1886, Adolfo Veber Tkalčević (1825–89) wrote how the Ottomans as an empire could not be expected to hold on for much longer because they sent all their money and resources to Mecca.[38] In his second and more famous travelogue documenting his journey to Plitvice, Tkalčević again insinuated that, once the revolution was under way, 'the Turk will feel it horribly in Medina (*Ali kad se digne motika i kuka, bit će Turkom po Medini muka*)'.[39] In some contexts, the image of Mecca and Medina was presented in exoticised terms, sometimes depicted as the future centre of the 'Turkish Empire', far away from Constantinople, which once again was to be occupied by a Russian king.[40]

The interest in the Hajj and the wider attention paid to Islamic rituals and customs was part and parcel of the self-conscious examination of the relationship between the heritage of the Muslim population and the Serbian and Croatian intellectual elite. It was, in a certain sense, a part of the revision process that included considering Bosnian Muslims apart from the Ottoman context and 'dealienating' them.[41] With the increase in journalistic publishing and the inclusion of a larger number of intellectuals in the same public sphere, topics related to Islam began to draw the attention of non-Muslim writers and translators, which was the reason why the stories about the Hajj and Hajjis start to appear on the pages of traditionally Serb journals and gazettes, such as

[37] Many Western myths regarding holy places in Islam were connected to anxieties surrounding the Prophet's body, which in these narratives was sometimes mistakenly placed in Mecca and given miraculous, yet deceptive properties. For more, see Suzanne Conklin Akbari, *Idols in the East: European Representations of Islam and the Orient, 1100–1450* (Ithaca: Cornell University Press, 2009), pp. 221–35.

[38] Adolfo Veber Tkalčević, *Put u Carigrad: Sa četrdset slika i tlorisom Carigrada* (Zagreb: Matica hrvatska, 1886), p. 208.

[39] Adolf Tkalčević, *Put na Plitvice* (Zagreb: Tiskom dra. Ljudevita Gaja, 1860), p. 58.

[40] R. T. Petrović Nevesinjski, 'Iz jedne srbulje', *Bosanska vila* 9 (15 May 1909), pp. 132–33.

[41] For an example of a self-conscious critique of the previous attitude of Serb intellectuals toward Bosnian Muslims and their cultural heritage, see Vladimir Ćorović, 'Muslimani u našoj ranijoj književnosti', *Bosanska vila* 3 (15 February 1912), pp. 33–34.

Bosanska Vila.[42] The inclusion of stories about the Hajj is inevitably connected to the exoticisation of Islamic culture so characteristic of this period. At one point, for example, *Bosanska Vila* included a story about a Bedouin caravan leader by Alexander Benitsky, a Russian sentimentalist author, translated from Russian by Sava Manojlović. The story reflected the broader interest in pilgrimage for a non-Muslim audience as well. The information about rituals including the Hajj was not always couched in orientalising discourse, but often conveyed a certain interest in the religious customs of 'our Muhammedans',[43] where the conflicting *(br)othering* movement could be discerned.

While the space of Mecca and Medina was closed off to prying non-Muslim eyes, observers could still see the pilgrims on their way. Their impressions were interwoven with anxieties regarding the nineteenth-century cholera pandemics. Although the cholera outbreak of 1865 began in Mecca,[44] journalists were aware of the effects of the pandemics in relation to the pilgrimage in Mashhad. Writing in 1871 for *Naša sloga*, a certain Dr Gržetić described the cause of the disease as stemming from the 'Oriental or the Easterner, who is disgusting by his very nature, eating a carcass on this occasion', the occasion being a pious visitation to Mashhad.[45] The presentation of Mashhad and Karbala, apart from Mecca and Medina, shows a vague awareness of other pilgrimages in Islam. The connection between pilgrimage and disease in popular culture manifested itself later in the twentieth century in the hugely popular Yugoslav movie *Variola Vera* (1982) which depicted the smallpox outbreak in 1972 and related it to returning pilgrims.

The anxieties surrounding the cholera and other diseases were reflected in the official gazette *Sarajevski list*, which was published in Sarajevo towards the end of the nineteenth century. In one instance, the gazette published a proclamation conveying an imperial message against pilgrimage, clad in sympathy with the local Muslim population. *Sarajevski list*, thus, asserted that while it was noble to protect one's 'ancestral faith (*pradjedovsku vjeru*)' – and

[42] Established by the Serb cultural and educational society Prosvjeta.

[43] 'Uz naše slike', *Bosanska vila* 2 (16 January 1889), p. 30.

[44] David Edwin Long, *The Hajj Today: A Survey of the Contemporary Pilgrimage to Makkah* (Albany: State University of New York Press, 1979), p. 69.

[45] Dr Gržetić, 'O kratelju iliti koleri', *Naša sloga* 2/18 (16 September 1871), p. 73.

although the Austro-Hungarian Empire supported this – it would be most wise if people stayed put in face of the new waves of the plague and if they abstained from the Hajj.[46] Proximity to the Asian Hajjis who could bring the disease to pilgrims from Turkey and Bosnia led to burning questions: how will such horrendous consequences be justified in the face of Europe?[47] While this remark was published in the official gazette and anonymised, Europe appeared as a yardstick for measuring progress in many of the period's texts. Thus, far from being only the outlet for hitherto marginalised voices, and 'far from creating an equidistant world, these technologies were linked to ideas of progress and Western superiority, and their spread created new inequalities'.[48]

Through the print media, with their focus on novelty and the unusual, the Hajj became a contested issue for Muslim and non-Muslim authors alike: it was secretive enough to warrant immediate attention and semantically ambiguous enough to avoid any kind of easy understanding. As such, travelogues, notices and descriptions of the Hajj often featured next to other sensationalist news, such as juicy details about the Miss Yugoslavia contest and gruesome news on the love triangle murders. Stories of European travellers who entered the Arab Peninsula were popular,[49] occasionally with a gendered angle where European women would be presented as cunning white intruders who used marital and sexual means to move through unknown spaces.[50]

[46] 'Nezvanično', *Sarajevski list* (22 January 1897).

[47] 'Nezvanično'.

[48] Asseraf, *Electric News in Colonial Algeria*, p. 5.

[49] The Serbian journal *Vreme* published excerpts from the Yemen and Hadramawt travelogue of Hans Helfritz (1902–95), presenting them as a foray into the lands of the Arabian nights, never before visited by Europeans and, importantly, places of slave trade. 'Jemen i Hadramaut – arapske države iz hiljadu i jedne noći – u čiju unutrašnjost nije još ušao nijedan Evropljanin', *Vreme* (14 March 1932), p. 2.

[50] *Vreme* also took an intense interest in the Hajj by publishing instalments from a travelogue by a Frenchwoman, which continued throughout the 1933: 'She is constantly under the veil, and willy-nilly participates in all the prayers and mystical exaltations of the Arabians. She is the only woman in all that mass of obedient Hajjis, who stink of tallow and filth, and whose eyes are constantly directed towards the holy city'. The Frenchwoman was also afraid that this journey would take her all the centuries back to Muhammad. 'Kao žena muslimana na putu za Sveti Grad (Avanture jedne Francuskinje među Arabljanima)', *Vreme* (19 December 1933), p. 6.

Given that the Hajj was a journey sealed off to non-Muslims, the media was always on the lookout for insider views, for a figure that could act as a native informant for the eager audiences, providing much needed information which then became an essentialised view of the 'self-consolidating other'.[51] This was the danger that Čokić and Krpo saw in Varatanović's travelogue: his view and experience of Mecca and Medina as places of vice and decay would be taken to present the norm by different audiences, and the degradation of the holy places would necessarily have negative consequences for the view of Islam and Muslims themselves. Through the profanisation of the holy places, the very nature of the pilgrimage was brought into question: is the Hajj journey indeed just like all other journeys?

The Hajj as a Modern Curiosity

The rise of organised travel, first through transportation supported by colonial powers (such as the Austrian Lloyd)[52] and then in the interwar period through agencies such as *Putnik*, enhanced the way in which the figure of the Hajji was bound to turn into a tourist in the popular media. Tourism was equated with leisure and comfort, which was contrasted with the premodern Hajj journeys that resembled 'a romantic endeavour [. . .] similar to the forays into the American wilderness'.[53] Unlike those times, however, as journalists wrote, 'now they [Hajjis] travel like civilised people, like true tourists without cumbersome effort and struggle'.[54] Closer to home, however, the image of Bosnian Muslims as more devoted than other Muslims was prevalent, with Hajj being depicted by some as an endeavor that carries no use and that should be replaced with travel to other regions (Fig. 3.3).[55]

If the Hajj was turning into a regular tourist journey, it posed a problem for more than one reason. Apart from the profanisation of the journey that

[51] Gayatri Spivak, *A Critique of Postcolonial Reason: Toward a History of the Vanishing Present* (Cambridge, MA: Harvard University Press, 1999), p. 131.

[52] Šehić, 'Putovanje bosanskohercegovačkih hodočasnika u Meku', p. 71.

[53] 'Umesto gusarskim lađama i kamilama, naši muslimani putuju na ćabu u pulmanovim kolima, automobilima i brzim lađama', *Vreme* (5 March 1932), p. 7.

[54] *Vreme* (5 March 1932), p. 7.

[55] 'Naše hadžije', *Bošnjak* 1/14 (1 October 1891), p. 1.

Na povratku s Hadža u Pireju pred lađom »Romanijom«
(Kasumagić, H. Baščauševič, Ekmečić, Krpo i Šehović)

Figure 3.3 Muhamed Krpo and his fellow Hajjis on the way back, in front of the steamship *Romanija*. Source: *Put na hadž*.

was felt by Krpo and Čokić, as outlined at the beginning of this chapter, there was a danger of the Hajj becoming yet another tourist attration, to be undertaken at whim, or superseded by journeys to other destinations. In an effort to overcome this problem, Krpo suggested the following:

> If the Muslims understood their Islamic duties correctly, none of the richer ones would spend several thousand dinars a year for nothing, travelling across various useless resorts, swimming places, parties and other trifling and meaningless places of culturally fake Europe. He would, instead, in respect of God Almighty, His Messenger and his elevated faith, use that money to go where God commands him to go, and do his religious Islamic duty and therefore contribute to and help building the magnificent mansion of the Islamic unity; with it he would help and strengthen his faith in God and thus God Almighty would strengthen and help him everywhere and in every sense, as God the Almighty says in the Holy Qur'an: '*In tansurullahe jansurkjum*' [if you support Allah, He will support you . . .][56]

[56] Krpo, *Put na hadž*, p. 299.

The unease with other types of journeys reflects a modernist reaction to new practices appearing together with greater physical and social mobility. Mehmed Handžić (1906–44), a traditionalist *ʿālim* and graduate from al-Azhar, wrote against honeymoon travel as a harmful innovation that made people travel far from home so that they could not perform or prepare for their religious duties.[57] The previous passage from Krpo's travelogue also indicates the importance given to the Hajj journey of wealthy Muslims. While having sufficient means is certainly one of the requirements for the pilgrimage, this emphasis on wealth pointed to insecurities regarding representation and power: the rich should invest their time and sources in the Hajj. Thus, the Hajj would increase in importance and global relevance.

At the same time, Hajjis utilised all the advantages of leisured travel. Muhamed Krpo himself enjoyed detours in Athens, Cairo and Damascus; urged fellow pilgrims to visit the Greek monuments (arguing with the Qur'anic injunction that one should travel and observe the world to see the fate of those who had passed before them); went to see the pyramids and a movie starring Umm Kulthum; smoked famous Greek cigarettes; and rented fast cars for sightseeing. Krpo was also an avid self-described 'amateur photographer' who took photos of places and people he saw on the way. His travelogue also contained reproductions of photographs, mostly of Egyptian women who were divided into 'types' (Fig. 3.4). And finally, the title page of his travelogue did not depict Mecca or Medina, but showed a caravan with pyramids in the background, indicating an emphasis on the journey rather than the goal.

The Hajj of non-Bosnian Muslims was a common topic of interest on the pages of budding Bosnian print.[58] News about faraway Muslim communities,

[57] Mehmed Handžić, 'Vaz o ulozi muža i žene u braku i njihovim dužnostima', *El-Hidaje* 1/9 (1937), p. 147.

[58] The interest in the international Muslim audience started at a fairly early date, to which the publication of journals exclusively in Ottoman Turkish (*Rehber*, *Vatan*) testify. Amzi-Erdoğdular, 'Alternative Muslim Modernities'.

Figure 3.4 Modern young Egyptian girl. Source: *Put na hadž*.

such as the Malay,[59] Chinese,[60] or Indian Muslims,[61] were frequent, together with notices on the state of Hajjis in regions where going on pilgrimage was becoming more complicated, such as in Turkey under Atatürk.[62] In many ways, the Hajj was becoming a litmus test for observing change in the new imperial and post-imperial worlds. At the same time, the view from the perceived peripheries of the Muslim World, such as China, pointed to potentialities of that world beyond the centrality of Mecca and Medina, through the emphasis on the number of Hajjis and their commitment.

While emphasising the vast diversity of Muslims on the Hajj was a common point in many journalistic reports and travelogues and became a constitutive element of new conceptualisations of the Hajj, as will be discussed below, seeing multitudes of Muslims on the Hajj sometimes led to unexpected interpretations of the ritual's inclusivity. A series of articles published

[59] Fehim Spaho, 'Panislamska ideja', *Behar* 9 (1906), p. 98.

[60] 'Veliki broj hadžija iz Kine', *Islamski svijet* 128 (1935), p. 3.

[61] 'Iz islamskog svijeta', *Hikjmet* 1/1 (1929), p. 32.

[62] Chameran, 'Jedan pogled na turske protuislamske reforme', *Hikjmet* 8/9 (1929), pp. 262–63; 'Turska i hadž ove godine', *Islamski svijet* 17 (1932), p. 4.

at the beginning of the twentieth century argued against the pilgrimage of poor people and suggested that the Hajj be performed only by the rich.[63] The sight of poor Moroccan Hajjis, who were in need of help on the streets of Jeddah, provoked an anonymous author ('One Turk') to ask what kind of benefit this pilgrimage would bring to Islam and Muslims. The same author suggested that the ulama should urge rich people to undertake the pilgrimage instead, in order to 'strengthen the brotherly link among Muslims, and to erect the iron wall against the enemies of the faith'.[64]

The diversity of Muslims on the Hajj was one aspect of the transformed interest in the geographies of the pilgrimage journey within a changing environment. As we could see in the previous chapter, Islamic geographies certainly mattered for Ottoman Bosnian Hajjis, who could collect blessings and earn spiritual awards while passing through places of *ziyāra* in Damascus or Cairo. Starting from the late nineteenth century, this geography radically changed for its observers, as pilgrims had to navigate physical borders and limitations, as well as the uneasy realities of the post-Ottoman world.

The Hajj between the Local and the Global

Despite all the comforts of the modern journey that Bosnian Hajjis enjoyed – such as trains, touristic detours, food and cigarettes while on steamships – their journeys were shaped by the restrictive state frameworks of the nineteenth and twentieth centuries. Passports, visas, stamps and different currencies became markers of the mobility of pilgrims, pointing to the state borders that now – instead of a set of *ziyāra* – defined modern pilgrimage. These markers implied the '*channelling* of mobility [. . .] the differentiation, regulation and bureaucratisation of different kinds of movement'.[65] While Bosnians could afford

[63] 'Could the Hajj and Zakat, two major duties in Islam, be carried out without capital?' was one of the questions asked. H. Kulinović, 'Pitanje "kadera" ili sudbine (Po istočnim izvorima)', *Gajret* 4 (1924), p. 59; 'think of the Hajj, be thrifty, work like a bee' was another set of advice to a potential Hajji given by Ibrahim Hakki Čokić; see his 'Hadž i Kurban Bajram', *Hikjmet* 2 (1929), p. 34.

[64] Jedan Turk, 'Hadž (Razmatranja)', *Behar* 9 (1906), pp. 98–99.

[65] Valeska Huber, *Channelling Mobilities: Migration and Globalisation in the Suez Canal Region and Beyond, 1869–1914* (Cambridge: Cambridge University Press, 2013), p. 3.

to go on pilgrimage in larger numbers than ever before, their experience was fundamentally different from their Ottoman predecessors. The modern Hajj was impacted by the colonial realities of the wider world which they were traversing and the pressures of the states to which they were bound. At the same time, post-Ottoman continuities pervaded both experience and writing, proving how devotional, spiritual or intellectual links were not necessarily dictated by state pressures and limitations.

Hajj journeys always started with farewell ceremonies, which showed the emotional connection of the local communities to Mecca and Medina. The customs were varied: in some parts of Bosnia Hajj-stones were erected to mark the year of the Hajji's departure and the place where the future pilgrim gave a speech (Fig. 3.5).

Figure 3.5 Hajj stones denoting a Hajji's name, birth date and the year of pilgrimage have been popular throughout the twentieth and into the twenty-first century. Photos by the author.

Local customs were a popular subject of postcards, featuring different cities. At the same time, the ruling states used the seeing-off of the pilgrims as a means to publicly show their own support. With the rise of print, this gained additional echo, as shown by the following description in the official gazette *Sarajevski list* in 1890:

> The farewell to the Hajjis in Sarajevo was remarkably solemn and the people followed them to the railway station in such huge numbers, as has not been remembered from the Occupation onwards. Many horsemen and an innumerable string of coaches with Muhammadan citizens and Rais-ul-'ulama Hilmi efendi Omerović and almost all other notables showed off these Hajjis to Ali-pasha's mosque on the way out of the city, where Hajjis performed prayer. All the way from the front of the palace of the National Government to Ali-pasha's mosque stood dense rows of Muhammadan citizens, men and women. After the prayer, the Hajjis and other notables went to the grand hall of the National Government. There the suzerain of this country, His Highness the Baron Appel, waited for the Hajjis, to say goodbye to them on their way out of the city. Together with the governor, there was his deputy, His Highness Baron Kutschera, the administrators of the national government, Sirs Sauerwald and Eichler, and numerous higher clerks from all the government departments who gathered for this solemn ceremony.[66]

Information on the interaction between the authorities and the Hajjis appeared in Bosnian journals throughout the Austro-Hungarian period and later. Sometimes those were shortened into brief notices mentioning the departure or arrival of the Bosnian Hajjis,[67] and sometimes they were expanded into elaborate reports on farewell customs for the Hajjis.[68] Over time, in the descriptions of these farewell ceremonies we encounter fewer state representatives.

In the interwar period, Bosnian Hajjis had to undergo a set of procedures, and those procedures, especially in the 1930s, often included travelling to

[66] Mali vjesnik, *Sarajevski list* (11 June 1890).

[67] Mali vjesnik, *Sarajevski list* (5 June 1889); Mali vjesnik, *Sarajevski list* (30 May 1890); Mali vjesnik, *Sarajevski list* (30 September 1891).

[68] Mali vjesnik, *Sarajevski list* (17 May 1891).

cities such as Belgrade to obtain the necessary documents. Belgrade was not a neutral place: it featured not only as an administrative centre, but also as a necessary transit point on the way to and from Mecca and Medina. As seat of the Islamic Religious Community in the early 1930s, it symbolised the power taken away from Sarajevo, and this exacerbated the already stressful journey that Bosnian Hajjis had to undertake, even after the Islamic Religious Community regained some of its autonomy after 1936.[69] In 1937, for example, the Hajjis were taken to prison on their return from the pilgrimage, based on the accusation that they were smuggling goods into Yugoslavia.[70] Muhamed Krpo, a reluctant saviour, managed to rescue the Hajjis by appealing to Mehmed Spaho (1883–1939), a minister in the government of the Kingdom of Yugoslavia and a key figure in the interwar years. Belgrade also carried a note of hostility: in their debate with Ismet Varatanović, Krpo and Čokić were aware of the power of the press published there and the effect that it could have on Muslims across Yugoslavia – a sentiment that would continue deep into the twentieth century.

The Hajjis would soon be able to continue their onward journey, stopping occasionally in different cities on the Balkans, such as Skopje. Further on, Muhamed Krpo's travelogue gives a rather lengthy description of his sojourn in Greece. Krpo's stance is that of a sympathetic observer: he tries to put himself not only in the position of the Hajji, but also of an ethnographer who is not passing quick judgement on the people he saw. When talking to common people in hotels or on the streets of Athens, Krpo does not clearly side with the Greek people – pitted as they are against the Turks in the narrative – but presents their grievances about the position that they had occupied during the late period of the Ottoman Empire, which was now irredeemably lost with the establishment of the Turkish Republic. The Ottomans were a constantly 'present absence': Krpo emphasised the positive role of Sultan Abdulhamit II, under whose rule these Greeks allegedly had held the highest

[69] For more on the related changes that happened in the mid-1930s, see Adnan Jahić, 'Obnova autonomije Islamske zajednice u Bosni i Hercegovini 1936. godine', *Prilozi* 37 (2008), pp. 95–111.

[70] Krpo, *Put na hadž*, pp. 376–82.

positions.[71] Krpo sympathised with the plight of the Greeks who were made to leave Turkey in the course of the population exchange and the sufferings that the population exchange entailed for both the migrant and the local population.

Their passage through Greece placed Bosnian Hajjis in an unusual position: apart from observing, they were also being observed. Being the object of a gaze meant having one's clothes, appearance and even skin colour laid out for scrutiny. In that process, Bosnian Hajjis keenly noted how they were seen: they were often mistaken for Turks, such as in the following excerpt that describes the encounter between Krpo and an angry Greek youth who wanted to punch him:

> In a secluded place, a young man approached me with his fists clutched and a horrid look in his eyes and yelled: 'Turk musun sen?' 'Yok, ben Yugoslavia'dan', I answered. Hearing that, he smiled cheerfully, patted me on my shoulder and said: 'I apologize; I thought you were a Turk from Kemal's Turkey [. . .][72]

Since the steamships allowed for pilgrims to interact with other Muslims, as well as with non-Muslims, the post-Ottoman traces are also present in descriptions of Bosnian Hajjis through their curious encounters and conversations with other passengers, as much as through the constant awareness of the modern state's rupture. On one occasion, Krpo's contemporary Ibrahim Čokić met two young Turks on a Turkish boat named *Ankara*. The youths started vigorously arguing about the need for reforms and translations. This interaction sparked a longer commentary about the nature of the Qur'an and the impossibility of its translation, continuing into a debate on the language reform and the so-called 'Kemal's alphabet', referring to the social and cultural changes initiated by Mustafa Kemal Atatürk. On the steamboat, the author also met a couple of Turkish Jewish women and remarked on their Arabic proficiency.[73] In these descriptions, we can discover what made the authors from this period so anxious about their Turkish fellow travellers: it was the

[71] Krpo, *Put na hadž*, p. 28.

[72] Krpo, *Put na hadž*, p. 27.

[73] Ibrahim Čokić, 'Moje putovanje na hadž', *Hikjmet* 4/40 (1932), p. 113.

looming danger of a secularised and watered-down religion with which they could not come to peace and which they considered to be unnatural for the Turkish citizens themselves, as indicated by their struggle with language and script reform. Unease manifested itself in a negative perception of reforms in dress, script and language, forays into translation and the use of the Turkish language in unexpected places. The use of Turkish phrases in this period (as well as the occasional references to Arabic) in the overwhelmingly Bosnian travelogue appeals to the sentiments of a shared Ottoman heritage, as a living testament to a past world now divided by the borders of nation-states.[74]

Encountering post-Ottoman others was not the only way in which Bosnian Muslims found themselves as the subject of the gaze. Encountering others on the streets of the Eastern Mediterranean or on ships often provoked comments on the inherent difference between Bosnian Muslims and others, because the former were seen as European.[75] When roaming the streets of Alexandria, Krpo and his companion felt afraid that the locals ('the natives') were observing them with suspicion, because of their skin colour and clothes that appeared visibly Western.[76] On another occasion, however, Bosnian Hajjis felt snubbed by Syrian Muslims and tried to better themselves in the recitation of the Qur'an.[77] With their perceived Europeanness, the Hajjis sometimes acted as commentators on the 'progress' of the countries of the Middle East through which they were passing.[78] Paradoxically, the travelogues showed that the more the unity of

[74] The use of Arabic in travelogues, however, remains a constant because most of the Hajj travelogues contain Qur'anic verses and prayers related to the rites. Thus, the persistence of Arabic is tied to 'sensational forms' (Meyer, 'Introduction', p. 13), formulas that were fixed and gave a recognizable religious and devotional character to the text.

[75] The idea of Bosnian Muslims as European had already appeared in the late nineteenth century in print and gained popularity throughout the twentieth century, to culminate at the time of the agression on Bosnia in 1992–95, which will be discussed in Chapter 5.

[76] Krpo, *Put na hadž*, pp. 51–52.

[77] Krpo is told by his fellow Bosnian Hajja: 'For the love of God, recite something from the Qur'an, so that these Arabs know that a Bosnian knows something'. Krpo, *Put na hadž*, p. 338.

[78] For example, when Krpo came to Cairo and saw the railway station, he admitted that it was comely but not in line with 'our European' expectations. Krpo, *Put na hadž*, p. 57.

Muslims was affirmed, the more diverse and different the Muslim world indeed seemed to be.[79]

Whether European or not, Bosnian Hajjis felt the same limitations on their mobility as other pilgrims during the journey. The worst part of it was the quarantine, which was set up for all incoming Hajjis. In that regard, the Hajjis seemed to be victims of a system that included native Egyptian authorities who appropriated the 'white mask' of oppression:

> The attitude of the Egyptian Consulate in Piraeus and the attitude of the police and health administration in Alexandria to the quarantine and afterwards [. . .] is the result of the Egyptian administration's lack of education and the attitude towards Hajjis inherited from Englishmen, which the Englishmen used to turn away the Islamic world from the Hajj and to minimise Islamic meetings around the Haramayn – and they wanted to reduce them even further, below the minimum because they are afraid for their haughty lordship in the Eastern, and especially Islamic regions, which serve for the import of their goods, and which they mercilessly suck and exploit. [. . .] Those 'tolerant' colonisers do not have nor do they know of quarantines and similar institutions for the pilgrims of different faiths – not for Asian and African Arabs, who make pilgrimages to Jerusalem, Rome (the heart of Europe) or some monastery – not even for the Shiite Mashhad in Persia. There are no quarantines for them, nor any health examinations, even after their return from the pilgrimage. But there is a quarantine and vaccinations and all kinds of injections for the *ahl al-sunna* when they are passing from Europe and other regions as well, not to mention when they are returning from the Hijaz during the Hajj season.[80]

The feeling of marginalisation and colonial oppression, culminating in the Hajj quarantine practice, was what ultimately led to a reaction. The time

[79] 'Muslim reformers embraced the notion of a united global faith to lessen their fear of actual diversity, which seemed to be a source of division and weakness'. Cemil Aydin, *The Idea of the Muslim World: A Global Intellectual History* (Cambridge, MA: Harvard University Press, 2017), p. 74. While Bosnian Hajjis were not necessarily self-avowedly modernist or bent on reformism at all, the language of unity permeated the whole discourse.

[80] Ibrahim Čokić, 'Moje putovanje na hadž', *Hikjmet* 4/41 (1932), pp. 148–49.

in quarantine prepared the pilgrims to imagine the spiritual unification of Muslims, through actions, institutions or states that might allow to reach such a goal:

> Those and other inhuman English acts opened the eyes of the Easterners, and they started resenting them. This resentment is reflected in the fact that all Arabs, almost without exception, ascribe to Englishmen certain unkind acts of the Egyptian authorities and organs. In my humble opinion, this means that the spiritual unification of the Arab, predominantly Islamic, regions is on its direct path to realisation.[81]

As travelogues became a popular genre that largely shaped interwar popular imagination, writing about major cities of Islamic geography on a Hajj journey was also a competitive and defensive act. While the Hajj itself was often liable to fantastic imagination by non-Muslim authors, as we could see earlier, cities such as Cairo also became an object of the Yugoslav outsider gaze. Jovan Dučić (1874–1943), a Serb poet and diplomat from Bosnia, left a number of travelogues, among which his 'Letter from Egypt' (1940) is well known. In this travelogue, Jovan Dučić presented a grim portrait of the city which he saw as divided between its pharaonic past and Islamic present. Accordingly, its inhabitants are uncouth and illiterate, almost robotic ('they know a few chapters from the Qur'an which they do not understand');[82] they are marked by neither wits nor beauty, having no morals nor family ideals like the Christians. Islam in Dučić's travelogue is anti-historic, which is why it seems to be antithetic, destructive and pernicious to the pharaonic past.[83] Muslims are geographically illiterate, too, since they are only familiar with the local places, without knowing the wider region or the world. The most scandalous part of the travelogue seems to be Dučić's insistence that all the

[81] Čokić, 'Moje putovanje na hadž', pp. 149–50.

[82] Jovan Dučić, 'Pismo iz Egipta', *Gradovi i himere* (Beograd: Politika, Narodna knjiga, 2005), p. 237.

[83] Dučić, 'Pismo iz Egipta', p. 238; after receiving complaints from Bosnian Muslims about this part of his travelogue, Dučić added Christianity as another possible pernicious influence. Tamara Rakić, 'Stereotipi o arapskom svijetu u srpskim rukopisima (od 1850. do 1940. godine)', *Književna istorija* 130/38 (2006), p. 576.

cities of the Muslim East, from Morocco to India, share the same frightening framework of stagnation and decline, with nothing to entice European heart and mind.[84]

Writing against this background, Krpo and Čokić promoted a narrative opposite to Dučić's. Cairo was the place of traditional Islamic devotions, yet also the abode of a budding Egyptian nationalism. For Čokić, it was a refuge for the late Ottoman ulama, such as Mustafa Sabri (1869–1954), and a place that defied the onslaught of harmful modernity. Turkish nationalism was frowned upon in the travelogues because of its secularist component, while Egyptian – or Arab nationalism – was very much approved of and considered a potential model for Muslims in Yugoslavia. However, the attitude towards the political situation among the Egyptian population was deeply ambiguous:

> While on the one hand indolence, laziness, apathy and decadence rule, on the other a totally new life is being created, a new epoch of Egypt is beginning, new generations are rising [. . .] this is a religiously and nationalistically conscious, well-organised and disciplined Egyptian youth.[85]

This enthusiasm obtained another dimension in descriptions of Mecca and Medina.[86] In accordance with progressivist narratives, Hajjis usually lauded the order, organisation and control of the Hijaz as created by the Saudis. Sometimes, however, these descriptions would show cracks, as the authors struggled to withhold criticism of any bad occurrence in the holy places and still show the honesty that they thought they owed to their readers and potential pilgrims. Even more so than in Cairo or Damascus, traces of material modernity assumed confusing visibility and ambiguity. The following excerpt is the depiction of a novelty in Mecca, which astonished Krpo who struggled to understand it:

> Everything in the Hijaz, the state administration, the absolute security of life and property, the lack of all which is disgusting, evil and forbidden by

[84] Dučić, 'Pismo iz Egipta', p. 239.

[85] Krpo, *Put na hadž*, p. 39.

[86] Muhamed Krpo could not afford to visit Medina, but he left a long description of its locations and holy sites as guidance and instruction for his readers and future Hajjis.

> the Sharia, as well as everything else, is laudable, but (and there is one but everywhere) – there is one novelty which cannot be tolerated at all, let alone be approved, because it does not agree with tradition, and it is not in accordance with the Sharia as well. [. . .] That night, when Abd al-Aziz came, his retinue and the more noble Hajjis who joined the retinue in Baghdad, rich Egyptians and different nobles, made their 'Sa'y' between Safa and Marwa in cars. Sitting comfortably in the seats of their limos, they passed between Safa and Marwa seven times and that was their 'Sa'y'.[87]

Despite this misstep, Islamic unity was not merely idealised, but in the travelogues appears to have acquired the contours of actual reality, embodied in the new Saudi Kingdom. Large parts of both travelogues were committed to the description of the new state and to refuting different Orientalist and other contrarian ideas. Still, such an idealised version of the Saudi Kingdom necessarily came with a certain ambiguity, which is especially visible in conflicting relationships of belonging. The authors of the interwar period were negotiating their multiple allegiances – to the Ottoman heritage that they cherished, to the authorities emerging in the newly formed countries of the Middle East and to the nation-state in which they lived. Both Čokić and Krpo supported the changes that resulted from the turmoil in the Hijaz in the 1920s and early 1930s. Čokić's journal *Hikjmet* fiercely defended the *Ikhwān*,[88] and his view is best illustrated with a poem composed for the group by Muhamed Seid Mašić and published in *Hikjmet*:

> **To Arabia**
> To Mecca, Medina, ruler of genius and the war band 'Ichvan' [. . .]
> Oh Ummul Kura, holy city,
> Nobody can threaten you
> Because Allah will bring revenge
> On all those who threaten you. [. . .]

[87] Krpo, *Put na hadž*, pp. 221–22. The interwar period seems to have seen a short outbreak in car usage around holy places, such as in Camino de Santiago; see Marco Túlio de Sousa and Ana Paula da Rosa, 'The Mediatization of Camino De Santiago: Between the Pilgrimage Narrative and Media Circulation of the Narrative', *Religions* 11/10 (2020), p. 480.

[88] The army of Ibn Saud (1875–1953).

Oh Arabia, you are now ruled
By a ruler of genius
Who would not let Europe
Dig its claws into you:
Ibnus Suud Abdul Aziz
A great protector of the glorious faith: London, Moscow, Rome and Paris
Have to pay attention to him.
[. . .]
Oh Arabia, early dawn! Homeland to Al Ichvan!
You have been lauded more
Than any other land.[89]

Since the journal *Hikjmet* was already publishing sequels of Čokić's travelogue, there exists the possibility that it influenced the composition and publication of the pro-*Ikhwān* poem. In the travelogue itself, the positive changes seen in the Saudi Kingdom and the 'Wahhabi' rule mostly relate to the eradication of innovations (*bidʿa*)[90] and the improvement of road safety,[91] which was usually contrasted with the previous state of turbulence and chaos during the Ottoman period. In Krpo's travelogue, the phrase 'Hajj as an all-Islamic congress' is repeated often, but the author also stresses that the 'congress' was the reception at the court of King Abdul-Aziz (Ibn Saud), which gathered 'all notables and more conscious representatives of all countries'.[92] The heroic image of King Abdul-Aziz persists throughout the narrative, and his photograph is part of the travelogue, along with that of one of his sons.[93] His physical appearance is described in flattering terms, as is his treatment of guests and visitors at the audience ceremony.[94]

The progressivist narrative presented only one approach to the holy places under Saudi rule. Ismet Varatanović, whose travelogue was scrutinised by

[89] Muhamed Seid Mašić, 'Arabiji', *Hikjmet* 6/8 (1935), pp. 238–39.

[90] The eradication of tombs was mostly evoked in this context: Krpo, *Put na hadž*, pp. 105–6; Čokić, 'Moje putovanje na hadž', *Hikjmet* 5/58 (1934), p. 301.

[91] Krpo, *Put na hadž*, p. 290.

[92] Krpo, *Put na hadž*, p. 300.

[93] Krpo, *Put na hadž*, pp. 285 and 287.

[94] Krpo, *Put na hadž*, pp. 284 and 286.

Krpo and Čokić, offered a sunken view on the post-Ottoman realities of the Hijaz. Varatanović's narrative offered a gloomy outlook on the chaotic social situation in the post-Ottoman world:

> All the doors are closed, the premises are empty and restless spiders have made cobwebs in every corner. Still, the square in front of the station is alive. Dozens of cars, lined up in a straight line, are bathed in a multitude of the sun's rays, and flocks of pigeons are landing on them, having made their nests under the domes and around them, in sculptured or carved ornaments. It is a sad image of former better times and strivings to make this city and its environments more accessible and to enliven it. The sad picture of the Hijaz railway, which today is demolished in many places; partly during the World War, to impede the transport of the troops to various strategic points, and partly because of the rebellious tribes, and mostly because of the enmity towards the modernisation of the country. [. . .] There are piles of iron pieces, planks, rails, all kinds of bars and nails. Millions and millions lie there and rot. It's rarely looked at. Nobody looks at this enormous wealth, nor regrets its decay. The lizards are the only ones there, dancing their eerie dance over the piled wealth, while the nation moans under the burden of life and lacks even bread. There is a road from the square in front of the station, across the main entrance to the centre of the city, in the midst of which there are still rails firmly pressed into the iron tracks. The train has not crossed over them for more than a decade. Will the train ever cross it? – it is hard to predict, although during the congress of Muslims in Jerusalem two or three years ago, a board for the renewal of the Hijaz railway was elected.[95]

The Hijaz railway project was a symbol of Muslim unity, combining mobility related to the pilgrimage with new technological developments, to which Muslim coreligionists across the world contributed.[96] As Varatanović reminded his readers, only several decades later it was laying in decay, reminding the passers-by of its former glory. On another level, this passage

[95] Ismet Varatanović, 'Sa puta u Meku', *Jugoslovenska pošta* 5 (14 October 1933), p. 13.

[96] On Bosnian Muslim contributions to the Hijaz railway project, see Hamza Karčić, 'Supporting the Caliph's Project: Bosnian Muslims and the Hejaz Railway', *Journal of Muslim Minority Affairs* 34 (2014), pp. 282–92.

communicated the pervasive decline of the holy places, something which neither Krpo nor Čokić could take lightly. Signs of decay in Mecca and Medina signified that there was something wrong with the current state of Islam; on the fierce battlefield of images, this could lead to detrimental consequences for Muslims, too.

The idea of unity during the Hajj, however, was alive and resisting, and once it was set in motion in the early twentieth century, it continued to be one of the dominant ways in which Mecca and Medina were portrayed. On a practical level, the unity was articulated through the emotional connection that linked all Muslims 'as one body'. And yet, despite the polemics and assertion of the social value of the Hajj, the holy places also retained the same emotional significance that they had held for generations of pilgrims. The moment of separation from the Kaʿba was filled with immeasurable sadness, which affected minds and bodies:

> Saying goodbye to Bayt Allah is heavier on a true and honest pious Islamic believer than separating from the one dearest to him, and especially when, after all seven circles of *tawaf*, and after kissing al-Hajar al-Aswad for the last time, he stops in front of Bayt Allah, leans on 'Multazam' [the wall of the Kaʿba between al-Hajar al-Aswad and the doors of the Kaʿba], kisses the threshold of the Kaʿba, leans with his right cheek, chest and stomach on 'Multazam', sobbing, from the depths of his tumultuous heart and soul, in tears of sincere regret for his sins and separation. In that state, everyone is asking the Almighty to forgive them numerous sins, to make it *nasib* to come there once again, to accept his effort and Hajj, and to make him come home safely.[97]

As the interwar Bosnian authors grappled with an imagery of the Hajj and the Islamic geography that was appropriated and interpreted in journalistic contexts, there existed a pressing need for them to define the meaning of the Hajj. The anxieties pertaining to the nature of the Hajj were not taken lightly. It was not just a matter of the profanisation of the journey by different, sometimes non-Muslim authors, or it being equated with a common tourist trip; the very meaning and significance of this pilgrimage had repercussions on the

[97] Krpo, *Put na hadž*, pp. 294–95.

way in which Islam itself was conceived and, consequently, how it affected Muslim lives. But the meaning of the Hajj remained stubbornly elusive to any firm grasp, threatening to be misunderstood as meaningless or as a sign of fanaticism in ill-intended media, or to be regarded as lost and forgotten to many Muslim authors. The next section will examine the struggles over the significance of the Hajj that occupied many Bosnian Muslim authors from the first half of the twentieth century.

The Significance of the Pilgrimage

Like his brother a feisty and argumentative person, Adil Čokić (1888–1954) was embroiled in a fiery debate during the 1930s, this time with Osman Nuri Hadžić (1869–1937), a writer and thinker with a long polemical record. At the crux of the critique was a recently published book by Osman Nuri Hadžić, *Muhammad and the Qur'an*, which aimed to refute Western claims on the Prophet and Islam, as well as to offer an overview of the Prophet's biography to a wider readership. Osman Nuri Hadžić had previously spent a large part of his career refuting the claims of Serbian Orientalists, as evidenced not only in *Muhammad and the Qur'an*, but also in the polemical work *Islam and Culture* (1894). The latter was written as a reposte to Milan Nedeljković, who had attacked Islam in the publication *Letopis Matice Srpske*. In these books, Hadžić was replying to deep-seated prejudices against Islam, which were in many ways veiled critiques of Bosnian or Ottoman Muslims. Yet, his presentation of Islam, its beliefs and rites, as well as its history, did not sit well with some of the Bosnian traditionalists.

Publishing in several journals – such as *Hikjmet* (established by the Čokić brothers), *Novi Behar* and *Gajret* – Čokić and Hadžić wrote back and forth about the issues they deemed controversially explored at the other end: the personality of the Prophet Muhammad, the status of the hadith in comparison to the Qur'an, the role of miracles and intercession, as well as afterlife. Their debate was fierce and unapologetic, partly because it represented the polarising stance of a self-awoved traditionalist theologian and a modernist thinker who fought for the right to interpret Islamic beliefs, history and practice, as well as to offer guidelines for social action in the Islamic framework.

One of the controversial questions was the issue of the Hajj, more specifically its origins. In his book *Muhammad and the Qur'an* (1931), Hadžić noted the pre-Islamic roots of the pilgrimage, adding that Islam had only 'consecrated' it, leaving the majority of the rituals untouched.[98] Without engaging the Islamic sources regarding the pre-Islamic period, Hadžić was leaving open the interpretation of the pilgrimage to historicism and the suggestion that Islam did not claim the Abrahamic past as its own, thus bringing into question the universality of Islam and its diachronic expanse and significance. Several other points were also controversial: misidentifying the place of the Prophet's Tomb, which indicated that people could pray at or over it; suggesting that the Maqām Ibrāhīm was a cave which could be climbed by pilgrims and that the Kaʿba contained a statue of the Prophet Abraham; and mistaking the name of the Medinan mosque where the shift of the *qibla* happened. Finally, the insinuation that the ultimate object of the ritual was the Kaʿba, a stone temple, and that al-Hajar al-Aswad was 'the highest Arabian relic'[99] once again seemed to emphasise the pagan roots of the Hajj and to imbue it with the meaning of focused devotion. Limiting the universality of Islam to the circumscribed genius of 'Arabianness' not only reflected the Orientalist discourse of the age, but also served as a deterrent for any potential accusations of religious fanaticism from the Serb and Croat side, because it offered a graspable rationale for the rites.

Adil Čokić's response, which was published over several years between 1931 and 1933 on the pages of *Novi Behar* and in his own journal, *Hikjmet*, reveals several anxieties that overlapped with the topic. Čokić's major criticism revolved around Hadžić's usage of sources regarding the history of the holy places and the ritual: Čokić insinuated that Hadžić barely used the Qur'an, discarded the hadith or used weak ones, and abundantly perused the works of non-Muslim authors.[100] Yet, perhaps most frustrating for his ideological adversaries was the authority with which Hadžić undertook the writing: he did not have the classical 'theological' training and seemed to look down on the ulama as untrained and ignorant and thus unaware of the new scientific

98 Osman Nuri Hadžić, *Muhamed i Koran: Kulturna Istorija Islama* (Beograd: Izdavačka knjižarnica Gece Kona, 1931), p. 107.

99 Hadžić, *Muhamed i Koran*, p. 17.

100 A. Adil Čokić, 'Muhamed i Koran: Kulturna istorija Islama', *Novi Behar* 11–12 (1931), pp. 166–71.

breakthroughs that offered a new yardstick for everything, including religion. Čokić's retort in response to this was accordingly relentless: he painstakingly corrected Hadžić's mistakes, including one about the invented ritual where the Hajjis stand on the 'cave' at Maqām Ibrāhīm (to which Hadžić, again, replied with 'So what?');[101] he indicated the sources that should have been used (hadith, *sīra*, chronicles); and he discouraged the use of works by non-Muslim authors as an authoritative tool for explaining Islamic beliefs and history. The major points of Čokić's criticism regarding the ritual could be subsumed under his insistence that the Hajj is not a ritual with pagan origins – it did exist in the pre-Islamic period but was incorporated into an Islamic framework. Similarly, the Hajj was not a 'consecrated' pagan ritual. And most importantly, Čokić stressed that the Hajj was not a ritual directed to the Kaʿba, but instead a single binding rite, which is the act of standing at Arafat.

The debate between Čokić and Hadžić reveals several faultlines in the new conceptualisations of the Hajj. The disintegration of traditional religious authority led to the appearance of new actors claiming the power of interpretation: Hadžić was intent not only to offer his own, but also to correct other alternative approaches to the topic. Beyond and before the debate with Čokić, Hadžić had been involved in refuting the claims of Serbian Orientalists about Islam. At the same time, Čokić's role was not apologetic or defensive or even weak, as modernist discourse would have it. His strong engagement with the journalistic media (his brother even owned one!) indicates that, as Indira Falk Gesink shows, the traditionalists engaged with the modern with the same vigour as the reformists.[102] Yet, the debate indicates that, while . . .

> . . . religion has been part of the restructuration of practical times and spaces, a re-articulation of practical knowledges and powers, of subjective behaviors,

[101] A. Adil Čokić, 'Mudafea i objašnjenje povodom odgovora g. Hadžića na moju kritiku njegove knjige "Muhamed i Koran" (Nastavak 4)', *Hikjmet* 43 (1932), p. 205; Osman Nuri Hadžić, 'Muhamed i Koran', *Gajret* 13/6–7 (1932), p. 102.

[102] Indira Falk Gesink, '"Chaos on the Earth": Subjective Truths versus Communal Unity in Islamic Law and the Rise of Militant Islam', *The American Historical Review* 108/3 (2003), pp. 710–33; see also Junaid Quadri, *Transformations of Tradition: Islamic Law in Colonial Modernity* (New York: Oxford University Press, 2021).

> sensibilities, needs, and expectations in modernity [. . .] that applies equally to secularism, whose function has been to try to guide that re-articulation.[103]

Consciously or not, all the participants in the debate were aware that religion – Islam – had become the crucial object of a wider debate that permeated discussion on a range of other issues, such as women's rights, clothing, or civic status. Consequently, as Islam was reshaped, the Hajj was scrutinised as well, and 'as a social, religious, medical, political, and economic phenomenon was starting to be fleshed out at this time'.[104]

The debate over the nature and the meaning of the Hajj shows that neither was fixed and certain. The historicised vision of the Hajj where its Islamic origins were blurred was challenged by the traditionalist stance on the pervasiveness of the Islamic framework in the pre-Islamic context. Similarly, the view that the purpose of the Hajj was only visiting the Kaʿba was refuted by Čokić's insistence on pilgrimage as going beyond the pre-Islamic form – it was not about the structure, but about obeying God's command. However, authors such as Hadžić represented a new wave in interpreting Islam and its rituals, a way to offer a new practical vision for believers. In that process, Islam, as well as the Hajj, was defined and redefined, explained for different types of audiences and presented as not only a 'locus of collective connection',[105] but also a space of collective action. The underlying assumption was that Islam had to be aligned with the criteria of science and rationalism, and a part of that process included explaining the essence of rituals and rites, which often were attacked by outsiders as evidence of dogmatism and formalism. What was novel in this discourse is that, for all participants in the debate, Islam was a fixed and unchanging reality, reified and thus liable for assessment and comparison with other phenomena of the modern world.

Discussion on the nature of the Hajj, however, often turned into an explanation of its benefits.[106] In the modernist turn to functionality, the Hajj was

[103] Talal Asad, 'Reading a Modern Classic: W. C. Smith's *The Meaning and End of Religion*', *History of Religions* 40/3 (2001), p. 221.

[104] Tagliacozzo, *The Longest Journey*, p. 254.

[105] Charles Taylor, *Varieties of Religion Today: William James Revisited* (Cambridge, MA: Harvard University Press, 2002), p. 25.

[106] Fehim Spaho, 'Panislamska ideja', *Behar* 7/3 (1906), p. 26.

depicted as having dual use: the otherworldly and elevated, and this-worldly and practical.[107] The pilgrimage was a meeting point of Muslims from all parts of the world, where they would exchange ideas. In the ordering of rituals, the Hajj was given prominent social importance; together with fasting, almsgiving and prayer, it was among the most important outer signs of one's faith. And faith, according to Mehmed Handžić, was a matter of the heart.[108]

Unlike previous depictions of the Hajj and *ziyāra* in *faḍā'il* literature and other treatises, the newly emerging Hajj literature brought into the narrative awareness of the pilgrimage's social dimension. While the earlier pre-nineteenth century writings revealed fascination with and annoyance at the diversity of Muslims on the Hajj, the emphasis on unity was outside the focus. The diversity of different Muslims coming to the Hajj was noticed, but not politicised. With the turn of the twentieth century, the increasing numbers of Muslims on the Hajj under European imperial protection sparked unprecedented interest in the seeming unity-in-diversity. Thus, correspondingly, writing about the Hajj as a shared event for all Muslims was a modern development visible in travelogues of the twentieth century.[109] The idea of the unity of Muslims world through the Hajj became defined and delineated by the late nineteenth century, in the words of the Bosnian authors writing under the pseudonym Edhem Riza (Edhem Mulabdić and Riza Karabeg):

> Muslims are in blood, tribe and geographically dispersed and without any connection that would bind them altogether – apart from faith. However, this unity is also imagined ideally, so in order to keep the unity, and to strengthen it, as well as to help the harmony between them, they need a physical unity, which is accomplished only by the Hajj. Apart from that, from the first to the fifth century [AH] grand scholars gathered there during the Hajj, and used to evaluate the works of famous people, since to meet a scholar, to see whether he is good, diligent and famous, was valued even more by the fact that in this place *mujtahids* lived, the people who on the basis of the Qur'an, hadith and

[107] Durendiš, 'Vazovi jednog imama (drugi vaz)', *Behar* 7/17 (1907), p. 196.

[108] Handžić, 'Važnost vanjskih znakova sa šeriatskog gledišta', p. 81.

[109] Tagliacozzo, *The Longest Journey*, p. 253.

> philosophy set the Islamic rules. If the critics praised someone in Mecca or Medina, the whole world was inspired to use his knowledge.[110]

In imagining the unity of the Muslim world, Edhem Riza mention faith as a common denominator, but quickly pass on to the imagination of the unity. Several decades later, Krpo would elaborate on its *social* potential:

> Meeting one another, discussing the conditions and needs of the Islamic religious communities in all the regions of the world, reaching useful conclusions, establishing friendly trade relations, meeting the world, peoples and their customs, and in that way acquiring knowledge and expanding the horizons, etc. etc. – that is the main goal and purpose of the Hajj. Therefore, the Hajj is an all-Islamic congress, with which the unification of all Muslims of the world into one singular Islamic community takes place. [111] [. . . community] when it, God willing, is created like that, shall rule the world, as it used to rule the world, and will be the bearer of true, pure and unalloyed Islamic culture, civilisation, true (and not the fake, materialistic) progress and every happiness.[112]

One of the characteristics of the Hajj narratives of this period is their double orientation: the attachment to the idealised past is directly connected to the post-imperial attachments and the appreciation of Islamic history, as well as to the imagination of a future interconnectivity and the vision of a brighter post-colonial future for the *umma*. Both of the discourses imply an imagined unity which was disrupted by a turbulent present.

What did this mean for concrete visions of the Hajj? The Hajj had to be defined and explained for increasingly large audiences; however, many authors were also keen on offering an image of how the Hajj should look like in order to be socially useful. In many of these writings, the readers were offered a view of utopian comfort during the Hajj, which was then inadvertently contrasted with their own experiences during the pilgrimage. Throughout the first half of the twentieth century, many Bosnian Muslim authors likened the Hajj to a congress. Their imagination of the congress,

[110] Edhem Riza, 'Put na Meću', *Nada* (15 March 1896).

[111] Krpo, *Put na hadž*, pp. 10–11.

[112] Krpo, *Put na hadž*, pp. 298–99.

pictured in the shiniest colours possible, remained confined to the realm of the idealistic. One of the illustrative examples is *Hikjmet*'s presentation of the Hajj as a congress in 1929, in the poem titled 'Hajj and Eid al-Adha (*Hadž i Kurban Bajram*)':

> Arafat is the meeting of Muslims from the whole world,
> Arafat is a grand congress of the whole Islamic world,
> A Muslim goes to the congress upon the command of his Faith.
> Nation is irrelevant in that grand congress.
> A Muslim is a brother, whoever he is, Arab or non-Arab,
> For that congress, everyone has only white garb.[113]

The use of the concept of congress for the betterment of the Muslims' state appeared frequently on the pages of religious journals such as *Hikjmet*, even in relation to micro-level issues and the position of Muslims in neighbouring countries. A *Hikjmet* article from 1930, which lamented the non-existence of congresses similar to the Eucharistic congress held in Zagreb, indicated that the inspiration for the idea of a congress as solution to the community's problems stemmed not only from the pan-Islamist discourse of the period, but also from contemporary social tendencies among the region's non-Muslim communities. The author, A. Nametak, delved into the topic of Muslims in Serbia, who were in grave danger of assimilation because they did not have mechanisms similar to the Eucharistic congress for preserving their religion.[114]

While the idea of the Hajj provided a large conceptual space for mediating the experience and socio-political visions, around the same time Hajj writings began to point to the idea that pilgrimage was 'losing' its importance and aim and becoming a type of a 'humorous formality'.[115] These writings

[113] Čokić, 'Hadž i Kurban Bajram', p. 34.

[114] A. Nametak, 'Misli uz Euharistički kongres u Zagrebu', *Hikjmet* 17 (1930), pp. 151–52; this was not the only case where a Christian model of organisation was observed in a positive light. Muhamed Krpo, while in Egypt on his way to the Hajj, praised a Christian youth organisation and lamented the current state of Muslim youth in Yugoslavia, who was wasting its time on sports activities. Krpo, *Put na hadž*, pp. 39–40.

[115] 'Nekoliko pouka iz islamske prošlosti: Predavanje povodom Nove muslimanske godine', *El-Hidaje* 5/4–5 (1942), p. 109.

pointed to the need of underlying ideals such as equality and brotherhood, which, as they claimed, were inherent in the Hajj, yet unrecognized by contemporary Muslim elites. These conceptualisations were not simply products of authors' musings, but reactions to an increasingly restrictive reality that led to the transformation of the Hajj experience into encounters with state-imposed restrictions, colonial regulations and growing hostilities. In the process, Hajj writings transformed into social commentaries. The idea of the Hajj as an unfulfilled potential would become especially prominent in the postwar period, as we will see in the next chapter.

Conclusion

On the eve of the Second World War, a Bosnian Hajji wrote in his (still unpublished) diary how the pilgrims read the *khatm* of the Qur'an for the 'victors in Palestine', while praying together with the 'Muslims of Gumuldjina' in Mecca.[116] The unity of Muslims during the Hajj, a dominant way to normatively describe the Hajj in the late nineteenth and early twentieth centuries, seemed to have acquired the contours of an emotional community that was especially visible at breaking points and through the medium of prayer. In the world of crumbling empires and rising nation-states, the Hajj, as a ritual and as a journey, was envisaged as the authentic Islamic answer to encroaching modernity.

Yet, the Hajj itself was a part of modernity, as testified by the struggles over the nature and meaning of the Hajj that were part and parcel of larger debates concerning the renewed role and function of Islam in the modern world.[117] More than just the change and proliferation of media that affected the way in which the Hajj was imagined, this period witnessed an overarching and systematic re-evaluation of the concept of Islam by and for multiple audiences. Its effects expanded temporally and geographically,

[116] Kulenović (?), Pr-1875 (Gazi Husrev-bey's Library), fol. 8a.

[117] 'Over the course of the 20th century, modern Islamic discourse elaborated a meaning of Islam in relation to modernist and postmodernist discursive traditions. The meaning of Islam was thoroughly debated, and the entire process yielded a space in which an Islamic modernity was posited'. Armando Salvatore, in Abdulkader Tayob, *Religion in Modern Islamic Discourse* (London: Hurst, 2009), p. 15.

and more people than ever participated in the formation and consumption of the discourse surrounding the pilgrimage. They were, however, part of a larger conceptual metamorphosis: in the fashion of a conceptual Russian doll, the reification of religion led to a similar process related to the concept of Islam, which then, consequentially, also influenced the way in which rituals were conceived. The intellectual and cultural roots of this transformation were varied; however, the urgency of explaining the religion and its rites stemmed from the challenges posed by non-Muslim, in many cases Western European, writings about Islam.

The debates were inter-Muslim as well. Rather than seeing them as conflict between old and new, we could see the negotiations regarding the origin, nature and significance of the pilgrimage as part of the mediative tension that engendered not only new meanings, but also new sentiments tying Bosnian Muslims to their coreligionists. The next chapter will look at the dis/connections generated by Hajj in the second half of the twentieth century.

4

DIS/CONNECTIONS

Many Hajjis describe the summon at Mount Arafat, the crucial mount and place of a major Hajj rite, as a foretaste of Judgement Day. The heat and the vast mass of people in one place often provoke feelings of belonging to a wide unified body of believers, whose numbers and strength in their eyes represents an untapped human potential, a pool of unbreakable solidarity and a firm link between all Muslims. Hasan Ljubunčić, one member of a tiny Yugoslav group of Hajjis travelling in 1949, was not overly impressed by this idea. The difference between Muslims was stark at Arafat: Turkish Hajjis meticulously pondered over every single detail of the ritual and marvelled at the things that the Yugoslavs told them about freedom of religion in their homeland, raising their hands in prayer for the long life of Marshal Tito. Indonesians tearfully recounted their struggles against the colonisers and asked for help. Ljubunčić dejectedly thought how the mission of gathering all Muslims in Mecca for the purpose of knowing and learning from each other had somehow failed, since to him it seemed that it only served to support the poor in this desert region.

The Hajjis were invited to a dinner at King Ibn Saud's court. The instructions for the attendance were clear: the guests were asked not to request songs or music, and they were to abstain from giving speeches. The dinner was served in 'European style' yet simple: whole roasted sheep and turkeys, with cold water for drinks. Hasan Ljubunčić noted the high-ranking guests that flocked around the king: one of them was Amin al-Husseini (1895–1974), a former Palestinian mufti who, as the author recalled, had helped with forming the infamous Handžar division in Bosnia during the Nazi occupation. Ljubunčić added that the Yugoslavs had extremely bad memories of al-Husseini.

Just a few days later, the Yugoslav Hajjis were attending the Eid reception at the king's court. Waiting in the tent in the courtyard, the Hajjis were sipping lemonade in the scorching heat. Ljubunčić observed the guests: one, who seemed like a 'maharaja', wore an elegant turban made of translucent pink silk. Ljubunčić thought he was a bit haughty and proud, like a peacock. Yet, as the young man turned, the Hajjis could see his somewhat dirty clothes, and that ruined the image. The Hajjis were finally allowed into the spacious room where the other guests were already seated. The Yugoslav delegation realised that they were bestowed the particular honour of being seated close to the king, from where they could watch other Hajjis as they came to kiss his hand and greet him.

Then came the time for speeches, to which the Hajjis listened with great interest, observing the reactions of the king. The unnamed speaker from Hadramawt attracted everyone's attention, as he passionately and somewhat irreverently addressed the king. The Muslims are in a dire state! It was especially difficult for the Muslims in Bulgaria and the Soviet Union, he stressed. And then he proceeded to touch a nerve for everyone in the room: the Palestinian question, 'the greatest shame of all Arabs'. Shaken, he urged the king to do something, considering that he had the authority to do so and a reputation to upkeep. The king wanted to protest, and repeated '*esma* (listen)!' Yet, the speaker would not stop. When the king finally spoke, he seemed dumbfounded and vexed. 'There is no freedom without struggle!' he shouted. Freedom does not come on a silverplate and is not given freely. In the end, the king broke into tears and said that he prayed to be taken from this world so he could forget the disgrace.

The guests dispersed in silence. The Yugoslav Hajjis went back to their thick-walled premises overlooking a busy street with people selling books, trinkets and lemonade, where they could get some respite from the dust and heat. The Hajjis talked for a long time about the reception. What exactly passed between those walls is impossible to know – but according to Ljubunčić the Hajjis spoke about the grand liberation struggle that the Yugoslavs had experienced, which 'had no precedent in the history of the humankind', and they felt proud that they belonged to such a nation. Yugoslavia, they thought, had the unique reputation of a country who had paved the way of struggle for 'all the other smaller and enslaved nations'. Its respective peoples fought for their freedom and equality. Likewise, the Muslims who lived in Yugoslavia enjoyed full rights, like as any other citizen of the country. Ljubunčić felt that the common people whom they had met on their journey recognized its value; however, this contrasted with the propaganda that was being spread about the state of Muslims in Yugoslavia and that the Hajji delegation was bent on countering. It was a heavy burden, and the Hajjis were tired; at nighttime, under the starry sky, they would talk for long periods of time about the gentle climate of their country, yearning to go back. Some even fell ill. It seemed to Ljubunčić that everything, including the animals' movement, became slower in Mecca. Home seemed far.

Hasan Ljubunčić and his group were the first Hajj delegation to travel to the Hijaz after the Second World War. As we will explore below, their Hajj was a profoundly political affair, designed to counter different rising propagandistic narratives that threatened the postwar Yugoslav reputation and could potentially endanger the relationship with its allies. The two travelogues penned by Hasan Ljubunčić in 1949 and 1954 served another purpose as well: they showed the local Muslim readership that the new socialist rule was not limiting their rights. In continuation of the earlier trend, the travelogues functioned as a means of ideological reassurance for the reader; in Ljubunčić's case, moreover, this evolved into a full mediating device between the state which aimed to assert its authority and the Muslim population which needed to be managed. For at least some time, this was the dominant discourse about the Hajj, as the Hajj journey became an important asset in Yugoslav foreign policy. However, it coexisted with other modernist nuances of meaning to the pilgrimage: the emphasis on the utilitarian and rational explanation of the rites, as well as the exotification so often driven by the journalistic demands that served growing Yugoslav audiences. Yet, other ways of conceiving of the Hajj (such as the Sufi interpretation of the rites) persisted deep into the twentieth century as well, testifying to the porousness of imposed categories and dictated discourses.

This chapter will look into the imaginations and conceptualisations of the Hajj as a highly contested tool that connects believers to the holy places, the ritual and other Muslims. The Yugoslav authors who are the subject of this chapter reveal the complex ways in which the Hajj was fleshing out the contradictions between multiple belongings and connections: to Mecca and Medina, to Yugoslavia, to other believers and to multiple reading audiences. In the process, the elaborations on the ritual fell in line with its perceived utility and social use. While most of the authors writing about the Hajj did so from an emic (that is, insider) perspective, seeking to find the right meanings of the pilgrimage and then use it for the benefit of the wider community, there were others, such as Zuko Džumhur, whose depictions of Mecca, the ritual and the pilgrims corresponded to Orientalist imaginaries fit for general Yugoslav consumption. This perspective seemed to come close to what Krpo and Čokić had feared in the 1930s: that the Hajj would become yet another tourist attraction for the rich, decreasing in value and enabling outsiders (non-Muslims, but more importantly those who objectify Islam) to denigrate this crucial ritual. The anxiety over the ritual is propelled by the invading presence of sensationalist media, leading to defensiveness and struggle over meanings ascribed to the Hajj.

These Hajj discourses did not remain in the domain of the abstract but were firmly embedded in the world that shaped pilgrims' experiences. Among the socio-political events and developments that marked the second half of the twentieth century, one stood out: the Palestinian plight undermined the image of Muslim unity and sparked debates on the economic, social and cultural state of the Muslim World. While previous authors, as we could see above, believed in the immediate potential of the Hajj to engender better connectivity among Muslims, the postwar period led many to doubt the power of the Muslim World and to seek for alternative ways to imagine the active present and future of Muslims, especially Yugoslav Muslims.

The Yugoslav Muslims were not debating the meanings of Hajj in a vacuum. The second half of the twentieth century witnessed a rise of exploratory forays into the idea of pilgrimage as a starting framework for decolonial, anti-imperial and liberatory projects. From Malcolm X (1925–1965) and Jalal Al-e Ahmad (1923–1969) to Ali Shariati (1933–1977), the Hajj presented revolutionary possibilities for overturning racism, secularist indifference and oppression. Moreover, the writings of Jalal Al-e Ahmad and Malcolm X show the transformative power of the pilgrimage that engenders the 'possibility of a new politics through an engagement with Muslim practices and social worlds'.[1] The Hajj writings of these decades embody what to some spectators might seem a tension between the 'representational logic' and the 'instrumental framework'[2] – in other words, they use interpretative lenses (those stipulating a particular reading of scripture, or promoting a rational view) in order to also fashion a certain type of individual or collective. In her study of pre-revolutionary Iranian thinkers' writing on the ritual, Fatima Tofighi stresses several ways in which rituals featured at the crux of social debates on rationality, and how they were instrumentalised in the creation of a new subject, including the cultivation of bodies through practices.[3] As we will see from Bosnian authors such as Husein Đozo, the Hajj became a reflective mirror for a modernist ethics that valued the inner feeling of faith and outward action over bodily obeissance. Yet, how successful was their effort?

Modernist efforts yielded modest results. With the expansion of travel, as well as rising rates of literacy that allowed more people to join the ranks of those writing about the Hajj, perspectives on the pilgrimage were expanding. People writing about the pilgrimage included the ulama who had been sidelined by the mainstream modernist discourse dominant in the decades following the Second World War in the highly controlled publications of the Islamic Community, and common believers, including women, who described their experiences of the Hajj in a more straightforward and less ideological fashion. In that way, 'different articulations of piety'[4] coexisted, enabled by the ever-expanding media.

While the previous chapter ended with a plea for the *umma* in a sentiment of proverbial solidarity, this one begins with the shattered illusion of the unified Muslim World. What follows is a journey through different facets of the

[1] Golnar Nikpour, 'Revolutionary Journeys, Revolutionary Practice: The Hajj Writings of Jalal Al-e Ahmad and Malcolm X', *Comparative Studies of South Asia, Africa and the Middle East* 34/1 (2014), p. 68.

[2] Fatima Tofighi, 'Religious Rituals as Civil *Hexis:* The Case of Modernist Interpretations of Islamic Rituals among Iranian Pre-Revolutionary Intellectuals', *Method and Theory in the Study of Religion* 32 (2020), p. 185.

[3] Tofighi, 'Religious Rituals as Civil *Hexis*'.

[4] Henig, *Remaking Muslim Lives*, p. 106.

Hajj imaginary of the second half of the twentieth century, which emphasised or deemphasised the connection of Yugoslav Muslims to the Hajj and to their Muslim coreligionists. The state regulation of the pilgrimage, popular responses, modernist interpretations and Sufi continuities all constitute a caleidoscope of religious experience captured by a growing body of writings.

Promoting Yugoslavia: Postwar Hajj Delegations

After the Second World War, the organisation of the Hajj was tied to the tightening state grip and control of religious practices. With the Communist suppression of practices such as veiling and Sufi worship, the Hajj journey, which included physical travel outside the borders of Yugoslavia and exposure to external influences, was observed with increased caution. Yet, specific political alignments and ground-breaking events worked in the opposite direction as well and made the Hajj an asset for the nascent socialist Yugoslav state. In 1948, the tensions between Yugoslavia's leader Tito and Stalin peaked, which led to the expulsion of Yugoslavia from the Information Bureau of the Communist and Workers' Parties (Cominform). The Yugoslav regime also encountered opposition from the wide and diverse body of exiles who fled Yugoslavia in the aftermath of the Second World War. The feeling of isolation was real, and the authorities sought ways to counter the propaganda that was damaging the Yugoslav reputation, especially in Middle Eastern countries that seemed to be useful allies. The Hajj was a perfect opportunity to accomplish several goals: crush the dissent from the outside, build a good image of Yugoslavia and regain trust with the local Muslim population.

State and imperial Hajj delegations who pursued political and financial gains were not a rare sight: in the interwar period, the Japanese Hajj delegation sought to further economic interests through a pan-Asianist framework.[5] In 1949, the year of the first Yugoslav Hajj delegation, there was also a delegation of Moroccan Muslims under the supervision of the Francoist regime.[6] Despite the delegation being chosen on the basis of their quietism (unlike the Yugoslav group which had proven their socialist credentials and was vocal about anti-colonialism), their motivations were somewhat

[5] Koyagi, 'The Hajj by Japanese Muslims in the Interwar Period'.

[6] Dieste, 'The Franco North African Pilgrims after WWII'.

comparable: political isolation pushed both states into seeking allies among Arab countries, and the fear of alternative discourses abroad (such as among the diaspora and émigré groups) shaped much of their itinerary.

To accomplish the task, the first Yugoslav Hajj delegation consisted of the *raīs al-ʿulamā* Ibrahim Fejić, the second-in-command Murad Šećeragić, Hasan Ljubunčić who was the president of the Religious Committee for Bosnia and Herzegovina, Šaip Šerif from Macedonia and Sinan Hasani from Kosovo. In a limited way, the group reflected the diversity of the Yugoslav Muslim population by bringing together Bosniaks and Albanians. The itinerary was tightly planned so that they could visit Egypt, Syria, Saudi Arabi, Lebanon and Turkey, avoiding Iraq where there were no Yugoslav exiles and refugees. Iraq was also seen as a place where Yugoslav Hajjis could be negatively provoked.[7] The Hajjis' tight schedule was organised such that they could visit religious dignitaries in the countries through which they passed, as well as meet with the press and émigrés from the region. The journey was closely monitored by Yugoslav diplomats who saluted the effort and reported back to say that the visit was successful, since it touched upon the religious sensibilities of the region and managed to foster a favourable public opinion about Yugoslavia abroad.[8] After the journey, the Hajjis themselves wrote a report which was sent to the Marshall Tito, and they also suggested some of the ways in which Yugoslavia could improve its relationship with Middle Eastern countries, including sending students to Al-Azhar, starting a journal on religious life for Muslims, establishing a diplomatic post in Saudi Arabia and maintaining connections with Yugoslav émigrés in Turkey (Fig. 4.1).[9]

Hasan Ljubunčić, one of the more prominent members of the delegation, wrote two travelogues, one documenting the 1949 journey, which took them onto a longer detour through Turkey on the way back, and the second one his Hajj journey in 1954, which focused more on the delineation of the Hajj-related rituals. While the itineraries were different, the travelogues document postwar transformations of technology and its impact on travel, as well as the increasing role that states played in the shaping of a national Islam. Both

[7] Radmila Radić, *Država i verske zajednice 1945–1970* (Beograd: Inis, 2002), p. 604.

[8] Radić, *Država i verske zajednice 1945–1970*, pp. 604–5.

[9] Radić, *Država i verske zajednice 1945–1970*, pp. 605–6.

Naše hadžije na izgradnji proširenja Haremi-šerifa u Medini

Figure 4.1 Hajjis on a construction site in Medina. Source: *Glasnik IVZ*.

travelogues also read as narratives in support of the nascent socialist Yugoslav state. The description of the preparations for the journey includes significant praise for the authorities and their goodwill in ensuring that the Hajj journey would not see any bureaucratic problems. The syntagm '*naše narodne vlasti* (our people's authorities)' was repeated throughout the narratives in relation to the easy circumstances of the journey, implying that the communist authorities managed to improve the political and social situation after the Second World War. The Hajj endeavour, however, was affected by changes on a global level as well. In the second travelogue published in 1954, Ljubunčić described how the establishment of a shipping route between Rijeka and Hongkong affected their own travel, since they were able to board a ship that took them to Port Sudan. Apart from the preoccupation with administrative technicalities (such as obtaining visas), the obvious problem was money in foreign currencies (Fig. 4.2).

Bosnia featured prominently in the narrative of Yugoslav socialist success. In the 1949 travelogue, Ljubunčić described the journey through Bosnia and further on to Dalmatia, reflecting on the heavy burden carried by Muslims in the past. As the Hajjis passed by a power plant under construction,

Figure 4.2 Hajjis on the steamship *Romanija.* Source: *Glasnik IVZ.*

Ljubunčić pondered its significance for the economic development and merrily exclaimed that 'Bosnia is no longer a downtrodden orphan girl (*Bosna nije više sirotica kleta*)' who had served as a bargaining chip in its difficult past. Bosnian Muslims, as Ljubunčić recalls, not so long ago had been second-class citizens in 'old' Yugoslavia, where they had been dehumanised, attacked and persecuted on account of their religion. According to the author, the situation was different in socialist Yugoslavia, as evidenced by the better economic position of Muslims and their access to jobs and positions. The Muslims, however, had earned their status within the Yugoslav state due to their participation in the People's Liberation Struggle, together with many non-Muslims whose heroic stories are embedded in the other travelogue as well.[10] The Muslims of Yugoslavia belonged to 'our people' – a non-religious designation which for Ljubunčić meant the multitudes of those who shared the same history of struggle, just like 'our country' emphasised indisputable belonging to Yugoslavia. Paradoxically,

[10] Hasan Ljubunčić, 'Istorija hadža u Bosni i Hercegovini sa putem na hadž u 1954 godini', *Glasnik Vrhovnog islamskog starješinstva u Federativnoj narodnoj republici Jugoslaviji* 6/1–2 (1955), p. 45.

the Hajj journey also became a tour of wartime battlefields which served to remind the reader of the significance of the People's Liberation Struggle. Furthermore, it became an opportunity to observe places of dispute and conflict.[11] Thus, what had once been a network of *ziyāras* to tombs in the case of seventeenth- and eighteenth-century travelogues, or a string of visits to religious scholars, as in the case of interwar Hajjis, now became a journey of remembrance of the struggle, with a clearly defined task of state promotion through meetings with state officials and journalists.

The urgency of the Hajj delegation could not be overstated. The end of the Second World War and the victory of the Communist Party of Yugoslavia ushered in a new age where many old actors – not only those who had previously been active participants in the system of the Independent State of Croatia, but also others who now were political or social undesirables for other reasons – fled the country and resided in places as varied as Egypt, Great Britain or the USA. A large part of the Yugoslav emigrant population was hoping for the Tito regime to be overthrown, but the Bosnian Muslims in the diaspora were not a homogenous group by any means. Despite being ethnically and politically diverse, the entire emigrant population was labelled as 'enemy' in Yugoslavia.[12] Some of them had indeed been aligned with the structures of the former regime, and they had fled from Yugoslavia to places as far as Argentina, such as Ismet Varatanović whom we remember from the previous chapter as the author of a provocative Hajj travelogue. Although unwelcome in the new Yugoslavia, these figures could still wreak havoc on the fragile international connections. Some of them remained faithful to their wartime ideals, and the possibility that they could spread their propaganda about the dire situation of Muslims in Yugoslavia seemed very real.

Thus, the Hajjis set on the mission to combat these narratives 'spread relentlessly by the enemies of our state and war criminals'.[13] At the same time, they also sought to visit the Balkan diaspora that was spread out across the

[11] In the second travelogue, the reflections on the Trieste Crisis (1953) serve as background to the description of the stops that the Hajjis made at the beginning of their journey.

[12] Mustafa Imamović, *Bošnjaci u emigraciji: monografija 'Bosanskih Pogleda' 1955–1967* (Zürich: Bosniak Institute, 1996), p. 78.

[13] Radić, *Država i verske zajednice 1945–1970*, p. 605.

countries of the Middle East, especially in Turkey, where waves of immigrants had settled in the aftermath of the demise of the Ottoman Empire. The journey of 1949 included a longer sojourn in Turkish cities with a large *muhajir* population, where the Yugoslav Hajjis tried to reconnect with Bosniaks and to see which types of links still tied them to their old homeland. Seeking Bosniaks in Turkey became a search for a third space – one equally far from homeland and holy land, where connections with the past as well as with potential for the future were sought:

> One can say that there in Turkey, there used to be a small, old Bosnia, which is diminishing from day to day. Today there are four generations of our expatriates living in Turkey. They are known in Turkey as 'Bosniaks'. Many feel pride in being one of those. However, the majority of them say that they are both Bosniaks and Turks. A smaller number of them says that they are just Bosniaks. And a tiny number of them says that they are only Turks, giving up Bosniakness [. . .] One should say that our people in Turkey are completely devoted to the Turkish state, and they love it sincerely, without pretending. Many appreciated its hospitality when they moved there. [. . .] The Turks do not consider them a minority. They consider them good Muslims, good citizens, good neighbours and Turks. [. . .] Their love for Bosnia, for their homeland, has turned into love for their new homeland, Turkey.[14]

In contrast to the travelogues from the interwar period, the image of Turkey received positive treatment in Ljubunčić's narrative, owing to the perception of its industrial progress and the backward past that it had apparently left behind. This image of Turkey fitted a particular desire for modernisation and an adversarial attitude towards the past. The following excerpt shows some of the key elements in imagining a modern present and a modern future:

> Around 9 pm we arrived in Adana. We stayed over an hour there, and were watching the people going by, there were lots of them on the platform, both men and women. There were officers and uniformed clerks, but there was no trace of the fez or full body veils, which one sought in Turkey unconsciously. This old physiognomy was lost in Turkey, and it [Turkey] became less attractive

[14] Ljubunčić, 'Put na hadž', *Glasnik VIS-a* 4/5–7 (1953), pp. 160–61.

> to foreigners because people do not look exotic any longer. It amazes all the cultured world with its progress. Somewhere behind the station one could hear a patriotic song sung by youth in a chorus. Turkey is no longer burdened by any prejudice that could hinder its progress.[15]

In this excerpt it is apparent that the author considered Western dress a symbol of progress and a sign of discarding the unwanted Ottoman past. However, what Ljubunčić also implies with the discarding of dress is the loss of exoticism and, hence, of its appeal to foreigners, while simultaneously – and paradoxically – this world itself is becoming more Western. The whole narrative on Turkey is imbued with the words 'progress', 'modernisation', 'democracy' and 'democratisation', although Ljubunčić sometimes exerts caution when, for example, he describes the democratic steps that Turkey had to introduce as slow and gradual. When commenting on the Turkish educational institutions, Ljubunčić warns:

> *Mekteb*s and madrasas, which hindered the progress and advance of the Turkish nation with their unscientific views of the world, were abolished by one of Kemal's decrees, and no regime after Kemal even thinks about bringing these back, because it would once again mean the stagnation of progress.[16]

Ljubunčić is interested in every aspect of social and technological development, so he lists the names of popular journals (*Cumhuriyet*, *Vakit* and so on), parks (Vamunecitlik) and more. The emphasis on modern media is especially relevant in the context of the state projects that aimed to create modern identities, as well as to foster visions of a common opponent or enemy. In that process, the centralised structure of mass media was often seen as a tool of unification.[17] The obsession with the modern in the narrative is also evident in how cities are described. In the case of Alexandria, Ljubunčić emphasises

[15] Ljubunčić, 'Put na hadž', *Glasnik VIS-a* 3/8–12 (1952), p. 265.

[16] Ljubunčić, 'Put na hadž', *Glasnik VIS-a* 3/8–12 (1952), p. 268.

[17] Dale Eickelman and Jon Anderson, 'Redefining Muslim Publics', in *New Media in the Muslim World: The Emerging Public Sphere*, ed. by Dale F. Eickelman and Jon W. Anderson (Bloomington: Indiana University Press, 2003), p. 3.

that this city has wide boulevards which make it similar to Western European cities, in contrast to 'Oriental' cities.[18] A peculiar case of positive modernity, as described above, is detected in Turkey, in which case the author even produces a photo of Ankara as a modern city.

The vantage point assumed by the Hajj delegation – where the Yugoslavs earned their position to observe, comment and enlighten others – was part of the broader spatial and political attitude that was developing in the decades after the Second World War. As Yugoslavia started to forge relations with an increasing number of countries, the travelogue became one popular genre for promoting the country and moulding a specific self-image. The authors included a range of diplomats and journalists, 'all former partisans, all Communists'.[19] The backdrop of other countries – in many cases African – served as a canvas against which a new Yugoslav identity could be formed. In a range of travelogues that have only recently begun to attract scholarly attention, Yugoslavia was presented as a key node in the global solidarity of nations that refused to be squashed between the West and the Soviet Union; yet, it remained thoroughly European.[20] In its contact with Muslim countries, the somewhat atypical national texture of Yugoslavia was recognized: "It is the land of Marshal Tito and there are no Russians there, but there are Muslims."[21] Muslims seemed like an ideal medium between Europe and the Third World.

The postwar world through which the Hajjis were passing was depicted and carved up according to the mixture of the pilgrims' experiences and preconceived expectations, with a strong awareness of the state lines that diminished different forms of attachment (such as the feeling of belonging to the *umma*) yet could not entirely erase them. While there was a reduced sense of political unity of the 'Muslim world',[22] the feeling of being part of a distinctive

[18] Hasan Ljubunčić, Hasan. 'Istorija hadža u Bosni i Hercegovini sa putem na hadž u 1954 godini', *Glasnik Vrhovnog islamskog starješinstva u Federativnoj narodnoj republici Jugoslaviji* 6/3–4 (1955), p. 112.

[19] Nemanja Radonjić, '"From Kragujevac to Kilimanjaro": Imagining and Re-Imagining Africa and the Self-Perception of Yugoslavia in the Travelogues from Socialist Yugoslavia', *Godišnjak za društvenu istoriju* 2 (2016), p. 83.

[20] Radonjić, 'From Kragujevac to Kilimanjaro', p. 65.

[21] Radonjić, 'From Kragujevac to Kilimanjaro', p. 65.

[22] Aydin, *The Idea of the Muslim World*, p. 179.

Yugoslav European society was strengthened throughout the journey. Despite the rise of airplane travel, which shortened the time and the procedure (albeit being stressful at times), Hajjis encountered increasing problems with borders and regulations, including their prolonged stays in the quarantine. Returning from the Hajj and landing in Beirut in 1949, the Bosnian groups was held in quarantine for fear of the plague that had appeared in Java that year. They unsuccessfully tried to protest by saying that they were Europeans who were mindful of hygiene, but still had to undergo the same procedure.[23] In the quarantine, the Yugoslavs were picky: they did not want to stay in joint dormitories with dirty linens but asked for separate rooms and decent service. Other Hajjis were surprised at this resoluteness yet, as Ljubunčić wants us to believe, admired them for being more diligent, more cultured and generally more persistent in asking for what they needed.

Mecca in the Postwar Imaginary

Even in Mecca, the feeling of distinctiveness did not disappear. Everything seemed different and abruptly distinct from the 'European life and world'.[24] Time was reckoned differently, which reflected the increased piety of the city's inhabitants.[25] Piety was posited as antithetical to the fast and uncompromising flow of modernity. The Hajj narratives emphasised Mecca as a place of faith more than anything else:

> Faith dominates everything in Mecca. Everything submits willingly to faith. Everything is marked by piety. Everyone utters prayers. Relations between people are coloured by religious tolerance. Everyone is obliged to fulfill religious duties. Faith in God is great. It controls everything. Many Hajjis who suffer from various diseases go on the Hajj, believing they will be cured that way.[26]

By presenting Mecca as a place of pure faith, the non-interfering, apolitical nature of the pilgrimage was pointed out and made the Hajj comparable to

[23] Ljubunčić, 'Put na hadž', *Glasnik VIS-a* 3/5–7 (1952), pp. 159–60.
[24] Ljubunčić, 'Put na hadž', *Glasnik VIS-a* 1/11–12 (1950), p. 342.
[25] Ljubunčić, 'Put na hadž', *Glasnik VIS-a* 1/11–12 (1950), p. 342.
[26] Ljubunčić, 'Put na hadž', *Glasnik VIS-a* 1/4–7 (1950), p. 136.

the pilgrimage practices of other religious traditions.[27] Faith was reified, and even its practices (such as 'uttering prayers') were made separate from other activities. Ljubunčić also stressed the role of tradition in the Hijaz. Tradition as a term was used to describe the preservation of a connection to the Islamic past, and especially to the early Muslim community. While it might come as surprise to a modern reader whose image of Mecca today is overshadowed by the domineering Royal Clock Tower, Ljubunčić stressed the Saudi preservation of the Prophet's house and the room of His daughter Fatima.[28] The Ottoman past of the built landscape existed in traces; with a hint of nostalgia, the Hajjis found out through their *dalīl* (guide) about the elaborate set of architectural monuments that had been destroyed by the ruling power in the Hijaz. Yet, apparently other things remained constant over time, such as the families who claimed descent from the Prophet and were held in special regard, as well as the transmission of knowledge, through learning the Qur'an and the hadith, and the recitation of the Qur'an.[29]

In a world of shaken trust in the unity of the Muslim World, where other models of belonging took precedence, the ritual remained the binding thread for believers. In his travelogue from 1954, which was less focused on the promotion of Yugoslavia and more on the historical and religious aspects of the pilgrimage and the holy places, Ljubunčić turned his attention to Mecca as a place that is immutable and beyond change:

> Hajjis go to Mecca with sincere religious feelings, which they strengthen and enrich there. They come to the city because of the worship, to which they dedicate themselves in full. One forgets everything in Mecca and does not think about worries or other things and focuses only on worship and good deeds. Spiritual religious life is very intense here. Religious rules are paramount, and

[27] A simple example of this would be the insistence on the usage of the word '*sveštenik* (priest)' while referring to a Muslim ulama member, even in the context of Mecca. See Ljubunčić, 'Put na hadž', *Glasnik VIS-a* 1/4–7 (1950), p. 136.

[28] However, he noted how Ibn Saud had destroyed all the other tombs which had no relation to the Prophet. Ljubunčić, 'Put na hadž', *Glasnik VIS-a* 1/11–12 (1950), p. 343.

[29] Ljubunčić mentions that this kind of preservation of knowledge exists in other parts of the 'pious Islamic world', but that there it is not preserved as strongly. 'Put na hadž', *Glasnik VIS-a* 1/11–12 (1950), p. 343.

> everyone willingly succumbs to them. Hajjis are in such a religious fever which they cannot experience anywhere else in the world. They become a part of an enormous religious mass, which carries them through religious events. Religious feelings get so enflamed in Mecca, that the boundary between this world and the other world seems blurry. [. . .] If someone mistakenly comes here, without those basic and sincere religious feelings, he cannot get used to it, he cannot understand the enormous religious strength that moves the Hajjis, and he is irrationally afraid and sees strange wonders and sensations in things which are normal and natural for a Hajji.[30]

This paragraph reflects some of the anxieties that we have already encountered in the interwar period: the fear that the rich and intense experience of the practitioners, which is bound to its specific habitus and its inner logic, will be revealed – perhaps violently – to outsiders who do not have the capacity to comprehend the attachment of the believers to the seemingly strange customs and sights of the pilgrimage. Even in times when the Hajj was used for nation-states' political agenda, spiritual allegiances could not be denied: the rituals were observed in accordance with the legal prescriptions, and the Hajjis respected the form which they shared with myriads of other coreligionists. Yet, Hajjis' worries were not unfounded: pilgrimage could indeed become a matter of dreaded touristic attention and journalistic sensationalism. As Yugoslavia used travel as a means of heavy self-promotion, there was also a rising interest in non-European cultures,[31] with a stream of diplomats and journalists flocking to different locales across Africa and Asia. As Yugoslav imaginative geographies swiftly expanded, it was only a matter of time when Mecca and Medina would also come into the focus of outsiders' curiosity.

[30] Ljubunčić, 'Istorija hadža u BiH sa putem na hadž u 1954', *Glasnik Vrhovnog islamskog starješinstva u Federativnoj narodnoj republici Jugoslaviji* 7/1–3 (1956), pp. 65–66.

[31] James M. Robertson argues that, despite the fact that these writings often 'relegated non-European cultures to a precolonial, premodern past', they nevertheless were not a simple expression of Yugoslav orientalism. James M. Robertson, 'Navigating the Postwar Liberal Order: Autonomy, Creativity and Modernism in Socialist Yugoslavia, 1949–1953', *Modern Intellectual History* 17/2 (2020), p. 410.

No Angels in the Desert: Zuko Džumhur in the Hijaz

Travelogues of the postwar era were in many ways a reflection of the perceived role that many Yugoslav public figures consciously imposed on themselves. In the preface to one of the first anthologies of Yugoslav travel writing, Fadil Hadžić (1922–2011) notes how postwar travelogues emerged from the journalistic tradition, aiming not only to inform the readership but also to add a literary value to the experience.[32] The travelogues written by Yugoslav authors 'revealed the state in the contemporary world'; they 'direct us politically, but at the same time paint people and events, describe the farthest places and landscapes, and deftly draw immense galleries of human fates spread across the meridians of this world – still unliberated from colonial politics and discrimination'.[33] Yugoslav authors entered those worlds as self-perceived experts, leaving them with hefty records that mapped tragic histories of 'small and backward' peoples.[34] Their treatment of race as a category of otherness has long passed under the scholarly radar, even though studies on race have now started to appear.[35] For a long time, race constituted a neglected subject in the study of Yugoslav history; yet, as we could see, it formed one crucial way to observe the Other. Yugoslav authors created racialised geographies, built on a particular 'temporal subordination'[36] which positioned Yugoslavs at the end of the developing line of history, through mechanisms we have already seen in the travelogues of Hasan Ljubunčić. Yugoslavs, in this framework, stood at the forefront of all other non-western nations, even when Yugoslavs saw themselves as European. The other geographies of interest to

[32] Fadil Hadžić, 'Put oko svijeta (uvod)', in *Put oko svijeta* (Zagreb: Novinarsko izdavačko poduzeće, 1961), p. 6.

[33] Hadžić, 'Put oko svijeta (uvod)', p. 6.

[34] Hadžić, 'Put oko svijeta (uvod)', p. 6.

[35] One of the recent studies dealing with race in the Yugoslav region is Catherine Baker, *Race and the Yugoslav Region: Postsocialist, Post-conflict, Postcolonial?* (Manchester: Manchester University Press, 2018).

[36] Ussama Makdisi, 'Ottoman Orientalism', *The American Historical Review* 107/3 (2002), p. 769; while Makdisi's artice deals with the particular late Ottoman modernist treatment of the imperial peripheries through the prism of progress, the term is applicable to the Yugoslav cultural production which aimed to create a progressivist socialist normativity.

Yugoslav authors were thus portrayed as lagging behind the Yugoslav path of progress, waiting for their light and guidance, being simultaneously connected and disconnected from it.

Written predominantly as a journalistic genre for the eager public, Yugoslav travelogues also tried to bring closer different spaces, while constantly reminding the readership of the local context. This double perspective found its representative in Zuko Džumhur (1920–89), a Bosnian author who earned fame through his illustrated travelogues and television travel show *Hodoljublje*. His most famous work – *Nekrolog jednoj čaršiji* (*Obituary to a Small Town*) from 1958 – was prefaced with an introduction written by Ivo Andrić, who would go on to receive the Nobel Prize in literature in 1961. Andrić himself noted the double perspective of Džumhur's travelogues: 'He is among those real travellers-travel writers [. . .] who do not forget who they are and what they are, where they come from and where they are supposed to return'.[37] Andrić also commended Džumhur's drawings that accompanied the travelogues and distinguished the author from other travel writers.

The collection contained several travelogues from Džumhur's travels around the world and, notably, two travelogues dedicated to Džumhur's visit to Mecca in 1957. Two travelogues titled 'Kamen crnog sjaja (The Shiny Black Stone)' and 'Putovanje po besmislu (The Travel in Nonsense)' depict Džumhur's sojourn through the Hijaz, from Jeddah to Mecca. 'Kamen crnog sjaja (The Shiny Black Stone)' is conspicuously lacking from the edition of *Nekrolog* which was published in 2004, reflecting according to some critics the falsification of Džumhur's work and its place in the post-war Bosniak nationalist narrative.[38]

The fact that Zuko Džumhur followed Hajjis in 1957 is not widely known in contemporary Bosnia. It was a smaller group of Hajjis, less than forty, consisting mostly of farmers, artisans and some members of the Islamic Religious Community. Yet, the Hajjis gained plenty of attention, even being hosted by the Egyptian president Gamal Abdal Nasser, who stated his support for

[37] Ivo Andrić, in Zuko Džumhur, *Nekrolog jednoj čaršiji* (Sarajevo: Svjetlost, 1958), p. 9.

[38] http://www.prometej.ba/clanak/kultura/prometejske-price-i-pjesme/zuko-dzumhur-kamen-crnoga-sjaja-originalni-tekst-sa-ilustracijama-2956 (accessed on 27 August 2021).

the politics of Yugoslavia and Tito.[39] The Hajj journey was, as had been the case earlier, heavily monitored and directed to promote Yugoslav rule. With Džumhur, however, the Hajj once again became the sensationalist topic that the interwar Hajjis had feared it would become.

In his characteristic style, Džumhur juxtaposed different images, producing a sense of the unfamiliarity and utter foreignness of the holy places. The Hijaz seems like a wonderland from a modern *Arabian Nights*: 'In small stores of good-for-nothings one can buy herbs that cure snake bite, talismans against evil eye, and the parade uniform of a Chinese emperor'.[40] Jeddah was a melting pot of people who were drawn by unknown fates and dark impulses, looking like a flashy gallery 'full of prayers, spices, and pilgrims'.[41] The travelogue essays contain a number of accompanying drawings: 'Putovanje po besmislu (The Travel in Nonsense)', which describes Džumhur's encounter with the desert and several holy sites, such as Jabal al-Raḥma, contains caricatures depicting women who were naked or in transparent clothing, with contours of minarets and domes in the background. Džumhur also drew street scenes, trying to capture their various layers from ascetics and beggars, over hustling traders and buyers, to covered women peeking out from windows that overlooked the alleys covered in Coca-Cola advertisements and photos of Arab leaders. Other drawings followed the narrative details more closely: a shaykh administering a punishment of multiple lashes, while a plane flies overhead, depicting a scene that Džumhur claims to have witnessed.

In his travelogues, Džumhur also noted the faces of women and Bedouins. Women would sometimes reveal their faces, and their eyes 'sparkled instead of stars',[42] yet would bashfully lower the gaze whenever the author intrusively looked at them. One of the Bedouins, however, looked as if 'someone [had] spilled a bottle of the cheap paint across his face'.[43] They all loved poetry and their language. In Mecca, Džumhur seems not to have

[39] Radić, *Država i verske zajednice 1945–1970*, p. 607.

[40] Džumhur, 'Kamen crnog sjaja', p. 80.

[41] Džumhur, 'Kamen crnog sjaja', p. 80.

[42] Džumhur, 'Kamen crnog sjaja', p. 82.

[43] Džumhur, 'Kamen crnog sjaja', p. 82.

cared about the rituals; the city could have been 'a colourful filigree box full of old gems hidden by a giant hand in the heart of desert'.[44] Mecca, and indeed the whole of Arabia, seemed to be a place that hides the most bizarre of the old and the modern: Swiss watches and German machines, French cosmetics and Pakistani ascetics. Yet, the long listing of different wonders covers the ultimate flatness and unchangeability of human lives in Arabia, and ultimately their absolute otherness. Džumhur does not describe his Hajji co-travelers at all; there are only small and scattered mentions of Yugoslav geography in the travelogue.

Abdel Rahim Hadi is the only companion whom Džumhur mentions in more detail, but even he has a name too long to write in full: 'Abdel Rahim learned to pronounce the name of my country, and that is how we became friends'.[45] Abdel Rahim, his native interlocutor and informant, knew all the global and local trivia and proved very useful to Zuko, with whom he spoke in a 'strange language [. . .] made up from Italian, English, French, international words and Serbian and Arab fingers'.[46] Through him, the author found out that this country forbade painting and sculpture, play and music, and alcohol and gambling. This lacklustre place crushed all hopes: Zuko Džumhur remembered a young prince from Hadramawt who was travelling with him from Cairo, lamenting the fact that he would no longer be able to sing *Mambo Italiano* in his hilly country, nor marry his belle from Napoli. Instead, he would wear white clothes and pray in a mosque.

Reiterating the interwar obsession with corporeal punishment in the Hijaz, a large part of Džumhur's travelogue is dedicated to the spectacle of public lashings and cutting of hands. The shaykh who supervised the punishments wore glasses and sipped lemonade with a straw, while Lufthansa and KLM planes flew above their heads. The utter corporeality of the scene (where those whose hand was cut off could choose whether to take it with them or leave it in the sand) is juxtaposed with the extreme indifference of the onlookers. But that is not the only contrast that Džumhur is trying to evoke: every scene he presents includes a detail of the encroaching modernity

[44] Džumhur, 'Kamen crnog sjaja', p. 83.
[45] Džumhur, 'Kamen crnog sjaja', p. 86.
[46] Džumhur, 'Kamen crnog sjaja', p. 88.

in the shape of Western food, luxury items, or transportation means. Yet, this modernity cannot change the essence of Arab life, as all the products of Western modernity will be consumed superficially:

> The cars of a rich Arabian are in the latest technological trend [. . .] As soon as the car arrives in his garage, the noble owner will hang the prayer beads soaked in the holy water 'Abu Zamzam' and draw the silk curtains that his wives sew to keep him from crashes and other traffic accidents [. . .] The owner will sit confidently in the driver's seat with his two, three or four wives veiled in black from head to toes and he will not respect any traffic signs or rules. [. . .] Women will sit behind the back of their strong husband, black and still like huge bottles of ink. Their rich husband is stern and strict when it comes to the rules of his country, but he is very gentle and attentive to his wives. He seldomly cheats on them and outside of his harem has no other mistresses.[47]

The stillness of Arab life and its unchangeability were also reflected in the unquavering fanaticism of the inhabitants of the Hijaz, those who would 'believe in a hoja's talisman the same way he believes in penicyllin'.[48] The Arab man, it seems, has taken over Western material goods, yet remained enchanted in ways that to the author seem incongruent with modern times. The form is the only thing that matters: 'Master's wives will all be illiterate and manicured. They will use Elizabeth Arden cosmetics and French undergarments under their horrendous black pellerines'.[49] Their food will remain the same, as well as their cleaning habits, despite springs of oil that miraculously flow on their fields. Their feelings are depicted as extreme as well: without providing any context, Džumhur points to Arab love towards Gamal Abdel Nasser and hatred towards David Ben Gurion which evolves into worship and hysteria. 'Had Arabs not been Semites, their hatred towards Israel would be antisemitism'.[50]

[47] Džumhur, 'Kamen crnog sjaja', pp. 98–99.

[48] Džumhur, 'Kamen crnog sjaja', p. 99.

[49] Džumhur, 'Kamen crnog sjaja', p. 100.

[50] Džumhur, 'Putovanje po besmislu', p. 79.

Even the descriptions of the holy places contain sarcasm. Describing Jabal al-Raḥma – or Mount Arafat – a place where Adam and Eve are believed to have united after long wanderings on Earth, Džumhur dryly comments how life in Arabia in those times 'must have been pretty hard, because oil had not been discovered yet'.[51] His characterisation of the austerity of the place is even more essentialist:

> The Italians would erect a church on this sacred hill, the Americans a base, the French a hotel, and the Lebanese a casino. The Bulgarians would build a huge academic institute for the fight against border superstition. The Turks would build a fort as is their custom, and those from Belgrade would open a 'Tavern at the First Sin'. The Arabians built nothing.[52]

It seems utterly ironic that Zuko Džumhur accompanied a group of Hajjis to witness a ritual he found completely foreign. The city seemed to be a place where 'the general rehearsal of hell took place'.[53] So what did all these Hajjis – interchangeable and indistinguishable because of their fanaticism – look for in this place? Ultimately, Džumhur found futility in their striving:

> This morning Indians, Javanese, Moroccans, Turks and Afghans asked for forgiveness of their sins and those of their predecessors, raising their hands into the incandescent sky.
>
> This morning the columns of people under green Mohammad's flags shouted oaths to Allah and fell under the wise glow of the holy meteor.
>
> This morning the money changers counted their cloths full of green American notes like spinach.
>
> This morning the streets were pestilent from hundreds of corpses that in the warm night released their final pious shout and repented for the hundredth time for the sins never committed.
>
> The August day burned the roofs of the city, the columns of skeletons and green banners of the righteous believers.

[51] Džumhur, 'Putovanje po besmislu', p. 74.
[52] Džumhur, 'Putovanje po besmislu', p. 74.
[53] Džumhur, 'Kamen crnog sjaja', p. 100.

> In front of the shop that sold German medicine, an old man sighed his last. He could have been an Indian, or Arab, or Persian.
>
> In his open eyes was reflected a part of the desert sky that was disappearing. There were no angels in the vicinity.[54]

Džumhur's travelogue mediated between both postwar Yugoslav self-promotion and new audiences eager for sensationalism. The Hajj as a ritual that was close enough – since Yugoslavia had a considerable Muslim population – yet out of reach for most and therefore ultimately prone to exoticisation and sometimes extreme stereotyping. Džumhur's position thus was that of both insider and outsider, allowing him to provide access to the prying eyes of the Yugoslav public. Džumhur was writing on the eve of the formation of the Non-Aligned Movement; his travelogues had become very popular, and he even made a televised show on his travels. His observations of Arabs and Hajjis in general, thus, fit the label of 'consumerist Orientalism',[55] Orientalism of a kind that would several decades later produce rock songs evoking the ever-other, never changing Orient, as in the case of the hugely popular 1981 hit song *Mustafa* by Bebi Dol (Dragana Todorović, 1958–) and turbo-folk depictions of oil-rich exploitative Arabs, as depicted in the 1985 song *Šeik* by Lepa Brena (Fahreta Živojinović, née Jahić, 1960–). It seems no wonder that much of the translation of racial and ethnic stereotyping into the cultural register happened through figures such as Lepa Brena, who was observed as in-between: both Muslim in origin and well established in Belgrade, the centre of Yugoslav and Serbian might.

The implication of religion in cultural representations within popular culture continued to perplex the worried believers. In 1972, the readers of the newly established biweekly journal *Preporod* (*Revival*) were embroiled in a heated discussion about an article that had recently appeared in a Belgrade journal. The journal had published an interview with Vahida, a young Bosnian Muslim woman, who owned a discotheque and was married to an Orthodox Christian. Those two things were already somewhat controversial for a Muslim audience, but specifically the fact that the interview revolved around the recent

[54] Džumhur, 'Kamen crnog sjaja', p. 101.

[55] M. Keith Booker and Isra Daraiseh, *Consumerist Orientalism: The Convergence of Arab and American Popular Culture in the Age of Global Capitalism* (London: I. B. Tauris, 2019).

Hajj experience of Vahida stirred strong emotions. According to the rendering of the interview, she claimed to have gone on the Hajj as tourist, for a road trip to see the countries of cultural significance to the Muslim tradition. During the Hajj performance, she was allegedly attacked for being white and different from other pilgrims. The photograph that was taken to accompany the interview showed her in a miniskirt. The sensationalism of the news item, which stressed that a young Muslim woman, whose father was an imam in Bosnia, went on the Hajj as if it were a random exotic journey, was disturbing to many people who contributed to the debate. The more the popular media in Yugoslavia claimed to have access to the Hajj, the more foreign and exotic it was presented to the general public, and this was producing a disconnection from those pilgrims who felt that their experiences were not accurately represented.[56]

Yet, even outside the realm of the sensationalist, the Hajj was a matter of intense debate. What did the Hajj mean to modern Muslims and how connected did Bosnian Muslims feel to their coreligionists at a time when the state controlled most public expressions of religion? The next section will discuss the contested and opposite meanings of the Hajj in the works of Husein Đozo and Fejzulah Hadžibajrić, indicating the feelings of profound disconnection, as well as the persistence of the religious and spiritual links that could not be broken by the firm state grip.

Against Empty Form: 'I Do Not Kneel to You, Nor Do I Worship Thee'

In sharp contrast to the first half of the twentieth century, when a range of journals and publishing venues offered creative spaces for Bosnian Muslims, religious publications were severely curtailed and censored in the socialist period. The reading public was informed through official publications of the Islamic Community – *Glasnik*, as well as, from the 1970s onwards, *Preporod* (*Renewal*). The Islamic Community (until 1969 called the Islamic Religious Community) in many ways was a 'disciplining institution' that regulated 'the

[56] For more on this case, as well as the contested visibility of Muslim women in the Hajj discourse of this period, see Dženita Karić, 'Bosnian Women on Hajj', in *Muslim Women's Pilgrimage to Mecca and Beyond: Reconfiguring Gender, Religion, and Mobility*, ed. by Marjo Buitelaar, Manja Stephan-Emmrich and Viola Thimm (New York, London: Routledge, 2021), pp. 147–65.

form and content of acceptable Islam',[57] in a manner that was compliant with the compartmentalised role of religion in the public sphere and within the normative boundaries of the modern state, as seen in the travelogues of Hasan Ljubunčić. The alignment with the authorities, however, was not the only dominant framework through which religious topics, including rituals, were observed and evaluated; just as it was the case in many Muslim societies in the twentieth century, the dominant discourse created and shaped by the Islamic Community was profoundly reformist. Over several decades, *Glasnik* and *Preporod* published fatwas, essays, travelogues and reports on the Hajj, which aimed not only at providing the readership with necessary information on the pilgrimage, but also at fashioning a distinct attitude towards the ritual that would translate into other parts of a believer's life. Meaning-making processes were still dynamic: through questions raised in the journals' fatwa sections, readers' comments and reports, common Bosnians could also shape and shift the Hajj discourse (Fig. 4.3).

Naše dvije hadžince na Arefatu

Figure 4.3 'Our Hajjas on Arafat'. Source: *Glasnik IVZ*.

[57] Kevin Reinhart, *Lived Islam: Colloquial Religion in a Cosmopolitan Tradition* (Cambridge: Cambridge University Press, 2020), p. 137.

The reformist line in the above-mentioned journals was spearheaded by Husein Đozo (1912–82), a scholar trained at al-Azhar, who had served in a Nazi corps in World War II and been exonerated by the Communist authorities after the war, becoming President of the Association of ulama of Bosnia-Herzegovina in 1964. Under Đozo's leadership, much of the religious discourse was shaped in the characteristic progressivist attitude, and with a staunch resistance to whatever was perceived as superstition or formalism. Apart from numerous essays, Đozo also wrote columns in *Glasnik* and *Preporod*, where he issued different fatwas and answered questions from his readers. Throughout several decades of his editorship of the gazette, Đozo very clearly delineated the contours of the discourse on progress. The crux of this discourse was ritual, with Đozo proposing how it should be observed and valued, as well as pruning those ritual practices and attitudes that, according to him, constituted excess and superstition.[58]

Much of Đozo's vision of the ritual is framed as a critique of the modern state in the Muslim World. The Hajj, in that way, became a mirror image of the perceived decline of Muslims in history. This decline, according to Đozo, was caused by an emphasis on the form and ignorance of Islam's essence. In his 1967 essay on occasion of Eid al-adha, Đozo wrote that there had been certain progress concerning the material aspects of the Hajj ritual: Hajjis were now using modern transportation, and their comfort level had increased. However, he was not interested in discussing this aspect of the Hajj, but the neglected perspective of where the Hajj was:

> A general annual meeting of Muslim representatives from all sides of the world, where they analyse the state of all Islamic countries and communities, reach necessary conclusions and discern responsible measures, as that is the main purpose of the Hajj.[59]

[58] The majority of Đozo's fatwas were related to 'acts of worship, including ritual ablutions, prayers, fasting, charity, pilgrimage, funerals and so on'. Sejad Mekić, *A Muslim Reformist in Communist Yugoslavia: The Life and Thought of Husein Đozo* (Abingdon: Routledge, 2017), p. 125.

[59] Husein Đozo, 'Uz ovogodišnji Kurban-bajram', *Glasnik IVZ* 30/1–2 (1967), pp. 1–4, in Husein Đozo, *Izabrana djela 3 (Publicistički radovi)* (Sarajevo: El Kalem/Fakultet islamskih nauka, 2006), p. 192.

Like Hasan Ljubunčić, Đozo expressed resignation about imagining Mecca and Medina as points of departure for progress in the Muslim world. Đozo separated the idea of the Hajj (*misao hadža*), which he considered to be actual and relevant at all times, and perhaps even more relevant in his own time,[60] from its realisation at the crossroads of history. Đozo described this state of liminality between the Hajj as an ideal and the Hajj as a realisation as stemming from the lack of unity (the lack of a 'healthy joint ideological platform').[61] The Hajj in its current form was simply a ritual that inspired without a deeper purpose, which made the Hajji turn towards the past instead of the future. Đozo was trying to reverse the paradigm, making the pilgrim look for inspiration in the past, while at the same time search for a (better) future.[62]

This vision was still somewhat elitist. Đozo was aware that his idealism was not shared by many, and he was irritated by the committment of the general populace to the literalist interpretations of the Hajj. Moreover, he was looking with pity at certain customs that pilgrims practiced while in the vicinity of the Prophet's grave.[63] His rejection of literalism should not be interpreted as quest for an esoteric understanding of the ritual: Đozo was simply protesting the blind following of rites without comprehending their inner meaning. This meaning was subsumed under progressive social action, which, according to Đozo, was sorely lacking among modern Muslims. While discussing the rite of throwing rocks on the pillar symbolising Satan (*ramy*) in his essay titled 'The Iftar in the Haram-i Sharif', the author commented:

> People, not God, need our sacrifice. If a person needs to sacrifice himself, then [he should do so] only for people and society but in the name of God, because in that case every selfishness and ignoble motifs and goals are excluded.[64]

[60] Đozo, 'Uz ovogodišnji Kurban-bajram', p. 193.

[61] Đozo, 'Uz ovogodišnji Kurban-bajram', p. 194.

[62] Đozo, 'Uz ovogodišnji Kurban-bajram', p. 195.

[63] Đozo, 'Na grobu posljednjeg Božijeg poslanika', *Glasnik* 32/5–6 (1969), pp. 193–200, in Husein Đozo, *Izabrana djela 1 (Islam u vremenu)* (Sarajevo: El Kalem/Fakultet islamskih nauka, 2006), p. 275.

[64] Đozo, 'Iftar u Haremi-šerifu (I dio)', *Preporod* 6/123 (1975), p. 5, in Husein Đozo, *Izabrana djela 3 (Publicistički radovi)* (Sarajevo: El Kalem/Fakultet islamskih nauka, 2006), p. 506.

While much of Đozo's critique was directed against empty formalism, what surfaces is an essentialised view of the religion and, metonymically, its rituals and rites. This implies that religion has a core which is not readily available and visible to a common believer – not because of mystical secrecy, but because of the inability of the modern world to crack it open and resolve it. Religion is directed towards the believer, making him the centre agent of action; this is reflected in the rituals:

> It is not enough to come to Harem, to pray and circumambulate the Ka'ba. Such spiritual refreshments are very necessary, but it is not everything. [. . .] It is true that these rituals have their mystical side in which the soul finds its peace, joy, delight and refreshment. However, one should not ignore the fact that these rituals have another side, a deep sense of life. [. . .] The human being is God's representative on earth. The whole phenomenal world has been placed at his disposal. He will be a sinner lest he accomplishes this mission.[65]

With a certain patronising distance, the author observed other pilgrims carrying out rituals: these were for him the masses who expected the Mehdi – their saviour – and did not use their spiritual strengths that are full of potential for social change. Đozo is pained by the following question: what are the sources of the enormous spiritual force that impels people to undertake certain painful rituals, and can this force be used otherwise (for rational, beneficial goals)?

Apart from the disillusionment with the masses who were well-intended and sincere, but not led in the right direction, Đozo was frustrated with the lack of any overt political use of the Hajj, especially against the backdrop of the Palestinian question, which he expressed in several essays. The political changes and tumultuous history of the 1960s brought attention to another sacred place in Islam that had not figured before in the same manner: Jerusalem/al-Quds. In this context, al-Quds became a focal point for political debates revolving around issues of imperialism, Muslim decline and revival, which were evident from clashes between conservative and progressive thought. Jerusalem/al-Quds is presented as the place of the first *qibla* and

[65] Husein Đozo, 'Iftar u Haremi-šerifu (II dio)', *Preporod* 6/124 (1975), p. 5, in *Izabrana djela 3 (Publicistički radovi)* (Sarajevo: El Kalem/Fakultet islamskih nauka, 2006), pp. 510–11.

the Prophet's Night Journey (*isrā* and *mi'rāj*). The authors of this period, and most notably Đozo, were appealing to the sensitivities of Yugoslav Muslims in order to draw their attention to the Palestinian plight.[66] In that regard, Đozo sometimes referred to the acts of violence committed against Muslims and, even more prominently, Islamic architecture of great religious significance. Thus, in one of his essays, Đozo referred to the burning of the al-Aqsa Mosque in 1969 by Denis Michael Rohan. In this context, this holy place for Muslims in Jerusalem was both a physical structure and an idea. As a building, it was prone to damage and attack; however, as a symbol, or a receptacle of the spirit, it was not easily destroyed. Al-Aqsa Mosque (or, rather, its idea), similar to Mecca and Medina, presented for Đozo 'a great latent and potential strength (*predstavlja veliku latentnu i potencijalnu snagu*)'.[67] In this case, there was a considerable difference between Hasan Ljubunčić's lukewarm attitude towards the Palestinian issue and Đozo's proactive stance. The rising interest in Palestine appeared especially after the events of 1967 and the burning of the al-Aqsa Mosque in 1969, which was seen as a key moment in awakening the Islamic spirit, beyond nationalist categorisation and nationalism.[68]

While Đozo addressed the Yugoslav Muslim public, the anxieties revealed in these essays actually belonged to the broader 'discourse of crisis',[69] which reverberated across (mostly, but not exclusively) Arab intellectual circles in the aftermath of the military defeat of 1967. The defeat provoked ruminations on the perceived stagnation and decline of the Arab and Muslim World, leading to a search for potential enemies to progress and obstacles on the path to the modern present. Some thinkers, such as Mohammed Abed al-Jabri, sought the culprit in the 'gnostic mode of knowledge that stresses spiritual revelation',[70]

[66] Husein Đozo, 'Geneza kriza na Bliskom Istoku', *Glasnik* 32/1–2 (1969), pp. 7–10, in *Izabrana djela 3 (Publicistički radovi)* (Sarajevo: El Kalem/Fakultet islamskih nauka, 2006), pp. 269–73.

[67] Husein Đozo, 'Povodom paljevine Džamije el-Aksa u Jerusalemu', *Glasnik* 32/11–12 (1969), pp. 546–51, in *Izabrana djela 3 (Publicistički radovi)* (Sarajevo: El Kalem/Fakultet islamskih nauka, 2006), p. 284.

[68] Đozo, 'Povodom paljevine Džamije el-Aksa u Jerusalemu'.

[69] Mohamed Wajdi Ben Hammed, '(Dis)Enchanting Modernity: Sufism and its Temporality in the Thought of Mohammed Abed al-Jabri and Taha Abdurrahman', *The Journal of North African Studies* 26/3 (2021), p. 553.

[70] Wajdi Ben Hammed, '(Dis)Enchanting Modernity', p. 555.

the intellectual and religious developments that resemble the object of Đozo's critique. And while Đozo's dissatisfaction with intellectual and cultural currents in the modern Muslim World was broader, at least some of his criticism was directed at Sufi practices, including those related to the Hajj.

Modernist Disconnections: Objections to Sufism

Despite nominally being outside of the public discourse (with *tekke*s closed and Sufi orders banned after World War II), Sufism began to appear as a common topic in fatwas from the 1970s onwards. Đozo answered numerous questions about Sufism posed by his readers, and in his answers framed Sufism in line with New Age spirituality,[71] through the comparison of the images of Sufi and Yogi, and the emphasis on the foreign origins of Sufism. When evaluating Sufism, there was a certain instability and imbalance between two opposing thoughts: Sufism, according to Đozo, took care only of the spirit and neglected ritual form; on the other hand, Sufism took care of the form only through visits to shrines and intercession. By its perceived utter neglect of the body, Sufism failed to be a moving force for modern times, just as the formalists – which according to Đozo consisted of the old and stagnant ulama – insisted solely on ritual form. Sufism was seen as being opposite to the Sharia and neglecting its formal precepts:

> One of the gravest delusions and misinformations is their teaching about personal inner experience as the highest measure and criterium. There are some Sufi orders that claim that the Sufi who authentically penetrated divine depths and who lives from secret mercy has the right to take as criterium his own experience and to act upon it. The Sharia stops being valid to them. Hallaj[72] claimed that the Hajj can be performed in his room.[73]

Yet, at the same time, according to Đozo, Sufism seemed to be obsessed with form. In 1969, a large group of religious dignitaries, including both Đozo and the Bosnian Qadiri shaykh Fejzulah Hadžibajrić (1913–90), headed

[71] Husein Đozo, 'Pitanja i odgovori', *Glasnik* 39/4 (1976), pp. 431–33.

[72] Mansur al-Hallaj (ninth/tenth century), a Sufi known for his martyrdom.

[73] Husein Đozo, 'Pravi put i stramputice tesavufa', *Glasnik* 41/3 (1979), p. 239.

towards Mecca, in what would be a rare bus trip that took Bosnian Hajjis across Kuwait and Iraq. Both men – Đozo and Hadžibajrić – penned travelogues of the journey, offering profoundly different views on the ritual itself. While Hadžibajrić's travelogue will be treated in the following section, we are here turning to Đozo's reflections on the ritual written several years later. In a series of essays dedicated to normative rituals, Đozo also analysed the Hajj in the context of the modern age. These writings transformed into a full-fledged critique of the state of the pilgrimage, its unused potential and the preoccupation of modern pilgrims with devotional rituals that stifle their progressive spirit:

> I watched with my own eyes and listened with my own ears how Hajjis stand for hours, kissing the walls of the Kaʿba and the walls of the tomb of the Prophet, uttering various prayers and seeking answers to their wishes. I observed the same scenes in Istanbul, Konya, Baghdad, Karbala, Damascus, Cairo, etc. At first, I was struck by this behaviour. I asked myself, what are these people seeking from Ansar Ayyubi in Istanbul, Jalal al-Din al-Rumi in Konya, Shaykh Gaylani in Baghdad, hazrati Husayn in Karbala and Cairo, Sayyidina Badawi in Tanta, Shaykh al-Akbar Muhyiddin al-Arabi and Pamun Baba in Damascus.[74]

The image and the vision of Islam, according to Đozo, had been ruined by deformities, mystifications, formalism and the focus on the non-living.[75] For Đozo, it was the death-oriented practices that prevailed among the masses, a consequence of their continuous and futile wait for something to change. Because they were not offered any alternative, and because they had lost faith in the 'living saviours', they had turned to the dead, seeking the 'Mehdi' and 'the second coming of Jesus'. In a vein similar to Ali Shariati, who claimed that in his time the Qur'an was being read at graves and to the dead more than to the living,[76] Đozo also tried to direct Islamic ritual towards a better use for

[74] Husein Đozo, 'Islam – hadž', *Glasnik* 35/3–4 (1972), pp. 113–21, in Husein Đozo, *Izabrana djela 1 (Islam u vremenu)* (Sarajevo: El Kalem/Fakultet islamskih nauka, 2006), pp. 390–91.

[75] Đozo, 'Na grobu posljednjeg Božijeg Poslanika', p. 275.

[76] Ali Shariati, *Hajj*, trans. by Ali A. Behzadnia and Najla Denny (Zürich: Indo Oriental Publ., 1980), p. VII.

society. He felt that Muslims were utterly disconnected from their reality and from each other. The only positive example he saw was that of the Yugoslav Muslims who, unlike their religious counterparts, managed to rid themselves of misconceptions from the past and have a clearer and more correct vision of Islam than others.[77]

This vision of the Hajj was ultimately anti-devotional. It was also not a solitary view, but a widely shared sentiment that corresponded to the twentieth-century scholarly and activist rejection of Sufism and Sufi practices as remnants of a shameful premodern past. Alija Izetbegović (1925–2003), a member of the outlawed Young Muslim Movement and later the first president of the independent Republic of Bosnia and Herzegovina, often criticised this type of formalism in his underground yet influential writings. Just like Đozo (whose alignment with the socialist state was frowned upon by the clandestine Young Muslims), Izetbegović also protested what he saw as reduction of the holy to the ritualistic and the mystical, as he stated in his controversial Islamic Declaration:

> Devotion to the Book did not cease, but it lost its active character while retaining what was irrational and mystic. The Qur'an lost its authority as law while gaining in sanctity as an object. [. . .] Under the constant influence of theological formalism, the Qur'an was read less and 'learned' [recited] more.[78]

But was this pessimistic vision of rituals, which both Đozo and Izetbegović espoused, the only one to which Bosnian Muslims ascribed or, in some way or the other, were exposed in the tumultuous socialist period? Numerous restrictions on religious publications seem to have placed the reformist view of rituals as the dominant one. Yet, if we fast forward to the late twentieth century, we are able to see a wave of publications of Hajj travelogues that were actually written between the 1960s and 1980s. The travelogues were written by women and men, scholars and commoners, and were often preserved in family archives and circulated among relatives and friends. The ever-rising

[77] Husein Đozo, 'Na grobu posljednjeg Božijeg Poslanika', p. 198.

[78] Alija Izetbegović, *The Islamic Declaration: A Programme for the Islamization of Muslims and the Muslim Peoples*, trans. unknown (Sarajevo: [n. p.], 1990), p. 19.

interest in the Hajj, and especially in the form of the travelogue, has led to a number of these writings being published decades after they had been written. Even when in some cases these travelogues were heavily edited by family members and descendants who had new audiences in mind, they can still offer some glimpse into the ways in which Bosnian Muslims conceived the Hajj beyond the confines of the official publications.

Some of these Hajj authors we have encountered in the introduction, such as Safija Šiljak and Hidajeta Mirojević, the two women who went on Hajj by car in the early 1980s. The others will be mentioned in the last chapter, since the fact that they were published at a later date speaks about the receptiveness of the twenty-first-century Bosnian public. However, before ending this chapter, I would like to turn to a travelogue that offers a vision of the Hajj which contrasts the dominant reformist discourse and perhaps in its tone and attention to emotions is more in tune with what ordinary Hajjis experienced. The travelogue of Shaykh Fejzulah Hadžibajrić was published for the second time in Sweden, outside of its Bosnian habitus. It fleshes out some of the alternative ways in which the Hajj was conceived, turning the readers' attention to the form of the ritual and its peculiar Sufi meanings through the prism of emotions. As such, it helps us to understand different forms of connection to Mecca and Medina, and to other coreligionists.

Kissing the Prophet's Tomb with One's Heart

In the decades after the Second World War, the Qadiri shaykh Fejzulah Hadžibajrić experienced a series of tribulations at the hands of the state. Throughout the postwar decades, Hadžibajrić struggled to reopen the *tekke*s, which remained closed because of state restrictions as well as the resistance coming from the dominant reformist circles in the Islamic Community. The major structures of the Islamic Community waged a war against 'superstition', which was often understood as activities of *tekke*s, shaykhs and talisman-makers.[79] Yet, despite his marginalisation, Hadžibajrić was still a known figure, working as a librarian, obtaining *ijāza*s of different Sufi orders

[79] Samir Beglerović, *Tesavvuf Bosne u vidicima Fejzulaha Hadžibajrića: Vjerski i kulturni razvoj bosanskih muslimana u prvoj polovini XX stoljeća* (Sarajevo: Bookline, 2014), p. 328.

and later becoming a shaykh of the Sinanova *tekke* in Sarajevo, as well as a *mathnavihan* – an interpreter of Rumi's *Mathnawi*.

In 1969, Hadžibajrić went on the Hajj with the same group as Husein Đozo, following the same itinerary that took the pilgrims on an unusual path through Turkey, Iraq and Kuwait. As it was the usual custom in the twentieth century, the representatives of the Yugoslav Hajjis usually met with state and religious dignitaries: for example, during this journey, Husein Đozo and a select few others met with the president of the Republic of Iraq. Hadžibajrić, however, used the opportunity to meet with Sufi shaykhs and religious figures, aiming to maintain the connections with Sufi communities along the way, to collect blessings and obtain more knowledge. For Hadžibajrić, visiting Baghdad presented an opportunity to reconnect with members of the Qadiri *tariqa* of which he was the head in Bosnia. This, again, provided an opportunity to present the state of Bosnian Muslims to his fellow Sufi audiences. Setting up and preserving various international links seemed to be a predominant motif in all twentieth-century Bosnian Hajj literature; what Hadžibajrić's travelogue added to it were Sufi networks. Hadžibajrić did not limit his connections to other Sufis: he was eager to meet with Shaykh Nasiruddin al-Albani (1914–99), a famous Salafi figure, whom he respected for his knowledge of hadith.

Somewhat resembling the premodern zeal of the *ziyāra* seekers, Hadžibajrić revived the coordinates of the neglected Islamic geographies through narratives about prophets, religious figures and saints that marked the space, interweaving them with factual information about cities and their spiritual value. Where Đozo saw indiscriminate masses intent on praying to the dead and the inactive, Hadžibajrić sought the traces of Sufi presence. This Sufi presence was visible through a renewed interest in the Ottoman past,[80] inquiries into connectivities about traditional ways of learning (teaching the *Mathnawi*),[81] references to Persian language and literature,[82] and *zikr* activities which the

[80] Fejzulah Hadžibajrić, *Putopisi i nekrolozi* (Stockholm/Tuzla: MOS-BeMUF/Harfograf, 2002), p. 18.

[81] Hadžibajrić, *Putopisi i nekrolozi*, p. 18.

[82] At one point, Hadžibajrić cites a Persian verse on the Kaʿba; Hadžibajrić, *Putopisi i nekrolozi*, p. 42.

Hajjis performed on the way, in addition to their meetings with a wider Sufi network.[83] Some spaces were present through their absence: although the Hajjis did not pass through Palestine on their way, Hadžibajrić devoted some attention to it, as he considered the fate of Palestine, and especially al-Quds, to be a punishment for Muslims. Palestine, just like in Đozo's narrative, presented a reference point for discussions on the failure and decline of the Muslim world. However, in Hadžibajrić's account, Palestine was also a place where 'one has to admire the persistence of the Jews to establish their state'.[84]

Although Palestine was not often frequented by Bosnian Hajjis whose travel arrangements had been organised by the Islamic Community, in the period before 1967, it was occasionally visited by pilgrims. In 1966, the hitherto largest group of Hajjis managed to visit Jerusalem/al-Quds and Hebron/al-Khalīl. A 'collegium of authors' wrote their impressions of the journey, which were published in *Glasnik*. They emphasised Jerusalem as the shared space of Muslims, Christians and Jews, admiring the ecumenical harmony of the place. The Hajjis were especially amazed at the sight of the Christian pilgrims, even recognizing some of them from Yugoslavia, who also came to celebrate 'the greatest celebratory days of life – the Hajj':

> We could see then that our proverb 'Blood is thicker than water' is full of wisdom and truth, because we shook brotherly hands and asked for our health, because we were closer to each other in this foreign land.[85]

The dominant lenses in Hadžibajrić's travelogue were openly Sufi. Embedding references to Sufism in the narratives on Islamic geographies had the purpose to delineate borders between Sunni and Shi'i sects and yet to point to their underlying unity,[86] as well as to carve out space for the Hanafi school. The importance of established schools became even more prominent

[83] Hadžibajrić, *Putopisi i nekrolozi*, pp. 22–23.

[84] Hadžibajrić, *Putopisi i nekrolozi*, p. 57.

[85] Kolegijum autora, 'Ovogodišnje putovanje na hadž', *Glasnik Vrhovnog islamskog starješinstva u Socijalističkoj federativnoj Republici Jugoslaviji* 29/5–6 (1966), pp. 213–14.

[86] The key difference between the sects, as Hadžibajrić states, is the question of leadership or *imamah*. Hadžibajrić, *Putopisi i nekrolozi*, p. 27.

in the later part of the travelogue; here, what Hadžibajrić saw as the Wahhabi assault on tombs was ascribed to their development in isolation from other Islamic legal schools of thought.[87] Through the focus on Islamic sects, the author tried to situate Sufism in religious narratives. To do so, crucial bits of Muslim history were given a Sufi interpretation. For example, Hasan, the Prophet's grandson who unlike his brother Hussain had decided not to fight the Umayad caliph Mu'awiya, was depicted as possessing a wisdom that inspired him to give up the fight for political and religious reasons. Consequently, he achieved the level of a spiritual pole (*qutb*) thanks to preventing a civil war.[88]

In sharp contrast to Đozo's dismissal of the past, Hadžibajrić tried to nurture the post-Ottoman links connecting Bosnia to the Hijaz, including finding similarities between the valley of Arafat and Sarajevo.[89] These links also included references to stories about Bosnian scholars in the Hijaz and Bosnian families who had settled in Arab countries over the course of the twentieth century. The Hajj, once again, became a foray into a lost past. Yet, the most distinctive difference between Đozo and Hadžibajrić's narratives was precisely the emotion that constituted the main channel of religious experience for the latter. The feeling of attachment and love, the ultimate devotion to God and the Prophet and, consequently, to the members of the Prophet's family, as well as the saints, and all that within the framework of the pilgrimage and Islamic geography, was gradually built up throughout the narrative. The emotions were thus something one *did*, and not just *had*:[90]

> [. . .] the voice came to me as if from the other world. Standing in prayer, watching the Ka'ba, listening to the sounds of the Qur'an, whose words were as if spoken by the heart, cannot be compared by grace to anything known by common humans. Allah sees you everywhere, wherever you pray you are in front of Him, but here next to the Ka'ba it is still different, closer and more

[87] Hadžibajrić, *Putopisi i nekrolozi*, p. 34.

[88] Hadžibajrić, *Putopisi i nekrolozi*, pp. 27–28.

[89] Hadžibajrić, *Putopisi i nekrolozi*, p. 35.

[90] Monique Scheer, 'Are Emotions a Kind of Practice (And Is That What Makes Them Have a History)? A Bourdieuian Approach to Understanding Emotion', *History and Theory* 51/2 (2012), p. 194.

> intimate. Still, in every moment there is awe (*mehaabet*) and that which is stronger than love (*mehabbet*). In Medina, next to Revzai-Mutahhera, love is stronger than awe.[91]

The comparison of Mecca and Medina reminds one of the hierarchical structures of *faḍā'il* literature, as described in the first chapter. For Hadžibajrić, Medina is even dearer to Bosniaks than the Ka'ba.[92] When in the vicinity of the Prophet's grave, Hadžibajrić translates the devotion to the Prophet into considerations of the human being's ultimate ontological status:

> The reality that you are in front of the Prophet is piercing, and it brings on a feeling of intimacy, which is not describable. It is not possible that a human being, who knows himself at least superficially, does not believe in God. The awareness that you are a being upon which virtues are bestowed uplifts one to the highest rank of nobility – the fact that you are a slave of God, and not of a human.[93]

The emphasis on servitude to God rather than to a human has to be interpreted within the context of the Saudi attitude towards Sufi orders and activities, which were often misinterpreted as tomb-worshipping. Thus, Hadžibajrić is preemptively explaining the Sufi approach to the *ziyāra* in order to avoid criticism. In the same way, he is against the profanisation of love for the Prophet's family (*ahl al-bayt*), which he thinks might stem from ignorance.[94] Descriptions of Medina are, again similarly to *faḍā'il*, related to the pervading feeling of love that overcomes any accusation of negative innovation (*bid'a*). As such, these feelings were expressed through the body, in an experience that culminated in the encounter with the holy:

> I prayed fajr, feeling as if I had a fever. [. . .] I walked automatically towards that holy place, where this worldly body of the pride of the worlds, of the last Prophet of God, Muhammad (s.a.w.s) was buried [. . .] I knew that only a

[91] Hadžibajrić, *Putopisi i nekrolozi*, p. 37.
[92] Hadžibajrić, *Putopisi i nekrolozi*, p. 51.
[93] Hadžibajrić, *Putopisi i nekrolozi*, p. 46.
[94] Hadžibajrić, *Putopisi i nekrolozi*, p. 48.

> few barriers stood between us. I was gushing with love, excitement and shame. My words broke in syllables, and like a toddler, I uttered *Assalamu alayka ya Rasulallah* . . . I believed and knew that he, God's Prophet, hears, sees and replies. Is there any greater joy and happiness apart from that? [. . .] I looked through the barriers and kissed with my heart the earth around the Rawda. My tongue uttered: *Shafaat* [intercession] *Ya Rasulallah, Shafaat, Shafaat.*[95]

Given the description of the bodily expression of strong emotions, Hadžibajrić's narrative could not be further from Husein Đozo's rationalisation of the ritual and its didactic flavour. At the same time, it resembles Hasan Ljubunčić's elucidation of the intense and incomparable emotional life of the holy places. Emotions, which do not feature greatly in Đozo's reformist discourse and which are exoticised and Othered in Džumhur's portrayal of the pilgrims, actually constitute a major medium through which the religious experience was expressed. Most of the Hajj narratives of the twentieth century and later – as we will see in the next chapter – describe overwhelming emotions that connect the pilgrims to the holy and to their coreligionists.

Conclusion

While the aftermath of World War II seemed to be a sharp temporal rupture that placed Bosnian (and Yugoslav) Muslims in a state of isolation – an image often favoured by historians of the region – the reality was quite different. When studying the discourses on the Hajj in the socialist period, it is possible to discern patterns of dis/connection towards the ritual, as well as coreligionists and fellow pilgrims. As the state framework tightened the media through which the Hajj experience could be expressed and interpreted, the focal point of the Hajj narrative increasingly became about the Yugoslav Muslims themselves. As was often the case in modern Hajj literature, the pilgrimage became a mirror image of whatever anxiety was carried by the authors themselves: it was an opportunity for Yugoslav self-promotion, a fulfilment of Orientalist fantasies, or a litmus test for Islamic reform.

Equal to the ritual, the journey also revealed the faultlines of dis/connection. As the authors lamented the state of the Muslim World, they sought old and

[95] Hadžibajrić, *Putopisi i nekrolozi*, p. 44.

new connections: meetings with *muhajirs* in Turkey and with Sufis in Iraq show that the cultivation of links of geographically dispersed Muslims was very much alive. Their links with non-Muslims grew stronger, too, often as result of the context of modern transportation. The opposite was true as well: Bosnian Hajjis felt modern and free and, as such, at the forefront of the global anti-colonial struggle, yet different from those who were still perceived as lagging behind. Palestine emerges as a present absence, a disturbing geography on the Hajj route which was visited rarely and simultaneously symbolised both the spiritual unity of Muslims and their perceived weakness and fragmentation.

Although being a mirror image for anxious conceptualisations, the Hajj constituted, perhaps predominantly, the time-space axis for the most powerful emotions. In that context, the pilgrims' writings added to the creation of an emotional habitus, just as their own emotions had been cultivated, connecting them to the holy and to other pilgrims that preceded and followed them. The emotions were not internalised, since we learn of Hajjis shaking, crying, pleading – in other words, using their bodies to act and experience the Hajj. And it is precisely this emotional body that will become crucial in the next chapter.

5

BOSNIAKS BETWEEN HOMELAND AND HOLY LAND

Munir Gavrankapetanović was thinking about God on a spring night in 1951, lying in his cell in the Central Prison in Sarajevo and bone-tired from a full day of forced labor on the construction site of the school for the State Security Administration (UDBA). The name of the security administration itself had a frightening ring to it and was often uttered half-jokingly as '*udba sudba*' – UDBA is your fate, referring to the seeming omnipresence of the intelligence service that monitored all the enemies of the state, like the KGB or Stasi. Yet, Munir knew that there was a more permanent and lasting presence that overshadows this earthly apparatus: God. He could not hear His words, but he knew God was there, and that He listened. His other cellmates were fast asleep, but Munir kept thinking about his friends and comrades who had perished over the past several years. Just like Safija and Hidajeta from the beginning of this book, Munir also was a member of the Young Muslim Movement, the religious organisation that had sought a more active political role in society but was crushed at the end of World War II: some of its members were executed, others jailed. In the years to come, the members of the movement and their extensive network were on the margins of social life in Yugoslavia; yet they were not completely silent. They maintained their family and social connections. More importantly, they cultivated the sentiment of being persecuted for their adherence and commitment to Islam. The feeling of marginalisation of religion – predominantly Islam – in

Yugoslav society created a growing subculture of non-comformists, and perhaps the most visible among these were the Young Muslims.

Gavrankapetanović was locked up in 1949, just one year after the Young Muslims branch in Zagreb to which he belonged published its last issue of the journal *Mudžahid* (*Warrior*). Back then, Munir had been a civil engineering student. His arrest had cut short his studies; instead, he was sent to do forced labor in several notorious prisons and construction camps across Yugoslavia. In a number of books and articles that he published much later in the 1980s, many under a pseudonym, Gavrankapetanović told of his encounters with other dissidents of the Yugoslav socialist project in prison: among them were the četniks, Serb ultra-nationalists with a terrifying record of crimes against Muslims in Bosnia and beyond. As we will see, this would not be Munir's last meeting with them, as things tended to repeat themselves in the twentieth century.

In the manner of many Muslim authors who suffered state persecution, such as the Egyptian author Zaynab al-Ghazali (1917–2005), in his spiritual biographies *Through the Strength of Faith to the Perfection of the Soul* (*Snagom vjere do savršenstva duše*, 1984) and *On the Path of Hope and Consolation* (*Na putu nade i utjehe*, 1990) Gavrankapetanović stressed perseverance and resoluteness stemming from his dedication to Islam at an early age. The hardships of prison life could not prevent him from praying, which he did in the dark, when everyone, including the guards, was asleep. Fasting was a struggle, however – in 1949 he was unable to observe Ramadan on the hot June days, but he decided to make up for it two years later. In order to avoid suspicion, Munir fasted entire days, twenty-four hours at a time. And on one of these nights when he recollected memories and conversed with God, right before dawn, Munir had a revelatory dream, the kind that happens once in a lifetime.

In the dream, Munir was standing in the midst of the Neretva, the strong and unpredictable river in Herzegovina, on a small pebbly island. It was summer, and the river was low. Suddenly, five or six enormous snakes emerged from the water, passing by him, but not doing him any harm. Behind them, they left human bones, ribs and skulls. To his left, Munir saw an amethyst rock in the form of a pyramid shining brightly. The snakes soon disappeared. As he looked downriver, Munir saw a desert hill behind the trees and shrubs, with two signposts indicating Mecca and Medina. And on the side of Mecca, the Ka'ba was rising, and many people were circumambulating it. Munir heard them praying and uttering *tekbir*. He felt exhilarated, and suddenly a loud voice thundered: 'Here, this is the Ka'ba!' The voice was so powerful that Munir startled up from his sleep and woke up a cellmate who was lying next to him.

Four decades after this dream, in 1994, Munir Gavrankapetanović was indeed on his way to Mecca. This time, the Hajj was not only a personal spiritual victory for Munir. The first organised wartime Hajj was an unprecedented event, the accomplishment of a greater dream for the Bosnian Muslim community and a symbol of resistance of Islam to past regimes and present threats. It seemed to resonate globally as well. A Hajj group consisting of 359 pilgrims was summoned and organised with the help of the Kingdom of Saudi Arabia. Even the first Bosnian president, Alija Izetbegović (1925–2003), mentioned in the previous chapter as the author of the *Islamic Declaration*, was one of these Hajjis. Just like Munir Gavrankapetanović, Izetbegović had also been a member of the Young Muslim Movement and had been imprisoned twice: the first time after World War II, and the second time during the infamous Sarajevo Process in 1983, for his active role in reviving the organisation in the 1970s. Izetbegović and his circle had been inspired by the Iranian Revolution; they were not content with the restrictions on religious expression in socialist Yugoslavia. At the same time, like many other reformists in the twentieth century, they sought new and effective interpretations of religion as an active force, in contrast to what they perceived as a stagnant and sterile monopoly on religion by the state-aligned ulama. It is not difficult to see the strong contrast between Hasan Ljubunčić's state-aligned narrative at the beginning of the socialist period and the dissenting and subversive opinions of the Young Muslims in the ensuing decades. Towards the end of the twentieth century, however, the tables had turned: the late 1980s had witnessed greater visibility of rituals such as the Hajj or the celebration of the Prophet's birthday commonly known as *mevlud*, as well as a greater presence of religious affiliations in the public sphere. While the state framework was not the only factor in shaping the visibility of religion, it certainly presented a way through which certain expression could be channeled.

The Hajj of 1994 was a simultaneously national and transnational event. For the first time in history, Bosnian Muslims went on pilgrimage under the banner of their independent state, with, as they stated, 'their own passport'.[1] The Hajj delegation was led by the Bosnian president, which added a certain gravity to the occasion.[2] The pilgrimage was accompanied by a number of journalists and cameramen, and it resulted not only in two travelogues, but also in a documentary movie that gained popularity among Bosnian audiences. The pilgrimage was an event that acknowledged the state's boundaries yet was not circumscribed by them. In that regard, the nation-state boundaries were at the same time recognized and ignored, through the existence of parallel 'universalisms' that framed this unique experience. Bosnian Muslims were leaving their war-torn country for the universalist call of Islamic pilgrimage; at the same time, in order to leave Sarajevo in the first place, the Hajjis needed the protection of UNPROFOR – a peace-keeping force that was 'neither enemy nor ally'[3] and that, more often than not, looked with indifference upon Bosnian Muslims. At the same time, the Hajjis were amazed at the silence and absence of artillery fire from Serb enemy lines: 'They must have been afraid of NATO'.[4] The Hajjis who went on pilgrimage in 1994 were not only Bosniaks, but also Arabs, some of them humanitarians and foreign fighters. In one of the two travelogues published in 1994, the Arab Hajjis were listed separately.[5]

Together with all the particularisms and universalisms, the Hajj of 1994 remained a deeply individual affair, which, in the manner of twentieth-century Hajj literature, took the form of an intimate self-narrative. Munir Gavrankapetanović's Hajj travelogue started with a dream narrative. Far from

[1] Amir Hodžić, 'Bošnjaci – Borci s predsjednikom na Hadžu', in *Odazivam Ti se Bože, Odazivam: Bošnjaci na Hadždžu 1414./1994.*, ed. by Mehmedalija Hadžić, Amir Hodžić and Jusuf Žiga (Sarajevo: El Kalem, 1995), p. 20.

[2] Hajj journeys of prominent politicians and state servants played a prominent role in twentieth-century Hajj literature. For example, the carefully crafted image of Suharto on the Hajj spurred the growth of Hajj travelogues in Indonesia. Bianchi, *Guests of God*, p. 199.

[3] Darryl Li, *The Universal Enemy: Jihad, Empire and the Challenge of Solidarity* (Palo Alto: Stanford University Press, 2020), p. 182.

[4] Munir Gavrankapetanović, *Kako sam obavio i doživio Hadždž 1414. h.g. – 1994. g.* (Sarajevo: Biblioteka Glasnika Rijaseta Islamske Zajednice u Bosni i Hercegovini, 1997), p. 28.

[5] The joint travelogue by Mehmedalija Hadžić, Amir Hodžić and Jusuf Žiga contains full lists of Hajjis at the end; see their *Odazivam Ti se Bože, Odazivam: Bošnjaci na Hadždžu 1414./1994.*, pp. 67–78.

being a rhetorical embellishment, dream stories such as Gavrankapetanović's were 'unique and pertained directly to the historical reality at that time'.[6] The dream was a medium that could 'open up sediments (of historical experience) that even diary entries cannot'.[7] And this narrative was embedded in a larger one related to the author's accomplished Hajj experience, thus making the whole narrative a layered set of mediations. Apart from the dream narrative, there were numerous other possibilities of self-narrative that were open to Hajjis in this period, including the confessional mode that often juxtaposed the prewar life of spiritual deprivation to the wartime and postwar changes in religious expression.

Munir certainly saw many close parallels between historical events and his own life, and he felt vindicated for his earlier suffering by the fact that he was going on the Hajj. He was an old man now, and the struggles of his youth had taken a toll on his health: he was in a wheelchair and had to be accompanied by his sons. Still, an inexplicable strength came to him while he was on pilgrimage: he was able to endure the arduous journey and excruciating heat, even though he and his fellow Bosniaks were unaccustomed to that climate, unlike the Arab Hajjis, who even fainted.[8] Tears of happiness flowed down his face; he was overwhelmed and could not sleep because of the excitement. Since he could not walk, during one of the rites his son pushed the wheelchair along the wider corridor of the building surrounding the Kaʿba:

> In the *tawaf*, I had a feeling that I belong to an unstoppable flow of believers circumambulating the Kaʿba and praising God not only in words, but in body, too. At the very edge of the floor, close to the fence, I prayed two *rakat*s looking closely at the Kaʿba. I was delighted that I belong to the nation of believers who in full commitment praises the God's Name and continues the covenant of the Prophet Ibrāhīm. I felt pride in my chest.[9]

[6] Reinhart Koselleck, 'Fiction and Historical Reality', in *Sediments of Time: On Possible Histories*, trans. and ed. by Sean Franzel and Stefan-Ludwig Hoffmann (Palo Alto: Stanford University Press, 2018), p. 14.

[7] Koselleck, 'Fiction and Historical Reality', p. 15.

[8] Amir Hodžić who was together with Munir Gavrankapetanović in the same group contrasts Munir's frail body in the wheelchair with the local able-bodied Arab Hajji who fainted. Hodžić, 'Bošnjaci – Borci s predsjednikom na Hadžu', p. 35.

[9] Gavrankapetanović, *Kako sam obavio i doživio Hadždž 1414. h.g. – 1994. g.*, p. 50.

Munir Gavrankapetanović's travelogue was not the only one documenting the experiences of the wartime Bosniak Hajjis. Three authors – Mehmedalija Hadžić, Amir Hodžić and Jusuf Žiga – also went on the Hajj with the group and wrote a joint travelogue presenting three distinct perspectives of the pilgrimage. Mehmedalija Hadžić wrote an essay in which he gave an overview of the major Qur'anic and hadith sources regarding the Hajj, as well as a clarification of its importance and emotional and spiritual impact on the pilgrims. Amir Hodžić wrote a travelogue recounting their experiences, while Jusuf Žiga gave lyrical impressions of the journey and the ritual. The second part of the travelogue, by Amir Hodžić, also contained statements by different Hajjis, thus making the travelogue at the same time a reportage. The writings were interspersed with direct instructions for future Hajjis (referring to *talbiya* and explaining the rites) and preceded by a joint introduction:

> At the time of writing this text, 'Bosniaks on Hajj 1414/1994', Serbo-Montenegrin aggression on Bosnia and Herzegovina still continues [. . .] around 200,000 murdered people, mostly civilians, over 30,000 raped women and one million people expelled, burnt villages and destroyed cities with recognizable Islamic architecture that gave a special charm to this region [. . .] are only one part of the Serbo-Montenegrin evil-mindedness in aggression on Bosnia and Herzegovina which started in April 1992. Despite this all, Bosniak Muslims have found the strength and possibility to go on the Hajj in times of a complete blockade [. . .] With this fact, which is objective, there is also a string of other reasons why the Hajj of Bosniaks in 1414/1994 has a special historical meaning. The texts speak about that.[10]

While still on the Hajj, Amir Hodžić tried to send some of the reports directly to Bosnia, for it to be included in the breaking and main news on national television. It was especially important to inform viewers about the Bosnian president Alija Izetbegović and his meetings with the Saudi officials who promised help and support for Bosniaks. The connection was not good because Bosnia was practically in media isolation: there were no satellite

[10] Hodžić, Hadžić and Žiga, *Odazivam Ti se Bože, Odazivam: Bošnjaci na Hadždžu 1414./1994.*, p. 5.

phones, and the reports faxed from Mecca and Medina had to pass through Riyadh and Vienna before reaching Sarajevo. Many of the reports never reached their destination.[11]

Regardless of the enormous difficulties experienced by the Hajjis – they were flying in cargo planes without normal seating, could not land immediately during their return flight (because, so they assumed, the Serbs shot at the plane or did not allow it to land)[12] and had an ugly experience with Ukrainian peace-keepers who refused to help the weakest among them to board – the successful completion of the Hajj had enormous symbolical resonance. The multiple meanings of the Hajj which were created throughout the twentieth century – the conjoining of the sacred and the political, the emphasis on the utilitarian function of the pilgrimage and the Hajj as catalyst of the self – were now subsumed under one defining moment. For Bosniak authors, the Hajj journey of 1994 assumed all these meanings; moreover, they were transformed and strengthened with the additional symbolical framework of the *hijra*: in the midst of war and genocide, Bosnian Muslims were going on the Hajj and making their own *hijra*. At the same time, as they headed to Mecca and Medina, Bosnia was rising as new spiritual and emotional centre.

This final chapter will look into the shift that occurred during the aggression of 1992–95 which placed Bosnia at the centre of the Hajj imagery, as well as in the postwar developments that recalibrated Bosnian Muslim ties to the ritual and the Islamic geography. In the process, the chapter will investigate the centrality of the body in this religious experience, the question of the non-Bosnian Other in the pilgrimage and the new sensibilities arising from the increased focus on the inner experience of the journey and the ritual. The Hajj writings of this period, thus, remained a constant mediating channel between the socio-political realities and the ritual, between Islamic history and present, as well as audiences that grew in unprecedented forms with the greater visibility of religious activities and, towards the end of the twentieth century, the internet. However, they also became a medium for conveying emotions in ways that had not been prominent in earlier periods. This, of course, does not mean that previous Hajjis had not experienced the same emotions; sometimes, as seen in

[11] Hodžić, 'Bošnjaci – Borci s predsjednikom na Hadžu', pp. 43–44.

[12] Gavrankapetanović, *Kako sam obavio i doživio Hadždž 1414. h.g. – 1994. g.*, p. 60.

both premodern and modern periods, the silence was indicative of the holiness of place or the proper *adab* related to the experience that occurred there. Yet, as the body became central in the Hajj narratives, emotions obtained greater visibility as well. Emotions are not spontaneous, sudden acts, devoid and outside of the body, but 'acts executed by a mindful body, as cultural practices'.[13] As such, descriptions of emotions had a cultivating role in their effort to elicit a proper bodily reaction in the reader. In this chapter, we will see how emotions and sentiments become public, not only conveying a connection to the transcendental, but also shaping the religious experience and expectations – the habitus – of future pilgrims and a wider readership.

Before turning to these issues, however, we will investigate the rising centrality of the Bosnian Hajji to the Hajj discourse in the first wartime pilgrimage. While the shaping of the Hajji persona was a constant factor in writings throughout the twentieth century, in the Bosnian context this process took on additional form: the Bosnian pilgrim was an active witness to the forms of the utmost devotion to Islam, not only through the pilgrimage, but also through the physical struggle for Islam in Bosnia. That is why, as Munir Gavrankapetanović and many of his contemporaries emphasised, the praise of God had to happen not only in words, but also terms of the body and physically. Bosniaks testified to their faith with their lives.

Bosniaks on the Hajj with their President

In many ways, in Bosnian writings the Hajj of 1994 held crucial significance, not only because it was the first time that a Bosnian president accompanied the Hajjis, but also because this president was Alija Izetbegović. His biography was striking: having spent multiple years in prison in two distinctive periods for his activities in the Young Muslim Movement and for challenging the Yugoslav state order, he also became a prolific writer who advised the creation of a 'folk pan-Islamism', which 'would be guided and influenced not by the project of liberal or socialist modernity but instead by an Islamic sense of belonging'.[14]

[13] Scheer, 'Are Emotions a Kind of Practice', p. 205.

[14] Piro Rexhepi, 'Unmapping Islam in Eastern Europe: Periodization and Muslim Subjectivities in the Balkans', in *Eastern Europe Unmapped: Beyond Borders and Peripheries*, ed. by Irene Kacandes and Juliya Komska (New York, Oxford: Berghahn, 2017), p. 61.

While dissatisfied with the way in which the socialist modernist project in Yugoslavia relegated religion to the social margins, Izetbegović's 'universalisation of the challenges that Muslims faced in Yugoslavia' was nonetheless inspired by Islamic decolonisation thinkers such as Jalal Al-e Ahmad (1923–69) and Ali Shariati (1933–77).[15] It is not a coincidence that these two authors penned their respective Hajj travelogues in the 1960s and 1970s, together with other luminaries of the decolonial struggle, such as Malcolm X. In recent years, critical attention has been given to the transformational power of the Hajj on the political, ideological and religious outlook of these figures, as well as to the effect which the bodily practice (of the Hajj ritual) had on the creation of new ideological and political interventions (Fig. 5.1).[16]

Preporod

ISLAMSKE INFORMATIVNE NOVINE

BOŠNJACI NA HADŽDŽU

PLANETARNO SVJEDOČENJE ISLAMA

BAJRAM ŠERIF MUBAREK OLSUN

Figure 5.1 The title page of the bi-weekly *Preporod* in 1994, announcing the first wartime Bosniak Hajj. Source: *Preporod*.

[15] Rexhepi, 'Unmapping Islam in Eastern Europe', p. 62.

[16] For example, Nikpour, 'Revolutionary Journeys, Revolutionary Practice'.

While it is possible to track the influence of decolonial thinkers on Alija Izetbegović's thought, the Hajj seems to have functioned in the opposite direction for the Bosnian Hajjis in 1994. The Hajj journey was a symbolic culmination of struggles against both the socialist Yugoslav limitations on religion and the Serbian ultra-nationalist attack on Bosnian lives. In both, Bosnian Muslims – at least those Hajjis who made up the group – saw themselves as victors. The Hajj was the reward, and the final point. It was the Bosnians who could intervene in the lives of other members of the *umma* on the Hajj.

As the aggression on Bosnia raged in the early 1990s, Alija Izetbegović was becoming a popular figure in the global press. Likewise, the image of Alija Izetbegović on the Hajj was striking for both local and wider audiences, and he was constantly surrounded by Saudi officials. While Izetbegović did not pen a Hajj travelogue, after some coaxing by the Bosnian journalist Amir Hodžić, he gave a long speech to the Bosnian Hajjis, which the former transcribed in full. The speech accentuated several points which have come to mark the modern Hajj imagery, and its incorporation in a larger travelogue in its entirety shows the overwhelming importance attached to his person. The speech started with the gratitude expressed to God and King Fahd, the organiser of the Hajj journey. The focus soon turned to the Bosnian Hajjis themselves, who were eagerly listening to their president:

> I am honoured to be here with you, and I feel somehow lesser than any of you because, unlike you, I have not lost any limb during the war. I could have been wounded, because I spent the whole time in Sarajevo, and I was not hiding too much. [. . .] There were days when even two thousand grenades fell on Sarajevo, but I remained unharmed. Some of you did not, and I feel lesser than any of you here who lost his arm, leg, eye.[17]

Alija Izetbegović was stressing the visual and symbolical centrality of maimed bodies on the Hajj, which was the focal point of the travelogues written about the 1994 Hajj journey. While maimed bodies will form the subject of the next section, it is important to indicate that the bodies of the soldiers

[17] Hodžić, 'Bošnjaci – Borci s predsjednikom na Hadžu', p. 25.

who were standing in front of their president testified to the highest ideal in Izetbegović's thought: action before words, and mobility as opposed to inertia.

Izetbegović's speech connected the Hajj with nation-making through references to memory. The pilgrimage, according to him, was a way of remembrance, which connected contemporary nations to their religious histories. Performing rites, such as *sa'y*, presented a way of remembering the prophets and their families. Memory, at the same time, served as a dividing criterion between 'civilised and cultured people' and those who were 'not cultured and primitive'. These cultured people had memory, and thus they 'had history',[18] which also implied continuity and persistence. The Hajj, thus, was a key component in cultivating and preserving that status, and it served to enhance the Bosnian cause.

Another important component of the Hajj emphasised by the president consisted of the symbolism of *ihram*, a cloth worn during the Hajj as well as a burial shroud pointing to the equality of all Muslims at birth as well as in death. The *memento mori* moment in the speech was followed by an emphasis on action and struggle, eerily reminiscent of the Yugoslav socialist narrative of people who had earned their freedom in Ljubunčić's Hajj travelogue. For Izetbegović, the struggle continued after the Hajj in the form of building a state that would further protect Islam:

> Life is a struggle, and only those nations that accept the truth have a chance of survival. Thank God for our fight [. . .] God willing, we are continuing our struggle for Bosnia and our nation. We want to have a state because a people without a state is like a family which has been cast out outside, and it is raining, and the family is without a roof over their head. [. . .] This is why we are resolute that, God willing, we should create our state, to have that house that can protect us against all these winds and storms. You [Bosnian Hajjis] have done for that the best you could do, and you sacrificed a lot, and we shall win, God willing. We will live in our state as we want. Nobody will tell us how to live, as it was the case earlier. One thing is certain: in this state, Islam will be respected.[19]

[18] Hodžić, 'Bošnjaci – Borci s predsjednikom na Hadžu', p. 25.

[19] Hodžić, 'Bošnjaci – Borci s predsjednikom na Hadžu', p. 27.

These words were greeted with *tekbirs*. However, back home in the Bosnian print media, the role of the Bosnian president on the Hajj was seen in a different light. In the midst of the wartime anxieties of siege and survival, the future and nature of Islam in Bosnia were debated by Western intellectuals who were flocking to Sarajevo in droves. Gilles Hertzog (1948–), who made a movie about Bosnia in 1994, also wrote an essay that was translated as 'Sarajevo Thought Well' and published in the daily *Oslobođenje* (*Liberation*) in early 1995. In that essay, the author identified Alija Izetbegović's Hajj journey as one of the examples of 'soft Islamism' condoned by the US, in order to prevent a stronger Islamist resurrection.[20] The Hajj was, according to this interpretation, a useful tool, a political means to present Bosnia in the light of popular pan-Islamism both at home and abroad, but with the aim of suppressing alternative and more radical expressions of religious zeal.

As shown throughout this book, the Hajj of Bosnian Muslims often became an object of interest for non-Muslim outsiders. The Hajj, as well as the visibility of religious expression in general, was here seen as a political move of the Bosnian pan-Islamist elites seeking allies for the nascent Bosnian state – a view that finds support in much of the contemporary scholarship on religion in Bosnia. This tunnel vision reflects a certain 'methodological nationalism' which is preoccupied solely with top-down religious processes, in such a way that it . . .

> . . . reduces a vast array of experiences with the divine into discourses on the politics of identity and/or difference, and silences and de-historicizes other ideas and practices that play an important role in villagers' as well as urbanites' articulations of what it means to be Muslim and live a Muslim life.[21]

In terms of the concrete example of the wartime Hajjis, this did not mean that various political and social forces did not affect the Hajj experience: after all, the first wartime Hajj journey was organised from besieged Sarajevo, and while their coreligionists from around the world enjoyed the privileges of proper air travel, Bosnian Hajjis flew in seatless cargo planes. In a century marked

[20] Giles Hertzog, 'Sarajevo je dobro razmislilo', *Oslobođenje* (1 March 1995), p. 9.

[21] Henig, *Remaking Muslim Lives*, p. 9.

by unprecedented mobility, Bosnian Hajjis met its other end of extreme and deadly restriction. And as much as the figure of Alija Izetbegović was popular in political or ideological imaginings of Bosnia's present and future, it was the people who physically fought for freedom who became the central element of the wartime Hajj imaginary, often in their own words.

Maimed Bodies on the Hajj

The last chapter showed how the reformist discourse often carried anti-body bias, through its condescending attitude towards devotional practices in *ziyāra*. In the wartime Hajj travelogues, the body returned with a vengeance. The bodies that constituted the focus of the Hajj narratives were not just praying, weeping, or sensing bodies, or what could generally be described as medium for religious experience. They had been maimed and wounded by shrapnel and bullets, testifying through the absence of their limbs to the presence of their faith. Through the examples of Munir Gavrankapetanović, who emphasised his devotion to Islam when he was able-bodied, and the images of wounded soldiers in the first Bosnian state-organised Hajj, the 'present body' is constantly juxtaposed to a 'habitual'[22] (able) body to show the greatness of the sacrifice performed for Islam.

In this context, these bodies, as feeble as they could be, were also mighty and did not provoke pity, but pride in fellow Bosnians and inspiration for other Muslims. Amazed at the number and visibility of the Bosnian Hajjis ('This is probably the unique case that such a number of those who were wounded in war pray together in front of the Kaʿba'),[23] Gavrankapetanović wrote:

[22] 'The habitual body casts a kind of aura around the physical body that shapes the subject's feeling of being in the world in the form of expectations regarding what the physical body is to encounter upon extending itself through its limbs and sensory organs'. Shahzad Bashir, *Sufi Bodies: Religion and Society in Medieval Islam* (New York City: Columbia University Press, 2011); p. 16; on bodies and disability in premodern Islamic contexts, see Kristina Richardson, *Difference and Disability in the Medieval Islamic World: Blighted Bodies* (Edinburgh: Edinburgh University Press, 2014), and Sara Scalenghe, *Disability in the Ottoman Arab World, 1500–1800* (New York: Cambridge University Press, 2014).

[23] Gavrankapetanović, *Kako sam obavio i doživio Hadždž 1414. h.g. – 1994. g.*, p. 35.

> I was overwhelmed with happiness that I will make *tawaf* with these brave youth, without arms or legs.
>
> The Almighty God has bestowed immeasurable bounty upon me.
>
> I will make *tawaf* with Bosniak believers. The old dreams from my youth are coming true. These believers are bringing freedom to Bosnia – so we can talk, write and think in freedom.[24]

The Bosnian wartime Hajj journey was intentionally visible. This visibility came in two interrelated forms. The first one was the presence of Bosnian Hajjis in general, which went against the perceived historical invisibility of the ritual under socialism and given the limited mobility during the war; the second was the visibility of the 'maimed bodies' that testified to the sacrifices that the Hajjis had had to make for Islam and Bosnia. The visibility of these bodies also had an educational role: it showed 'to the whole Islamic world [. . .] what kind of evil we are facing and what the aggressor did to people and our homeland Bosnia and Herzegovina'.[25] Since many of pilgrims had been soldiers, they were also young and would have been at the peak of their strength, had it not been for the war. Their youth was also seen in contrast to the expected stereotype that Hajjis should be 'exhausted old men who are crawling and coughing'.[26] This enhanced the way in which their sacrifice was seen; as stated, 'maimed bodies' became a matter of pride, and how they had been maimed or wounded was often described:

> In the elevator at the hallway and in front of the bus I am encountering dear friends . . . Mevrudin who lost both legs to a grenade, Mujo Borčak who is also an amputee whose one leg was amputated very high, then Ahmed, Omer, Vehid, Esad . . . all of them want to help me. I am proud for being a son of the Bosniak people! [. . .] This is the youngest generation of Hajjis that in the history of Bosnia came to the Hajj. [. . .] The days that followed showed that Bosnia became the centre of the Islamic world today, partly owing to these heroes who are with me. The lines of Muslims from all the continents are gathering around Bosnia and its sacrifice on God's path.[27]

[24] Gavrankapetanović, *Kako sam obavio i doživio Hadždž 1414. h.g. – 1994. g.*, p. 35.

[25] Hodžić, 'Bošnjaci – Borci s predsjednikom na Hadžu', p. 16.

[26] Enes Ratkušić, 'Dva i pol miliona ljudi, iz stotina različitih kultura, stopljenih u jednu misao . . .', *Ljiljan* 3/75 (22 June 1994), p. 23.

[27] Gavrankapetanović, *Kako sam obavio i doživio Hadždž 1414. h.g. – 1994. g.*, p. 41.

The Bosnian war was a cause that 'riveted the attention of Muslims worldwide'.[28] The systematic murdering of Bosniaks and the rape of women[29] provoked different types of symbolic and concrete responses by Muslims globally. The image of Muslims in Europe placed the Bosniaks' plight and suffering in comparison to the demise of Muslim Spain;[30] people came to Bosnia as humanitarians and fighters, defending the cause of Islam.[31] The Hajj of 1994 showed the centrality of Bosnia for the Hajjis and other pilgrims alike, through the visibility of wounded bodies, but it also triggered thinking about the diversity of the Muslim world that unified around the Bosnian cause. In the geographical imagination of the Hajjis, Bosnia and Mecca and Medina assumed the same centrality. Just as the pilgrims were uttering the *tekbir*, they also repeated 'Bosnia':

> Hajjis from all parts of the world were curiously stopping by us. They knew we were from Bosnia. This word was uttered with such pride. Many wanted to touch and kiss us and ask us how Bosnia was doing. Sincere tears of compassion flowed uncontrollably. We were suddenly in the centre here in Haram al-Sharif, just as Bosnia is in the centre of interest of the whole world.[32]

Still, the Hajjis faced many obstacles along the way. The amputees and those with paralysed limbs sought help from their able companions to put on their *ihram* attire, and by wearing the ritual clothing, they all testified in body, and 'not only in heart', to equality and brotherhood.[33] Such obstacles were quickly removed by the hosts: Gavrankapetanović mentions how he appreciated the

[28] Li, *The Universal Enemy*, p. 8.

[29] In his Hajj essay, Jusuf Žiga mentions the screams of 'bereaved mothers and humiliated Bosniak sisters'. Jusuf Žiga, 'Impresije sa puta u Meku', in *Odazivam Ti se Bože, Odazivam: Bošnjaci na Hadždžu 1414./1994.*, ed. by Mehmedalija Hadžić, Amir Hodžić and Jusuf Žiga (Sarajevo: El Kalem, 1995), p. 58.

[30] Džemaludin Latić, 'Muslimani moraju kazniti francusko-englesko-japansku pročetničku koaliciju', *Ljiljan* 4/131 (19 July 1995), p. 2.

[31] See Li, *The Universal Enemy*.

[32] Hodžić, 'Bošnjaci – Borci s predsjednikom na Hadžu', p. 32.

[33] Gavrankapetanović, *Kako sam obavio i doživio Hadždž 1414. h.g. – 1994. g.*, p. 30.

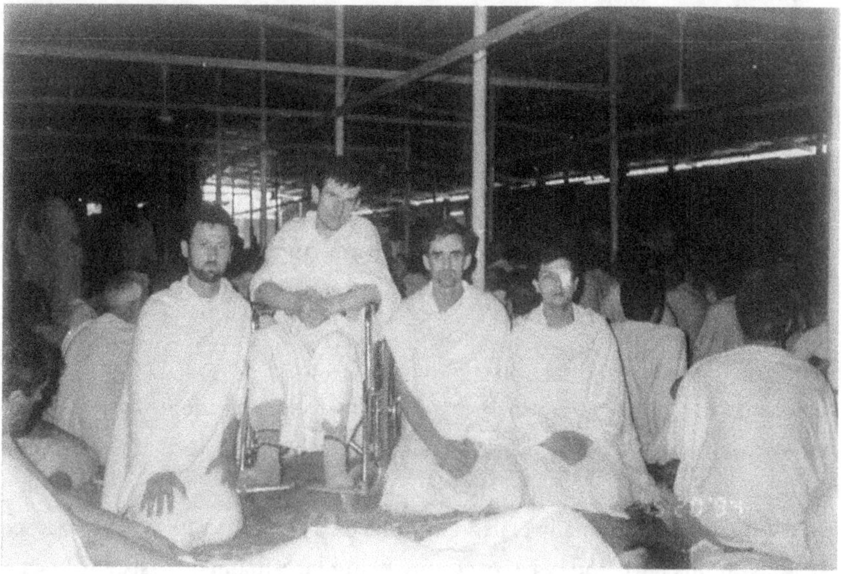

Figure 5.2 Bosniak Hajjis on pilgrimage in 1994. Source: From the family collection of the late Vehid Hodžić.

ramp in his hotel in Mecca,[34] which was an enormous relief compared to the time in Sarajevo when he attended an *ikrar* prayer in a mosque and sat behind everyone 'so that the wheels do not dirty the carpet' (Fig. 5.2).[35]

While performing Hajj in 1994, the Bosniak pilgrims were exposed to a number of hardships. So, what did the Hajj do for the wounded Bosnian pilgrims? The pilgrimage did not seem to be a culmination and end-point of their struggle, but it was 'a spiritual inspiration to become even braver and endure the havoc wreaked upon them by the aggressor'.[36] As the masses of pilgrims struggled to touch the wheelchairs of the Bosnian Hajjis, praying and weeping for them,[37] Bosnians felt invigorated, ready to return and continue fighting for their homeland: 'As soon as I return home, I will enlist in the army unit again. If I cannot march, at least I can fill the ammo and shoot

[34] Gavrankapetanović, *Kako sam obavio i doživio Hadždž 1414. h.g. – 1994. g.*, p. 33.

[35] Gavrankapetanović, *Kako sam obavio i doživio Hadždž 1414. h.g. – 1994. g.*, p. 7.

[36] Hodžić, 'Bošnjaci – Borci s predsjednikom na Hadžu', p. 16.

[37] Hodžić, 'Bošnjaci – Borci s predsjednikom na Hadžu', p. 55.

from the minethrower! [His leg had been amputated high above the knee]'.[38] For others, the Hajj was equal to rebirth, as in the words of one of the Hajjis who had been held by Serbs in several prison camps:

> I was first born when my mother gave birth to me. My second birth was when I was set free from the Chetnik torture camps in Batkovići close to Bijeljina and Kula near Sarajevo. And now, I feel that my third birth is coming to the Hajj and standing on Arafat. I would be the happiest if I died here.[39]

While earlier travelogues also included narratives from religious history related to the holy places, in the wartime travelogues some of these resonated even more. In Gavrankapetanović's travelogue, the story of the Prophet Ibrāhīm was especially emphasised: although the prophet was tortured on a pyre, threatened and finally exiled and forced to perform a *hijra*, he remained steadfast in his faith and 'with his entire being he remained persistent in calling [others] to Islam'.[40] Other episodes from the prophet's life were recounted as well, with a focus on trial and affliction and the ultimate perseverance and steadfastness in faith that prevailed.

The concerns of the emaciated and exhausted body often emerged unexpectedly in these travelogues. As the exhausted and impoverished Hajjis adjusted not only to the rites and the vicinity of the holy, they also roamed other spaces of Mecca and Medina:

> We were almost lost in the supermarket. We were taking coffee, tea, soups, oranges, bananas, toothpaste, toothbrushes, chocolates, candy, batteries . . . We have not been in a supermarket like this in ages. Since the aggression started, we missed everything, so we took what we needed and did not need. Whatever we looked at, we remembered there is no such thing now in Sarajevo.[41]

The war had irrevocably changed the Hajj discourse among Bosnian Muslim authors. The transformations were in line with the emergence of the Hajji as a

[38] Gavrankapetanović, *Kako sam obavio i doživio Hadždž 1414. h.g. – 1994. g.*, p. 59.

[39] Hodžić, 'Bošnjaci – Borci s predsjednikom na Hadžu', p. 36.

[40] Gavrankapetanović, *Kako sam obavio i doživio Hadždž 1414. h.g. – 1994. g.*, p. 20.

[41] Hodžić, 'Bošnjaci – Borci s predsjednikom na Hadžu', p. 44.

nodal point through which perspectives on the Hajj and the holy places were reflected. Moreover, Bosnian Muslim authors went a step further and through their emphasis on the visibility of the Bosniak struggle – the maimed bodies of soldiers – made Bosnia's image the centre of Islamic geography. Centring Bosnia and the Bosnian Muslims in the Hajj literature consequently implied their measurement and reflection against other Hajjis seen in Mecca and Medina. Writing in 1996, the Bosnian novelist Nedžad Ibrišimović (1940–2011) succinctly described this transformation:

> How can I describe the Hajj, when I only observed my Bosniaks. I could not get enough of it. I did bring the Kaʿba back home in my hands, preserving it as the most treasured thing in the world, but my soul is pierced by the faces of my Bosniaks who went on the Hajj with me. I have actually gone on a pilgrimage to Bosnia! Five-hundred people from Bosnia and Herzegovina and me, the tobacco smoker among them! That is the true value of my Hajj. I had to go to Mecca to find Bosnia in those people! Those are my Muslims, those are my Bosniaks, those are my compatriots! How did I look at people until then? Those are the best, the most chosen, Bosnians and Herzegovinians, those people, those soldiers, those heroes and fathers of martyrs from Gradačac, Cazin, Bužim, Žepa, Goražde, all the places in Bosnia [. . .] We did not go into a battle, but on a Hajj; we did not plow the land, but we went on a Hajj [. . .] everyone with their own *niyya*, their own struggle, their own prayers [. . .].[42]

The war ended with the Dayton Agreement in November 1995. As the centrality of the maimed bodies on the Hajj defined a new Bosnian Muslim perception of their own position during the wartime period, the postwar period witnessed a rising interest and engagement in reconnections with their coreligionists, often through corporal attitudes such as hospitality. The next two sections will examine more closely the Bosnian Muslim experience of the postwar Hajj journey and the multiple spaces through which the pilgrims

[42] Nedžad Ibrišimović, 'Kako da opišem hadždž, kada sam ja gledao samo svoje Bošnjake odlomak iz hadžijskog putopisa *Ruhani i šejtani inspiracija*', *Stav* 16 August 2018, available at https://arhiv.stav.ba/nedzad-ibrisimovic-kako-da-opisem-hadzdz-kada-sam-ja-gledao-samo-svoje-bosnjake/ (accessed on 27 August 2021).

passed, as well as the descriptions of the ritual, both of which inextricably tied the holy to the visibility of other non-Bosnian Muslims.

Places without God's House

The awareness of the Bosniak Hajjis' unusual fate is a defining characteristic of much of the wartime and postwar literature. Such a perception necessarily led to a question of difference: how exactly were Bosnian Hajjis exceptional? Their perceived distinction from many other Muslims was constituted in a layer of perspectives, some of them related to the body. One of those was race – despite all the well-intentioned and frequent emphases on the feeling of unity-in-diversity in pilgrimage, race was a frequent differentiating factor, often brought to light and utilised. The physical appearance of other Hajjis who came into contact with the Bosnians (to admire them or take inspiration from them) was very important to the authors.[43] Through the question of physical difference and race, theirs and the others', the Bosniaks were actually carving out a space for themselves, not only among the Muslims on the Hajj, but also in their imagination of Europe which lingered in their pilgrimage writings. The visibility of difference, however, was not necessarily underpinned by hierarchical thinking: behind emphasis on variety, apart from wonder, there was often a genuine desire to connect and learn from other Muslims.

Because the pilgrimage is simultaneously a form of mobility and a ritual, uniting prescriptive commands and mundane realities, the Hajj provides the necessary lenses through which we can observe the shaping of racial discourse. Through these lenses we can also see how race reflected itself in the religious experience. As a recent study by Catherine Baker suggests, 'the notion that the Yugoslav region, the Balkans or eastern Europe could have entered the twenty-first century without exposure to the global dynamics of race is [. . .] unsustainable, when these spaces have so often been defined in relation to "Europe"'.[44] While Europe plays an ambiguous role in modern Hajj writings,

[43] Gavrankapetanović himself comments on an older female Hajji with 'slanted eyes' who whispered the name of Bosnia almost like a sacred chant. Gavrankapetanović, *Kako sam obavio i doživio Hadždž 1414. h.g. – 1994. g.*, p. 53.

[44] Baker, *Race and the Yugoslav Region*, p. 7.

oft juxtaposed to Islam, perceived as desired by wealthy Westernised Muslims, yet 'culturally fake',[45] the characterisation 'European' often carried a more positive note. Bosnian Muslims identified themselves as Europeans throughout the twentieth century, but that identification came in varying degrees and was sometimes pushed into the background by a more dominant 'Yugoslav' marker. Yet, in the 1990s, the need for a redefinition of belonging peaked in the reassertion of the 'European' character of Bosnian Muslims.

While reshaping the European identity of Bosnian Muslims, the Other was necessarily created. The way in which Bosnian Muslim Hajjis saw others was shaped by their traumatic experiences of the 1990s, as well as the complex racial histories of the non-aligned Yugoslavia, but at the same time their views of the Other were also formed by modern religious discourses. These discourses sought to grapple with and reconcile the visible diversity during the Hajj with the purported unity of the Muslim World.[46] All these, commingled with real-life encounters that often had their own inner logic, led to a prominence of non-Bosnian Hajjis in modern literature.

While European identity was in the focus of many wartime Bosniaks, another self-determining change was under way. Many Bosnian Hajjis felt that their position on the imagined map of the Muslim World had been negligent and almost non-existent during the socialist period. The war and the sacrifice of Bosniaks symbolically placed Bosnia as one of the nodes on this map once again. At times, the Hajjis felt that Bosnia had become the centre of the Muslim World and that the Hajj was transformed into another opportunity to realise this new exceptionality of Bosnian Muslims.

As the distinct image of the Bosnian Hajji emerged due to the new visibility of religious expression and the war trauma, and as the very experience of the pilgrimage was given a new meaning of physical and spiritual struggle, the postwar period brought a certain recentralisation of the pilgrim gaze. In the postwar period, other spaces reappeared in the Hajj writings, together with an increasing focus on the further exploration of geographical, cultural and racial differences, through encounters with numerous people who were engaged in the logistics of travel, people whom pilgrims met on the way to

[45] See Muhamed Krpo's characterisation of Europe in Chapter 3.

[46] Aydin, *The Idea of the Muslim World*, p. 74.

and from and, most prominently, through an exploration of the pilgrimage world with one's senses. The war remained one of the dominant elements in shaping this experience. However, curiosity and wonder, as well as the cultivation of emotions indicating a belonging to the wider Muslim community and solidarity with different Muslims, exhibit continuity with previous periods.

After the war, Bosnian Hajjis travelled in organised groups by airplane or bus, in tight groups, especially after the Islamic Community took over most of the control of the Hajj organisation.[47] External events, especially in the turbulent late 1990s, still affected the way in which Bosnian Hajjis travelled to the Hijaz: in the immediate aftermath of the war, the Hajjis could not travel through Serbia, but had to go through Hungary; they also needed to be accompanied by members of the special NATO forces, the 'Implementation Force (IFOR)', on their return; this prompted one Hajji to write that 'our guards were foreigners, but the land is ours'.[48] In 1999, the Hajj journey from Bosnia was not certain because of the beginning of NATO's military intervention in Yugoslavia over the bloodshed Serbs committed in Kosovo. The Hajjis still managed to fly, but they were stuck for days in Jeddah because they

[47] The monopoly of the Islamic Community over the organisation of the Hajj was sometimes challenged by private entrepreneurs. In 2009, Fehim Omerbašić through his organisation Sabur Uspjeh offered to take Hajjis for a considerably smaller price than the Islamic Community. The officials of the Islamic Community accused Omerbašić of cheating potential pilgrims. A. Bećirović, 'Naš je hadž jeftiniji', *Oslobođenje* (10 April 2009), p. 8. This case became even more bizarre when Omerbašić was found tied to the steering wheel of his car, on the day he was supposed to bring the passports of the Hajjis travelling with his company, which were to be stamped with Saudi visas. The Hajjis waited in vain the entire day. Accusations and insinuations of kidnapping were flouted around, as well as the characterisation of '*vehabije*' (often used as a derogatory term for Salafis). Dragan Pavlović and Asaf Bećirović, 'Hadžija u lancima', *Oslobođenje* (8 May 2009), p. 3. Soon it became clear that Omerbašić planned his own kidnapping because he could not get the visas on time. The representatives of the Islamic Community used the opportunity to stress that the only official channel for organising the Hajj journey (including the visa process) was the Islamic Community. Davud Muminović, 'Organizator hadža inscenirao svoju otmicu', *Nezavisne novine* (9 May 2009), pp. 4–5.

[48] Hasan Šestić, *Put na hadž '96 (dnevnik i utisci)* (Bošnjačka zajednica kulture 'Preporod' Zenica: Zenica, 1998), p. 177.

could not land in Sarajevo since the airport was closed.[49] One of the Hajjis, Muhamed Bikić (1973–), a journalist, felt ambivalent about the event, yet convinced that it presented God's punishment for the aggressors:

> I felt happiness from my toes and then through my body. Dear God, is it possible that the aggressors finally met a small warning for all that they had done in Bosnia and in Kosovo? As much as I am happy, I am consciously suppressing my joy – it is not alright to rejoice over anyone's misery. Yet, the target of the planes of NATO are not the innocent civilians, but military warehouses, artillery, those tanks that killed my comrade Adnan Midžić, and Feko and Mirza, and thousands of adults and children. I cannot not be happy.[50]

The Hajjis who travelled by bus immediately after the war fared even worse because they were mistreated at the borders.[51] As it was increasingly the case throughout the twentieth century, Bosnian Hajj travel was usually arrangement in cooperation with different air travel agencies, many from the Middle East. Bus and air travel shaped the journey in slightly different ways. Bus travel was a slower experience, which offered a rapidly increasing number of Hajjis a brief tour of the Middle East. Bosnians very often encountered hospitality: in 2005, Bosnian daily newspapers reported that, in Istanbul, the Hajjis were seen off with 'Turkish march music' all the way to the 'hanging bridge over the Bosphorus'[52]; they were offered citrus fruit in Mersin.[53] The postwar years brought reflection and resentment towards the socialist past of the region: Hasan Šestić (1931–), a businessman from Zenica who performed Hajj in 1996, was not not happy about the gray-looking architecture in Romania and Bulgaria, unlike the 'beautiful Arab architecture' in Tebuk in Saudi Arabia.[54]

[49] Generalni servis ONASA, 'NATO odobrio slijetanje na Sarajevski aerodrom aviona 'Air Commerca' (8 April 1999).

[50] Muhamed Bikić, *Hadžijsko drvo* (Studentska štamparija: Sarajevo, 2000), pp. 29–30.

[51] Bosnian Hajjis were held on the Croatian border for hours upon their return because of the fear that they might carry malaria. Šestić, *Put na hadž '96*, p. 175.

[52] A. M., 'Bh. hadžije iz Istanbula ispraćene uz turski marš', *Dnevni Avaz* (25 December 2005), p. 4.

[53] T. L., 'Hadžije odmarale u Mersinu', *Dnevni Avaz* (14 December 2006), p. 8.

[54] Šestić, *Put na hadž '96*, p. 48.

The emotional relation to the sacred places of Mecca and Medina was often cultivated based on the wider imagery related to the Middle East and North Africa. This type of imagery was sometimes the starting point for nurturing greater attachment to the Hijaz, and it was created through an appeal to the senses. It was also an imaginative byproduct of the multiple connections developed between the Balkan region and the Arab countries during the Non-Aligned Movement:

> [My father Asim] always told me about the endless beauties of the Islamic countries – Iraq, Libya . . . He was a few times there for shorter periods, as an employee of 'Energoinvest'. He told me about grand mosques, the loud *ezan* that calls believers to prayer from every corner, about unbearable heat and how Arabs drink hot tea in summer and eat ice-cream in the winter. That was the strangest to me. This is why, ever since I knew, I wanted to visit what is called the Islamic World. Later, with my religious maturation, it turned into a conscious intention, and I knew that going to Saudi Arabia and performing the Hajj is the fifth duty of every Muslim believer.[55]

Yet, the Hajjis were also aware of the difficult and complex realities of the countries through which they passed. In Turkey, the sight of bootleggers and the fast pace of life confused the pilgrims,[56] but they admired the technological developments of the late 1990s, such as the 'hanging bridge',[57] and several years later, Turkey seemed like a rising giant.[58] However, they seemed to see through the propaganda of the Syrian regime and were bothered by the many posters of Assad's family in the country.[59] Wherever the Hajjis went, they were welcomed by the local population.

In the period before the onslaught of social media and communication-enhancing tools (such as google translate), some Hajj literature also incorporated short dictionaries with lists of the most important phrases and words

[55] Bikić, *Hadžijsko drvo*, pp. 10–11.

[56] Šestić, *Put na hadž '96*, p. 20.

[57] Šestić, *Put na hadž '96*, p. 21.

[58] Jusuf Pajević, *Hadžijski dnevnik: Autobusom na hadž i hadž u praksi* (Svendborg: published by the author, 2010), p. 11.

[59] Šestić, *Put na hadž '96*, p. 38; Pajević, *Hadžijski dnevnik*, p. 12.

in Arabic with Bosnian translation. Fikret Arnaut, the imam of a Bosnian community from Germany, composed one such treatise with a small dictionary. Written in simple language, the dictionary showed the major preoccupations of Bosnian Hajjis: introducing oneself, asking for prices, the names of food items. The dictionary did not use a strict *fusha*, but the vocabulary was adjusted to be understood by a common person on the street.[60]

The cities and villages of the Middle East were quickly traversed. For the Hajjis on buses, just like those who travelled by car in the 1980s, such as Safija Šiljak and Hidajeta Mirojević from the beginning of this book, some of the most striking sights were encounters with the desert upon crossing into Saudi Arabia. The desert, which simultaneously frightened and fascinated Bosnian authors, thanks to its vastness was a sign of the wonder of God's creation. With its bareness and lack of infrastructure – even mosques – it turned into a powerful sign of human fragility and God's omnipotence. The believers could pray to God without any external obstruction to the senses:

> All those numerous people who are passing here do not pray only in the mosque. If there is no House of God around, and it is time to pray, people perform the prayer wherever they can. One group of travelers, I do not know from where, did the same. Right by the road I saw several cars, and next to them the *džemat* in two rows, men and women. It was noon. It was such a dignified sight, one which I have never seen even on the photos. The sun is shining mercilessly, the sand is red-hot and incandescent, but those who are praying are not paying attention at all. Only humility and piety can be seen in their posture.[61]

Unlike that of cities and their inhabitants, the spatial framework of the desert did not inspire Hajjis to write about the ethnic or racial identities of the others. The desert was a place 'in between what is familiar and what is far, what is the World of the Unknown, Otherworldly, Unreachable',[62] and often they did not comment on the particular identities of the people they met there. Instead, they preferred to stress the common humanity and equality of all people in front of

[60] Fikret Arnaut, *Vodič na hadžu i umri* (Minhen: An-Nur, 2009), pp. 78–85.

[61] Šestić, *Put na hadž '96*, p. p. 49.

[62] Enes Karić, *Crni tulipan: Putopis hodočasnika iz Bosne* (Sarajevo: Tugra, 2009), pp. 94–95.

God, and in complete submission to Him. Therefore, this was a prelude to the spaces of Mecca and Medina and the experience of rites.

Rites and Close Encounters

Much of the contemporary discourse on the Hajj is influenced by Malcolm X's (1925–65) description of the unity-in-diversity in pilgrimage, a 'transformative experience [. . . and] a lesson in the hope Islam provides for racial and political justice'.[63] In Hajj narratives, this is compounded by the feelings of separation from respective homelands and the pervading anonymity of all pilgrims.[64] Indeed, it seems that the modern expectation of equality in diversity was as much a part of the habitus that cultivated the attachment to the holy places as the religious narratives that offered an interpretative framework for many rites.

Until the Arab Spring, which started with the self-immolation of Mohamed Bouazizi in Tunisia in 2010 and caused a chain of revolutions across the Middle East, the Bosnian Hajjis often travelled by bus, in addition to plane. The type of transport frequently was a decisive factor whether the pilgrims visited Medina or Mecca first. After spending some time in Mecca, authors describe how the Hajjis rushed to reach Arafat. For Hajjis who spent much of their time on buses with their fellow Bosnians, the sight of thousands of white tents produced feelings of confusion and awe, reminding them that the purpose of this rite was to remember the Day of Judgement and, thus, they needed to recite the Qur'an and perform the *salawat* as much as possible to repent for their sins. The focus on individual salvation stood hand in hand with curiosity at the multitudes on the mount:

> [On the Arafat] we met Hajjis from all over the world: Pakistanis, Chechens, Turks, Bulgarians, Russians, Americans, Iranians . . . All in one place. We are

[63] Sophia Rose Arjana and Rose Aslan, 'Red, White, and Blue: American Muslims on Hajj and the Politics of Pilgrimage', in *Muslim Pilgrimage in the Modern World*, ed. by Babak Rahimi and Peyman Eshaghi (Chapel Hill: University of North Carolina Press, 2019), p. 113.

[64] Seán McLoughlin, 'Pilgrimage, Performativity, and British Muslims: Scripted and Unscripted Accounts of the Hajj and Umra', in *Hajj: Global Interactions Through Pilgrimage*, ed. by Luitgard Mols and Marjo Buitelaar (Leiden: Sidestone Press, 2015), p. 52.

> communicating in different ways. [. . .] But, in any case, we are all speaking the same language here – the language of faith and *ibadat*.[65]

The experience of Arafat, as well as of the other rites in Mecca gave pilgrims the opportunity to reflect on their own individual lives and what was familiar to them (such as remembrance of relatives and loved ones through prayers), the larger community of Bosnian Muslims to which they belonged and the large *umma* of pilgrims unknown to each other.

> On Arafat, I prayed to Almighty God for all that I had prayed before, after my prayers at home or some other place. I prayed to Him for all who came to visit me before I went on the Hajj, and those who are my family, my parents, my relatives, my friends and neighbours and my country. [. . .] The flag of our country was raised high in our tent camp, which was a true joy for me. [. . .] The heat felt here is the warmth of time, of bodies, feelings, joy, happiness, exhilaration and excitement. The Almighty has given everything to His guests and invitees, so we the pilgrims could feel His Mercy and be thankful to Him, our Creator, performing the rites in this transitory world.[66]

The space of contemplation about the meanings of the Hajj and the prayer for forgiveness that Arafat offered was followed by the journey to Muzdalifa, and then to Mina. The experiences of these places were varied: some Hajjis reflected on the meaning of the stoning of the Shaytan; others were preoccupied with performing the act fast, in fear of getting hurt by the masses of other pilgrims. Some, like Muhamed Bikić, physically – in his nose – felt the presence of Satan which needed to be expelled.[67] Hence, daily occurrences and bodily contacts often displaced customary attitudes by 'unscripted'[68]

[65] Bikić, *Hadžijsko drvo*, p. 45.

[66] Ferid Šmigalović, *Ibrahim a.s. preci i potomci* (Tuzla: published by the author, 2006), pp. 32–33.

[67] Bikić, *Hadžijsko drvo*, p. 53.

[68] '"Living Islam" participants' accounts of "being there" also reflect many unscripted performances that qualify, destabilise, and sometimes contest dominant Islamic scripts. They highlight pilgrims' multiple time-space and lived-structural locations [. . .] in terms of age, health, ethnicity, education, responsibilities, and character on the one hand, and issues such as modernisation-versus-heritage on the other'. McLoughlin, 'Pilgrimage, Performativity, and British Muslims', pp. 53–54.

reflections on pilgrimage and other Hajjis. For example, performing the rites included a fair amount of anxiety, especially related to the frequent stampedes in which entire droves of Hajjis lost their lives. The bodies of other Hajjis were quite literally a potential death threat:

> The bodies of the Hajjis are more squeezed in *tawaf* around the Ka'ba, but almost no one gets hurt there. There are always great casualties at Mina. In *tawaf* all move in one direction, likewise in the *sa'y*, but in Mina one comes to *jamarat* and leaves from all sides, as they will. [. . .] A special problem is that specific groups of Hajjis, usually between fifty and hundred, all clutch each other tightly, and march towards the *jamarat*, do *ramy*, and in the same way, running heedlessly and without paying attention to those around, leave the place. In these groups they do *tawaf* as well. With their bodies, men make a strong circle and within that circle are women who belong to their group. This way of organisation of ritual performance particularly pertains to Indonesians and Malays. As one friend tells me, they practice it well before going on the Hajj, circumambulating a model of the Ka'ba which they have in their homeland. This is probably good for them but does great harm to the others.[69]

Despite the persistent rhetoric on the unity of Muslims on the Hajj, it seems that the physical proximity of the Hajjis' bodies, especially when organised in some way *against* other Hajjis, was a constant problem. The spaces of circulation around the Ka'ba, however, brought exhilaration and unexpected encounters that strengthened the believers' bond. Muhamed Bikić met an Egyptian pilgrim with whom he could communicate only in simple phrases. Yet, the man gave him prayer beads as a gift:

> When I said goodbye to the brother from Egypt, I accidentally looked towards the sky above Bejtullah and the Hajjis who were circulating. Hundreds of swallows were flying over the Harem in perfect and precise circles. Even though those who know say that birds follow people and voices, I still thought that swallows also make *tawaf* in their sky spaces, and, by circulating around Bayt Allah, admire the all-encompassing might of Allah.[70]

[69] Kenan Čemo, 'Putopis s hadža 2006', available at https://znaci.ba/tekstovi/putopis-s-hadza-2006 (accessed on 7 August 2021).

[70] Bikić, *Hadžijsko drvo*, pp. 66–67.

Beyond the rites, the Hajjis met others in mosques and resting places, airports and restaurants. The Bosnian Hajjis and their bodies not only were the object of other Muslims' attention, as in the travelogues of Munir Gavrankapetanović and other wartime authors. They also were among those who gazed and made observations as part of the religious experience. Some authors, such as Ezudin Kurtović and Kemal Zukić, even 'classified' the Hajjis according to their physical characteristics, thereby exhibiting fetishisation and imbedded stereotypes, as well as a racialisation of the bodies of other Hajjis – Kurtović wrote how the slender black bodies of pilgrims from Africa reflected 'the beauty of God's creation',[71] and Zukić differentiated between what he saw as masculinised black bodies and feminised Southeast Asians.[72] Still, such stark descriptions were not frequent. The Hajjis preferred to reflect on the shared humanity and unity in rites, even when the mobility of the bodies performing the rites turned out to be deadly.

Bodies and emotions remained at the centre of the postwar Hajj experience, through the focus on difference in the ritual and the journey. With the ever-increasing modes of writing, especially online texts that allowed instant and wide-spread participation in the creation of the Hajj discourse,[73] as well as with the publication of a number of travelogues written in the socialist period,[74] Hajj narratives in the form of diaries, travelogues, reportages, as well as facebook posts and blogs, became an expected part of the pilgrimage. With less timidity than ever, Bosnian Hajjis spoke about their emotional experiences in great depth, cultivating bodily responses in the process.

[71] Ezudin Kurtović, 'Putovanje na hadž 1999./1419. hg.', available at https://znaci.ba/tekstovi/putovanje-na-hadz-1999-1419hg (accessed on 8 August 2021).

[72] Kemal Zukić, *Odazivam Ti se, Bože moj, odazivam Ti se: Putopis sa hadždža* (Zenica: Minex, 2002), p. 120, and throughout the travelogue.

[73] On these transformations, see more in Karić, 'Online Bosniak Hajj Narratives'.

[74] Some of the examples include hadži Bećir Adilović, *Putopis – hadždž 1969. godine* (Zenica: Nedwe, 1998); Osman Kavazović, *Putopisi hafiza hadži Zaim-efendije Huskanovića* (Tuzla: OFF-SET, 2018); the travelogues of shaykh Fejzulah Hadžibajrić from the previous chapter and the travelogue of Safija Šiljak and Hidajeta Mirojević from the beginning of the book.

Traversing the Distance: The Hajj and the Self

Almost three decades after it had been published, Munir Gavrankapetanović's Hajj narrative is still being read, and sometimes played on radio stations as part of a programme dedicated to the annual pilgrimage.[75] The documentary movie that was made during the Hajj journey of 1994 has often been shown on local television. Despite the extremely limiting circumstances of the Hajj in 1994, it was multi-medial and reached the broadest audience possible. More importantly, it signalled a new change: the Hajjis had now taken over their share of public space and regained a new visibility in writing or producing content about the pilgrimage.

As we saw throughout this book, the impulse to write and share the experience and thus potentially prolong the effects of the ritual was present in different periods, according to the possibilities offered by material circumstances. What changed after the Bosnian war, however, was the sheer number of people shaping the Hajj discourse and its immediacy. Put simply, the Hajjis no longer needed venues such as the official gazette of the Islamic Community, nor access to printing presses; with the arrival of the Internet, anyone could now participate. This, of course, does not mean that previous generations of Bosnian Hajjis – those unprivileged or outside the ulama and intellectual circles – did not write about Hajj. They did, and many family libraries testify to shorter and longer itineraries written by Hajjis throughout the twentieth century, which remained confined to a readership of close family members. The wartime and postwar periods have moved these writings into the open: Safija and Hidajeta's diary, although written in the 1980s, was published only in 2014, by their children in a print shop. In the postwar decades, the Internet removed the mediating role of journals and editorship, as people from all walks of life can now write about their experiences directly. The archetypal Hajj author of the postwar period is a common person with no previous writing experience, often younger, and, in some cases, no longer even located in Bosnia, as result of the war and postwar mobility.

The shift towards visibility has brought more immediacy to writing about the experience. The Hajjis left no aspect of the journey unpacked and

[75] https://www.bir.ba/index.php/vijesti/item/7398-kako-sam-obavio-i-dozivio-hadz-u-programu-radija-bir (accessed 8 August 2021).

emphasised its emotional and internal aspects. The following pages will discuss how, through intimate discourse on the ritual, the postwar Hajj was felt and described by Bosnians. For Hajjis such as Hasan Šestić, writing about Hajj in the form of a diary was a way of 'traversing the distance' which he felt could not be fulfilled by a travelogue.[76] The same form was employed by many other Hajjis who posted their diary entries online.[77] Photos and videos, and occasionally the pictures of other Hajjis,[78] were a welcome addition to the textual core of diaries and travelogues. The photos most commonly featured Bosnian pilgrims who were friends of the author and photos of other non-Bosnian Hajjis whom they had encountered along the way, as well as the places they had visited.

Much like Munir Gavrankapetanović who had framed the Hajj within the story of his struggle against political repression and war on Bosnia, the postwar Hajjis tried to situate the Hajj within the larger story of their lives. Hasan Šestić spoke about his education and his family's reputation;[79] Muhamed Bikić explained how his family had resisted the pressures of the Yugoslav regime (his father lost his Communist party membership for naming his son Muhamed).[80] Others spoke about about a sudden feeling that had led them to plan the Hajj journey,[81] which could be interpreted as the popular notion of being invited to become a guest of Allah.

The emotions and the descriptions of the bodily experiences of the ritual are part of these new sensibilities. The Hajjis often felt overwhelmed and unable to express their feelings at crucial points of the pilgrimage: Muhamed Bikić mentions how his body was wrapped in an inexplicable feeling which he could not describe, but his thoughts were overcome by an 'untouchable serenity of patience'. He also felt tingling throughout his entire body.[82] At the same time, Bikić remarked that he could not cry when he was supposed to

[76] Šestić, *Put na hadž '96*, p. 5.

[77] For example, Pajević, *Hadžijski dnevnik*.

[78] Kemal Zukić painted Chechen Hajjis and included the image in his travelogue.

[79] Šestić, *Put na hadž '96*, p. 2.

[80] Bikić, *Hadžijsko drvo*, p. 9.

[81] Šmigalović, *Ibrahim a.s. preci i potomci*, p. 7.

[82] Bikić, *Hadžijsko drvo*, p. 38.

do so in the vicinity of the Ka'ba, unlike his fellow pilgrims.[83] The feeling of paralysis, he noted, was also valid.[84] Others simply claimed that the feeling could not be described in words, but must be felt.[85] Yet, noting physical sensations such as shaking, strong heart palpitations and even the shutting down of the senses (such as hearing loss)[86] is very common. Many Hajjis also tried to understand the anguish and despair and relief that came through the story of Hajar during the *sa'y*.[87] The Hajjis wrote about their companions and their reactions as well, and they also remembered those whom they had left at home, usually through the customary prayer upon first seeing the Ka'ba. Some Hajjis, however, also mentioned how they forgot all their human worries, including family connections, upon seeing the Ka'ba, and could not even articulate their prayers:[88]

> I have been preparing for this meeting for long. I know what I will ask from the Almighty when I see the Ka'ba. However, I forgot everything the moment I saw it. Oh, how much I loved the Ka'ba when I saw it! I still love it more than anything in the world. And I ask you, the Lord of the Ka'ba, now as I write these words, to love me the same way.[89]

Many Hajjis described love as the most extreme feeling upon seeing the Ka'ba; some, like Zehra Alispahić, found it to be the essence of the pilgrimage[90] while reflecting upon excerpts from Mustafa Mahmud's (1921–2009) Hajj travelogue and urging her fellow Bosnians to perform the pilgrimage at an earlier age. Fahira Fejzić likened the experience of encountering the Ka'ba for the

[83] Bikić, *Hadžijsko drvo*, pp. 57–58.

[84] Bikić, *Hadžijsko drvo*, pp. 55, 58.

[85] Pajević, *Hadžijski dnevnik*, p. 29.

[86] Đevad Koldžo, 'Putopis s hadždža 2008', available at http://www.islambosna.ba/putopis-s-hadda-2009-hadi-evad-koldo/ (accessed 8 August 2021).

[87] Kurtović, 'Putovanje na hadž 1999./1419. hg.'.

[88] Pajević, *Hadžijski dnevnik*, p. 29.

[89] Pajević, *Hadžijski dnevnik*, p. 29.

[90] Zehra Alispahić, *Hadž je i ljubav* . . ., available at https://znaci.ba/tekstovi/hadzdz-je-i-ljubav (accessed 8 August 2021).

Naše hadžije u Mekki
s čežnjom čekaju hadžske obrede

Nakon podne namaza u Haremu Poslanikove, a.s., džamije

Figure 5.3 'Our Hajjis in Mecca await the rituals with longing'. Source: *Preporod.*

first time to an 'inner intoxication' which is stronger and more permanent than any caused by substances (Fig. 5.3).[91]

The experience of the Hajj in travelogues, essays and diaries was also deeply gendered. The *sa'y* rite, associated with Hajar and her struggle to find water for her baby, was especially highlighted. Fejzić wrote that it is a 'typical female, gendered rite in Mecca',[92] and the permanent reminder of a brave woman and mother. The Hajj brought a reversal of gender roles, too: while waiting in line for one of the Zamzam wells, Fejzić was offered water by an unknown man, something that left her in surprise, because 'how can a man serve an unknown woman in the midst of Mecca'.[93] Like other encounters, this too was understood as the mercy of the Lord.[94] Fahira, whose travelogue was an account of her *umra* journey, also wrote about the gendered spaces

[91] Fahira Fejzić, *Putopisi – u susret znakovlju vremena i prostora* (Sarajevo: Connectum, 2011), p. 116.

[92] Fejzić, *Putopisi*, p. 119.

[93] Fejzić, *Putopisi*, p. 123.

[94] Fejzić, *Putopisi*, p. 123.

that she and her daughters had to navigate: small, crowded spaces where not much solidarity was left and where they felt pushed by other women who occupied more space.[95] However, once her daughter fainted, the other women rushed to help, bringing food and trying to bring her back to consciousness through 'ancient methods of healing'.[96]

The openness of the Hajj literature to exposition and inscription of the self allows for a multitude of perspectives to emerge. Bosnian Hajjis of the twenty-first century, just like pilgrims from other Muslim societies, interweave their religious experiences with their unique approaches to capitalism and materialism,[97] modernity and race. The emotive and the bodily are also more readily inscribed into the narrative, fully acknowledged as primary aspects of the religious experience and shared with online audiences. The Hajj experience acts as an omnipresent mirror that pulls pilgrims in different directions: at times they feel the infinite possibilities of the *umma*, and in other instances they are reminded of their isolating particularity as Bosnian Muslims and the importance of the mundane practices that keep Islam alive. After Bosnia having been the centre of the Muslim World in the 1990s, Bosnian Muslim Hajjis came to feel their marginal position once again:

> Being a Muslim here in Bosnia and in all other countries where Muslims are in minority is like being a part of the ocean of Islam on the periphery, on the limits, where after the low tide there are small lakes left. It is much easier to be a Muslim somewhere where everything invites to prayer, and where this worldly life stops for a while [. . .] for the first time after the Hajj, I prayed in our small mosque in Hrid. I came back, visited the pride and the glory of Muslims – the holy places. Life continues here, where there are no grand and shiny mosques, but our duty is to bring Islam into our lives in a true sense.[98]

Conclusion

From the highly publicised Hajj journey of 1994 to the annual pilgrimages of the postwar period announced on the local websites of tiny municipalities

[95] Fejzić, *Putopisi*, p. 127.

[96] Fejzić, *Putopisi*, pp. 127–28.

[97] Fejzić, *Putopisi*, p. 137.

[98] Kurtović, 'Putovanje na hadž 1999./1419. hg.'.

across Bosnia, the Hajj has obtained unprecedented urgency. The very act of this journey and the performed ritual during the wartime presented a stark break with the past, a very physical and bodily testament of obedience to God, and a straightforward connection to other Muslims who could help Bosnia. Unlike the Hajj delegations of the 1950s, the Hajj of 1994 also featured wounded soldiers, and as much as the pilgrimage affected the Bosniaks, the sight of their bodies also changed other pilgrims. This has placed Bosnia in the focus of a sacred geography. And although the rhetoric of the Bosnian struggle has subsided over the postwar years, the centrality of both the holy places and Bosnia for the imagination of Islam as it is lived or supposed to be practiced remains persistent in the Hajj writings.

With the new urgency of the pilgrimage, the Hajj writings remain one (but not the only) medium through which modern Bosnians have channelled their religious meaning-making impulse. The sheer vastness of Hajj travelogues, diaries and reports, as well as the variety of people writing about the Hajj, drawing or taking photos or videos, has shown their increasing relevance for individuals and the public. The visibility of the Hajj in the postwar period, enhanced by political, social and technological developments, made writing about the Hajj a key part of the pilgrimage experience. Still, it seems that the planned and structured meaning-making processes which seek a fixed, didactic and durable significance of the pilgrimage are a thing of the past. The Hajj writings increasingly aim to relate the individual perspective, conveyed through emotions and enacted by the peregrinating body, putting the ever-elusive pursuit of meaning on the backburner, instead focusing on the doing and being in pilgrimage.

CONCLUSION
THE PERSISTENCE OF DEVOTION

This book has spoken about the permanence and persistence of the Hajj in scholarly discourses and the everyday lives of Bosnian Muslims, as much as about their physical journeys to Mecca and Medina. This presence is especially seen in times of absence: as the current Covid-19 pandemic prevents Hajjis from going on a pilgrimage for the second year in a row, Bosnians have undertaken a number of activities to express their profound sadness at the impossibility of travel, sense of longing and attachment to the ritual. Apart from a number of personal reflections and photographs published online in the form of Facebook posts or through the webpages of daily newspapers and journals, the Hajj-deprived Bosniaks also organised events that kept the flame going. One of these events was held in summer 2021. The roundtable organised by the Rijaset of the Islamic Community in Bosnia aimed to 'maintain the awareness of the Hajj in the circumstances of the pandemics'. The event provided opportunity for attendees to learn more about the Hajj rites, as well as the significance of the ritual sacrifice and Eid. Special attention, however, was paid to the 'cultural and civilisational aspects of the Hajj', with the focus on the ways in which the pilgrimage had affected the Bosniaks in history. One of the participants of the roundtable, Ismet Bušatlić, a retired professor of Islamic civilisation, emphasised the long history of the Hajj in the history of Bosnia and stated that Bosniaks gained much with the Hajj, from dreams about the journey to its realisation:

Preporod
1970-2020.
Dova i nada iz Mekke:
Čovječanstvo će pobijediti pandemiju koronavirusa

Figure C.1 The title page of *Preporod* announcing the Hajj at the time of the pandemic. Source: *Preporod.*

> The Hajj has left a deep trace in the lives of Bosniak men and women, in our history and culture, poetry, literature, visual art, music. Our people went on the Hajj and composed poems about Baytullah, described their Hajj journey in travelogues and expressed their experience in painting. In a way, the Hajj has shaped the character of Bosniak men and women, our culture and history, remaining recognizable until today.[1] (Fig. C.1)

The Hajj discourse in the twenty-first-century Bosnian context, as seen from the example above, has reached a level of critical self-awareness and analysis that is rare for religious literature, particularly for writings about other normative rituals, such as fasting or almsgiving. Writing about the Hajj, in other words, is perhaps the most widespread means for conveying religious experience to different audiences. It is worth here reiterating the concerns from the introduction to this book: why did Muslims from all walks of life write about

[1] https://www.hadziumra.ba/okrugli-sto-u-susret-mubarek-danima-hadza-hadz-je-na-izvjesatn-nacin-oblikovao-licnost-bosnjaka/?fbclid=IwAR2oe0igw747pHnmZv74ia20UGdJkiu4MnAxeXmSy_scC5WzYG5OQ1T6QOo (accessed on 22 August 2021).

the Hajj more often than about any other religious experience? And secondly, how did the Hajj manage to mobilise ideas, thoughts, sentiments and feelings about the world, including Islamic geographies, Muslim coreligionists and Bosnian homeland? The answers to these questions pertain primarily to Bosnian Muslim Hajj writings, but they have wider implications for other spatial and temporal contexts as well.

Writing about the Hajj

The scarcity of opportunity to undertake the Hajj journey, the engagement of different audiences and the ritual structure that offers itself to different meanings, experiences and interpretations constitute the main reasons for the longevity of Hajj writings. The popularity and widespread writing about the Hajj are, paradoxically, tied to the rarity of the actual journey to Mecca and Medina. In premodern times, the journey undertaken by a small number of Ottoman Bosnians was certainly a once-in-a-lifetime event that brought pilgrims into contact with a multitude of other places and devotional practices, such as *ziyāra* to the tombs of the *awliyā* and scholars. Writings about the journey (in the form of travelogues and itineraries) thus contained practical valuable information on the circumstances and obstacles that a pilgrim might encounter, and they also indicated how the journey could be utilised best to obtain a number of blessings through devotional visits and practices.

Even when no longer such a rarity, the Hajj remains the powerful motivation and framework for much of religious writing today. The opportunity and ability to go on a Hajj journey have grown exponentially in the modern period; combined with the opportunities offered by print and literacy, this has produced an ever-increasing number of authors writing about and publishing their pilgrimage impressions. Scholars, journalists, engineers, housewives, all continue translating their experience into writing, photography and other media. The political pressures that had manifested themselves through censorship at certain points in the twentieth century, such as in socialist Yugoslavia, did not manage to stifle the zeal for writing about the Hajj. As the publications from the past several years show, Hajj travelogues were written in considerable numbers during the socialist period but gained visibility only over the past decades. Visibility through print, thus, is not always a reliable factor when investigating the Bosnian Muslim attachment to the Hajj.

While the Hajj is a duty incumbent on individual believers, writing about it has always implied an audience. Whether premodern or modern, authors were writing for an audience. Through various forms of writing about the Hajj, their experience was mediated to people who either could not go on pilgrimage themselves or were planning to do so in future. Relaying knowledge about the Hajj to larger or smaller audiences was regarded as a pious act, just as the very act of writing was supposed to prolong the experience and obtain spiritual reward. In the modern period, audiences grew considerably: Bosnian Muslim authors have written not only to inform, instruct and inspire, but also to correct wrong opinions and argue with those with differing opinions on rites and ritual. Their travelogues and reportages have reached broad readerships and tapped into different sensibilities, including the sensationalism surrounding much of the discourse on Islam in the twentieth century.

When considering Hajj writings and the popular appeal of writing about pilgrimage, the travelogue as a genre usually takes primacy. However, as the anxiety over the Hajj during the pandemic shows, Bosnian Muslim religious scholars have used a range of other genres to build and sustain the discourse on the pilgrimage and thus maintain the connection of believers to the ritual and the holy places. Through treatises and works in praise of Mecca and Medina, essays and fatwas, Bosnian ulama have built, shifted and pruned the discourse on the Hajj. Their cultivation of Hajj discourse was not always aimed at Bosnian Muslims exclusively, as the Arabic writings of ʿAlī-dada al-Būsnawī, ʿAbdullah al-Būsnawī and Ḥasan Imām-zāda al-Būsnawī demonstrate. The Hajj discourse, in other words, was not a local affair, and Bosnians, as members of the Ottoman learned elite, contributed to the scholarly treatment of the Hajj from imperial, legal or Sufi perspectives.

Yet, much of these writings that supported and bolstered the Hajj were directed at the local Bosnian audience. Exhortatory and instructive works were written to offer pilgrims guidance and knowledge about the rites and rituals. In the nineteenth century and later on, information about the Hajj was widely available in journalistic media in the Bosnian language. However, as this book has shown, these Hajj writings conveyed more than information about the correct performance of the ritual. From the exhortative works that encouraged Bosnians to perform the Hajj in the seventeenth century, to annual essays published in the official journals of the Islamic Community, particular visions of the pilgrimage were shaped. In Ottoman Bosnian writings, the Hajj was seen as a necessary duty, yet as something that is dependent on circumstances and thus tied to an ethical framework of human relations and obligations. In the twentieth century, the visions and conceptualisations of the Hajj changed drastically. The pilgrimage remained conceived as an obligatory duty, but this conceptual kernel is wrapped into layers of additional meanings. As religious studies scholars and scholars of Islam have noted, the symbolic 'emptiness' of the Hajj makes it more difficult to pin down one definite meaning of the rites in this pilgrimage. However, as we saw in the example of Bosnian Hajj literature, this lack of a fixed meaning has provided an opportunity to instil a variety of meanings within the Hajj framework. These gained a special urgency in the twentieth century, with the Hajj being a conceptual mirror for reformist projects that aimed at transforming the society.

In this context, this book did not set out to discover similarities between different periods in order to illustrate an unbroken continuity of Bosnian Muslim attitudes to the Hajj. Rather, it has observed the embedding of meaning into the Hajj structure (the fixed set of rites) which as a practice is continuous and becomes more visible through the proliferation of different media. While the first chapter carries the title 'Meanings', the book as a whole is engaged in uncovering meaning-making processes across several centuries. Yet, in order to prod and challenge the idea of the primacy of meaning, this book has also looked into how the Hajj was experienced through body and emotion. These different facets allow us to see the constancy of Bosnian Muslim devotion to the Hajj, which works alongside but still transcends the division of the modern and the premodern, meaning and experience, idea and emotion.

The Hajj and the World

Apart from being a ritual structure that allows people to weave and embed meanings into it, the Hajj is also a journey. As such, it nudges pilgrims into the world; at the same time, the journey redefines the relationship of pilgrims to themselves and their own communities. As much as the Hajj physically brought Bosnian Muslims closer to their coreligionists and shared spiritual places, it also actively reasserted the centrality of Bosnia in their religious imagination.

Bosnian Muslims moved through the spaces of Islamic geographies on their way to and from the Hajj. In Ottoman times, the Hajj journey included *ziyāra*s; in the modern period, these geographies became contested spaces of belonging and dissociation. Moving through spaces of sanctity reinforced Bosnian Muslim belonging to greater Hanafi and Sufi identities. These relations have not faded in the twentieth century; they have persisted in a subdued form, even when marginalised by nation-states' pressing identity-making projects. For interwar Hajjis such as Muhamed Krpo and Ibrahim Čokić, and later Šejh Fejzulah Hadžibajrić, the journey was an opportunity to rekindle these connections, whether through meeting with *muhajir*s (Bosnians and their descendants scattered across the Middle East), encounters with ulama and Sufi shaykhs, or participation in Sufi activities. For many Hajjis who wrote their travelogues, essays and diaries, the cities and places of Islamic geographies carried spiritual and cultural weight, the importance of which they aimed to convey to expecting audiences.

The appeal of the Hajj journey attracted different participants beyond practitioners and devotees. The possibility that the Hajj could turn into a tourist endeavour was one reason behind the persistent anxiety of the Bosnian ulama, who tried to disassociate the pilgrimage journey from a consumerist trip to exotic places. Yet, with the rise of sensationalist media, the Hajj journey became a tourist attraction, causing consternation not only among scholars, but also among common readers who often reacted to the exotification of the Hajj.

The Hajj journeys could, thus, enhance connection or create ambiguity of belonging. As the Hajjis passed through terrains of Islamic geographies, as well as geographies of post-Ottoman nation-states at a later point in time, their feeling of closeness to and distance from their coreligionists sometimes depended on social and political factors. For example, the changes occurring in interwar Turkey affected the way in which Turkish Hajjis were observed for much of twentieth-century Bosnian literature. As much as modernity enhanced mobility and the unprecedented encounters of different peoples, the nation-state framework shaped the amount and range of connections between coreligionists. Thus, the Hajj narratives show a constant tension between the imposed frameworks of borders and the spiritual and cultural connections that stubbornly persisted.

As much as the Hajj was a venture into the world, the literature about it showed that Bosnian Muslims engaged with their own position among their coreligionists and the wider world. While the Hajj literature was not exclusively written for Bosniaks, the consciousness of the local appears even in the earliest works on Mecca and Medina. Bosnia as a homeland and a frequent spatial referent appears in Ottoman Bosnian travelogues, indicating the author's origins and potential audiences. Over time, the greater emphasis on the specificity of Bosnian Muslims on the Hajj led to a feeling of exclusivity and the rise of the image of Bosnians as white Europeans, distinct from their non-Bosnian coreligionists. The constraints of the nation-state exerted itself on the most crucial ways in which Bosnians imagined themselves on the Hajj: as Yugoslavs and, later, as Bosniaks, citizens of the independent Bosnia and Herzegovina.

The Possibilities of Mediation

Studying Hajj literature as the ultimate channel of mediation opens up multiple possibilities for observing religious expression in other spatial and temporal contexts. Furthermore, Hajj literature as medium between the world and the transcendent inevitably enriches any conversation on diversity in Islam. In the context of the recent debate on the nature of Islam and the quest for the elements that bind together Muslims from around the world, Kevin Reinhart has pointed out rituals, and especially the Hajj, as crucial part of a 'Shared' or 'Koiné' Islam.[2] Despite the modernist desire to flatten the discourse on the Hajj and reduce it to its legal dimension, Muslims have dealt with its basic structure in a myriad ways, interlocked with local and colloquial understandings and contexts:

> All Muslims share the Koiné commitment to the Pilgrimage, but the *meaning*, and the *experience* of the hajj is determined by the colloquial, by the Lived Islam of its participants.[3]

[2] The term Koiné is used by Reinhart as part of his conceptual proposal that Islam could be observed as a language, with its Standard, Local, Koiné and Cosmopolitan variants.

[3] Reinhart, *Lived Islam*, p. 81.

The significance of the mediating role of Hajj literature cannot be overstated when attempting to understand the variety of Muslim religious expression, as well as normative meaning-making. Observing the variety of meanings that emerge from these writings across different genres, time periods and geographies offers ways to challenge a range of biases that still persist in Islamic Studies, area studies and religious studies. The focus on Bosnian Hajj literature has allowed us to see the forms (genres, but also images and symbols) deployed to express and sustain religious devotion to the pilgrimage and the holy places. While some of these forms are recognizable across wider – cosmopolitan – spaces, many are locally imbued and specific to Bosnia and its readerships. Thus, Hajj literature offers a unique insight into how Bosnian Muslims thought of and experienced their faith through the ritual, making them active meaning-makers who, even if inadvertently, challenge their perceived marginal status in the greater community of Muslims.

The diachronic depth of Hajj literature, however, allows us to see how the meanings and experiences of the pilgrimage have changed over time and under different circumstances. It de-essentialises any fixed meaning that could be given to the Hajj and, correspondingly, to Islam itself. Yet, what the persistence and proliferation of Hajj writings shows is the consistent devotion to pilgrimage, occasionally shaped by top-down pressures, while at the same time bypassing them. Bosnian Muslim pilgrims, once again, remain the protagonists of their own religiosity.

Finally, the variety of Bosnian literature on the Hajj and the unceasing interest in writing about pilgrimage tells us something about the wish of each and every pilgrim to inscribe themselves on one of the multiple paths to the holy, unique yet recognizable to their fellow Bosnians and Muslim coreligionists.

BIBLIOGRAPHY

Manuscripts

ʿAlī-dada al-Būsnawī, *Tamkīn al-maqām fi al-Masjid al-harām*, Esad Efendi 3814, Süleymaniye Library in Istanbul.

ʿAbdullah al-Būsnawī, *Kitāb al-yad al-ajwad fi istilām al-hajar al-aswad*, Carullah 2129, Süleymaniye Library in Istanbul.

Boro Efendi, *Manāzil min Foça ʿan Makka Mukarrama*, R-10309,2 Gazi Husrev-bey's Library in Sarajevo.

Ḥasan Imām-zāda al-Būsnawī, *Dalīl al-saʾirīn ila ziyārat Ḥabib Rabb al-alamīn*, MS 0719, Bosniak Institute in Sarajevo.

Ḥasan Imām-zāda al-Būsnawī, *Dalīl al-saʾirīn ila ziyārat Ḥabib Rabb al-alamīn*, Laleli 1363, Süleymaniye Library in Istanbul.

Ḥasan Imām-zāda al-Būsnawī, *Tashwīq al-labīb ila maḥabbat al-Ḥabib*, R-8584, Gazi Husrev-bey's Library in Sarajevo.

Ḥasan Imām-zāda al-Būsnawī, *al-Ilhām al-ilahiyya fi miʿrāj khayr al-bariyya*, no. 2302Y Rare Books and Special Collections, Islamic Manuscripts, Garrett Collection.

Jusuf Livnjak, R-7303, Gazi Husrev-bey's Library in Sarajevo.

Kulenović (?), *Putovanje na hadž*, Pr-1875, Gazi Husrev-bey's Library in Sarajevo.

Aḥmad Muʿadhdhin-zāda al-Mostārī, *Muḥarrik al-qulūb*, R-3731, Gazi Husrev-bey's Library in Sarajevo.

Muṣṭafā Mukhliṣī, *Dalīl al-menāhil wa murshid al-merāḥil*, Bağdatlı Vehbi 1024, Süleymaniye Library in Istanbul.

Muṣṭafā Novali, R-10310, Gazi Husrev-bey's Library in Sarajevo.
Anonymous, R-4342, Gazi Husrev-bey's Library in Sarajevo.

Printed Books and Articles

Adilović, Bećir. *Putopis – hadždž 1969. godine.* Zenica: Nedwe, 1998.

Alispahić, Zehra. *Hadž je i ljubav* . . . https://znaci.ba/tekstovi/hadzdz-je-i-ljubav (accessed on 8 August 2021).

Allen, Jonathan Parkes. 'Sanctifying Domestic Space and Domesticating Sacred Space: Reading Ziyāra and Taṣliya in Light of the Domestic in the Early Modern Ottoman World'. *Religions* 11/2 (2020): 59.

Allen, Jonathan Parkes. 'Up All Night Out of Love for the Prophet: Devotion, Sanctity, and Ritual Innovation in the Ottoman Arab Lands, 1500–1620'. *Journal of Islamic Studies* 3/30 (2019): 303–37.

A. M. 'Bh. hadžije iz Istanbula ispraćene uz turski mars'. *Devni Avaz* (25 December 2005): 4.

Arnaut, Fikret. *Vodič na hadžu i umri.* Minhen: An-Nur, 2009.

al-'Arnā'ūṭ, Muḥammad. 'Ṣūra Makka al-Mukarrama fī riḥlāt al-ḥajj li-l-bashāniqa: numūdhaj al-shā'ir Muṣṭafā al-Busnī'. In *Dirāsāt fī al- ilāt al-'arabiyya al-balqaniyya khilāl al-tārīkh al-wasīṭ wa-l-ḥadīth.* Bayrūt: Jadawel, 2012: 173–83.

Amzi-Erdogdular, Leyla. 'Alternative Muslim Modernities: Bosnian Intellectuals in the Ottoman and Habsburg Empires'. *Comparative Studies in Society and History* 59/4 (2017): 912–43.

Antrim, Zayde. *Routes and Realms: The Power of Place in the Early Islamic World.* Oxford: Oxford University Press, 2012.

Arjana, Sophia Rose and Aslan, Rose. 'Red, White, and Blue: American Muslims on Hajj and the Politics of Pilgrimage'. In *Muslim Pilgrimage in the Modern World*, edited by Babak Rahimi and Peyman Eshaghi, 112–30. Chapel Hill: University of North Carolina Press, 2019.

Asad, Talal. 'Reading a Modern Classic: W. C. Smith's *The Meaning and End of Religion*'. *History of Religions* 40/3 (2001): 205–22.

Asad, Talal. 'The Idea of an Anthropology of Islam'. *Qui Parle* 17/2 (2009): 1–30.

Asseraf, Arthur. *Electric News in Colonial Algeria.* Oxford: Oxford University Press, 2019.

Aščerić-Todd, Ines. *Dervishes and Islam in Bosnia: Sufi Dimensions to the Formation of Bosnian Muslim Society.* Leiden: Brill, 2015.

Aydin, Cemil. *The Idea of the Muslim World: A Global Intellectual History.* Cambridge, MA: Harvard University Press, 2017.

Azad, Arezou. *Sacred Landscape in Medieval Afghanistan: Revisiting the Fada'il-i Balkh.* Oxford: Oxford University Press, 2013.

Baig, Sohaib. 'Indian Hanafis in an Ocean of Hadith: Islamic Legal Authority between South Asia and the Arabian Peninsula, 16th–20th Centuries'. PhD diss., University of California, Los Angeles, 2020.

Baker, Catherine. *Race and the Yugoslav Region: Postsocialist, Post-conflict, Postcolonial?* Manchester: Manchester University Press, 2018.

Bashir, Shahzad. *Sufi Bodies: Religion and Society in Medieval Islam.* New York City: Columbia University Press, 2011.

Bećirović, Denis. 'O položaju Islamske vjerske zajednice u Kraljevini Jugoslaviji (1929–1941)'. *Historijska traganja* 2 (2008): 191–208.

Bećirović, A. 'Naš je hadž jeftiniji'. *Oslobođenje* (10 April 2009): 8.

Beglerović, Samir. *Tesavvuf Bosne u vidicima Fejzulaha Hadžibajrića: Vjerski i kulturni razvoj bosanskih muslimana u prvoj polovini XX stoljeća.* Sarajevo: Bookline, 2014.

Bell, Catherine. *Ritual: Perspectives and Dimensions.* Oxford: Oxford University Press, 2009.

Ben Hammed, Mohamed Wajdi. '(Dis)Enchanting Modernity: Sufism and its Temporality in the Thought of Mohammed Abed al-Jabri and Taha Abdurrahman'. *The Journal of North African Studies* 26/3 (2021): 552–71.

Bernards, Monique, 'Awā'il'. *Encyclopaedia of Islam*, third edition. Leiden: Brill, 2007.

Bianchi, Robert. *Guests of God: Pilgrimage and Politics in the Islamic World.* New York: Oxford University Press, 2004.

Bigelow, Ana. 'Introduction: Thinking with Islamic Things'. In *Islam through Objects*, edited by Anna Bigelow, 1–14. London: Bloomsbury Academic, 2021.

Bikić, Muhamed. *Hadžijsko drvo.* Studentska štamparija: Sarajevo, 2000.

Booker, M. Keith and Daraiseh, Isra. *Consumerist Orientalism: The Convergence of Arab and American Popular Culture in the Age of Global Capitalism.* London: I. B. Tauris, 2019.

Bracewell, Wendy. 'The Limits of Europe in East European Travel Writing'. In *Under Eastern Eyes: A Comparative Introduction to East European Travel Writing on Europe*, ed. by Wendy Bracewell and Alex Drace-Francis, 61–120. Budapest, New York: CEU Press, 2008.

Brunner, Rainer. 'The Pilgrim's Tale as a Means of Self-Promotion: Muḥammad Rashīd Riḍā's Journey to the Ḥijāz (1916)'. In *The Piety of Learning: Islamic Studies in Honor of Stefan Reichmuth*, edited by Michael Kemper and Ralf Elger, 270–91. Leiden, Boston: Brill, 2017.

Buljina, Harun. 'Empire, Nation, and the Islamic World: Bosnian Muslim Reformists between the Habsburg and Ottoman Empires, 1901–1914'. PhD Diss., Columbia University, 2019.

Burak, Guy. 'Between Istanbul and Gujarat: Descriptions of Mecca in the sixteenth-century Indian Ocean'. *Muqarnas* 34 (2017): 287–320.

Burak, Guy. 'Collating *The Signs of Benevolent Deeds*: Muḥammad Mahdī al-Fāsī's Commentary on Muḥammad al-Jazūlī's Dalā'il al-Khayrāt and Its Ottoman Readers'. *Philological Encounters* 4/1–2 (2019): 135–57.

al-Busnawī al-Mawlawī ʿAlī Dada. *Kitāb Khawātim al-ḥikam al-musammā bi-Ḥall al-rumūz wa-kashf al-kunūz.* Al-Qāhira: al-Maṭbaʿa al-Sharafīya, 1896.

al-Busnawī ʿAlāʾ-ad-Dīn ʿAlī Dada as-Sikitwārī. *Muḥāḍarat al-awāʾil wa-musāmarat al-awākhir.* Misr: al-ʿĀmira al-Sharafīya, 1893.

Campo, Juan E. 'Visualizing the Hajj: Representations of a Changing Sacred Landscape Past and Present'. In *The Hajj: Pilgrimage in Islam*, edited by Eric Tagliacozzo and Shawkat Toorawa, 269–88. Cambridge: Cambridge University Press, 2016.

Can, Lale. *Spiritual Subjects: Central Asian Pilgrims and the Ottoman Hajj at the End of Empire.* Palo Alto: Stanford University Press, 2020.

Chameran. 'Jedan pogled na turske protuislamske reforme'. *Hikjmet* 8/9 (1929): 260–63.

Chodkiewicz, Michel. 'Le Paradoxe de la Ka'ba'. *Revue de l'histoire des religions* 222/4 (2005): 435–61.

Conklin Akbari, Suzanne. *Idols in the East: European Representations of Islam and the Orient, 1100–1450.* Ithaca: Cornell University Press, 2009.

Coşkun, Menderes. *Bosnalı Muhlis'in Manzum Seyahatnamesi: Delîlü'l-Menâhil ve Mürşidü'l-Merâhil.* Isparta: Fakülte Kitabevi, 2007.

Coşkun, Menderes. *Manzum ve Mensur Osmanlı Hac Seyahatnameleri ve Nabi'nin Tuhfetü'l-Harameyn'i.* Ankara: Kültür Bakanlığı Yayınları, 2002.

Čehajić, Džemal. 'Šejh Abdulah Bošnjak "Abdi" bin Muhamed al-Bosnevi (um. 1054/1644)'. *Zbornik radova Islamskog teološkog fakulteta u Sarajevu* 1 (1982): 75–89.

Čemo, Kenan. *Putopis s hadža 2006.* https://znaci.ba/tekstovi/putopis-s-hadza-2006 (accessed on 7 August 2021).

Čokić, A. Adil. 'Mudafea i objašnjenje povodom odgovora g. Hadžića na moju kritiku njegove knjige "Muhamed i Koran" (Nastavak 4)'. *Hikjmet* 43 (1932): 203–7.

Čokić, A. Adil. 'Muhamed i Koran: Kulturna istorija Islama'. *Novi Behar* 11–12 (1931): 166–71.

Čokić, Ibrahim H. 'G. H. Ismeta Varatanovića prikazivanje puta u Meku'. *Hikjmet* 51 (1933): 93–96.

Čokić, Ibrahim H. 'G. H. Ismeta Varatanovića prikazivanje puta u Meku'. *Hikjmet* 52 (1933): 122–25.

Čokić, Ibrahim Hakki. 'Hadž i Kurban Bajram'. *Hikjmet* 2 (1929): 33–35.

Čokić, Ibrahim. 'Moje putovanje na hadž'. *Hikjmet* 4/40 (1932): 110–14.

Čokić, Ibrahim. 'Moje putovanje na hadž'. *Hikjmet* 4/41 (1932): 146–51.

Čokić, Ibrahim. 'Moje putovanje na hadž'. *Hikjmet* 5/58 (1934): 295–302.

Ćorović, Vladimir. 'Muslimani u našoj ranijoj književnosti'. *Bosanska vila* 9 (15 February 1912): 33–34.

Dallal, Ahmad S. *Islam without Europe: Traditions of Reform in Eighteenth-Century Islamic Thought*. Chapel Hill: UNC Press Books, 2018.

Dieste, Josep Lluís Mateo. 'The Franco North African Pilgrims after WWII: The Hajj through the Eyes of a Spanish Colonial Officer (1949)'. In *The Hajj and Europe in the Age of Empire,* edited by Umar Ryad, 240–64. Leiden, Boston: Brill, 2017.

Dučić, Jovan. *Gradovi i himere.* Beograd: Politika, Narodna knjiga, 2005.

Durendiš. 'Vazovi jednog imama (drugi vaz)'. *Behar* 7/17 (1907): 194–96.

Džumhur, Zuko. *Nekrolog jednoj čaršiji.* Sarajevo: Svjetlost, 1958.

Đozo, Husein. 'Geneza kriza na Bliskom Istoku'. *Glasnik* 32/1–2 (1969): 7–10, in *Izabrana djela 3 (Publicistički radovi).* Sarajevo: El Kalem/Fakultet islamskih nauka, 2006: 269–73.

Đozo, Husein. 'Iftar u Haremi-šerifu (I dio)'. *Preporod* 6/123 (1975): 5, in Husein Đozo, *Izabrana djela 3 (Publicistički radovi).* Sarajevo: El Kalem/Fakultet islamskih nauka, 2006: 504–8.

Đozo, Husein. 'Iftar u Haremi-šerifu (II dio)'. *Preporod* 6/124 (1975): 5, in *Izabrana djela 3 (Publicistički radovi).* Sarajevo: El Kalem/Fakultet islamskih nauka, 2006: 509–12.

Đozo, Husein. 'Islam – hadž'. *Glasnik* 35/3–4 (1972): 113–21, in Husein Đozo, *Izabrana djela 1 (Islam u vremenu).* Sarajevo: El Kalem/Fakultet islamskih nauka, 2006: 388–99.

Đozo, Husein. 'Na grobu posljednjeg Božijeg poslanika'. *Glasnik* 32/5–6 (1969): 193–200, in Husein Đozo, *Izabrana djela 1 (Islam u vremenu).* Sarajevo: El Kalem/Fakultet islamskih nauka, 2006: 273–82.

Đozo, Husein. 'Pitanja i odgovori', *Glasnik* 39/4 (1976): 431–33.

Đozo, Husein. 'Povodom paljevine Džamije el-Aksa u Jerusalemu'. *Glasnik* 32/11–12 (1969): 546–51, in *Izabrana djela 3 (Publicistički radovi).* Sarajevo: El Kalem/Fakultet islamskih nauka, 2006: 281–88.

Đozo, Husein. 'Pravi put i stramputice tesavufa'. *Glasnik* 41/3 (1979): 235–41.

Đozo, Husein. 'Uz ovogodišnji Kurban-bajram'. *Glasnik* IVZ 30/1–2 (1967): 1–4, in Husein Đozo, *Izabrana djela 3 (Publicistički radovi)*. Sarajevo: El Kalem/ Fakultet islamskih nauka, 2006: 192–95.

Edhem Riza. 'Put na Meću'. *Nada* (15 March 1896).

Eickelman, Dale and Anderson, Jon. 'Redefining Muslim Publics'. In *New Media in the Muslim World: The Emerging Public Sphere*, edited by Dale F. Eickelman and Jon W. Anderson, 1–18. Bloomington: Indiana University Press, 2003.

El Shamsy, Ahmed. 'The Social Construction of Orthodoxy'. In *The Cambridge Companion to Classical Islamic Theology*, edited by Tim Winter, 97–118. Cambridge: Cambridge University Press, 2008.

Falk Gesink, Indira. '"Chaos on the Earth": Subjective Truths versus Communal Unity in Islamic Law and the Rise of Militant Islam'. *The American Historical Review* 108/3 (2003): 710–33.

Faroqhi, Suraiya. *Pilgrims and Sultans: The Hajj Under the Ottomans 1517–1683*. New York: I. B. Tauris, 1994.

Fejzić, Fahira. *Putopisi – u susret znakovlju vremena i prostora*. Sarajevo: Connectum, 2011.

Filan, Kerima. *Sarajevo u Bašeskijino doba: Jezik kao stvarnost*. Sarajevo: Connectum, 2014.

Filan, Kerima. 'Turski jezik u osmansko doba'. *Anali GHB* 43 (35) (2014): 151–78.

Filan, Kerima (ed.). *XVIII. Yüzyıl Günlük Hayatına Dair Saraybosnalı Molla Mustafa'nın Mecmuası*. Sarajevo: Connectum, 2011.

Freitag, Ulrike. 'Heinrich Freiherr von Maltzan's "My Pilgrimage to Mecca": A Critical Investigation'. In *The Hajj and Europe in the Age of Empire*, edited by Umar Ryad, 142–54. Leiden, Boston: Brill, 2017.

Gade, Anna M. 'Twelve Zamzam Water: Environmentality and Decolonizing Material Islam'. In *Islam through Objects*, edited by Anna Bigelow, 189–204. London: Bloomsbury Academic, 2021.

Gavrankapetanović, Munir. *Kako sam obavio i doživio Hadždž 1414. h.g. – 1994. g.* Sarajevo: Biblioteka Glasnika Rijaseta Islamske Zajednice u Bosni i Hercegovini, 1997.

Gavrankapetanović, Munir. 'Allahu Ekber! Allahu Ekber!' *Preporod* 25/7:566 (1994): 20.

Gavrankapetanović, Munir. 'Bosna je ćilimom zastrta.' 25/9:568 (1994): 20.

Gavrankapetanović, Munir. 'Odazivamo Ti se, Bože, odazivamo!' *Preporod* 25/8:567 (1994): 18.

Gazić, Lejla (ed.). *Katalog arapskih, turskih, perzijskih i bosanskih rukopisa*. Sarajevo: Orijentalni institut Sarajevo, 2009.

Gelvin, James L. *The Modern Middle East: A History*. Oxford: Oxford University Press, 2011.

Gelvin, James L. and Nile Green, 'Introduction'. In *Global Muslims in the Age of Steam and Print*, edited by James L. Gelvin and Nile Green, 1–22. Berkeley: University of California Press, 2013.

Generalni servis ONASA. 'NATO odobrio slijetanje na Sarajevski aerodrom aviona "Air Commerca"'. (8 April 1999).

Grenier, Carlos. *The Spiritual Vernacular of the Early Ottoman Frontier: The Yazıcıoğlu Family*. Edinburgh: Edinburgh University Press, 2021.

Gruber, Christiane. *The Praiseworthy One: The Prophet Muhammad in Islamic Texts and Images*. Bloomington: Indiana University Press, 2019.

Gržetić. 'O kratelju iliti koleri'. *Naša sloga* 2/18 (16 September 1871): 73–74.

Hadžibajrić, Fejzulah. *Putopisi i nekrolozi*. Stockholm, Tuzla: MOS-BeMUF/Harfograf, 2002.

Hadžić, Fadil (ed.). *Put oko svijeta*. Zagreb: Novinarsko izdavačko poduzeće, 1961.

Hadžić, Mehmedalija, Hodžić, Amir and Žiga, Jusuf. *Odazivam Ti se Bože, Odazivam: Bošnjaci na Hadždžu 1414./1994*. Sarajevo: El Kalem, 1995.

Hadžić, Osman Nuri. *Muhamed i Koran: Kulturna Istorija Islama*. Beograd: Izdavačka knjižarnica Gece Kona, 1931.

Hadžić, Osman Nuri. 'Muhamed i Koran'. *Gajret* 13/6–7 (1932): 100–7.

Hajdarović, Rašid. 'Medžmua Mula Mustafe Firakije'. *Prilozi za orijentalnu filologiju* 22–23 (1972): 301–14.

Hajdarpašić, Edin. *Whose Bosnia? Nationalism and Political Imagination in the Balkans, 1840–1914*. Ithaca and London: Cornell University Press, 2015.

Halevi, Leor. *Modern Things on Trial: Islam's Global and Material Reformation in the Age of Rida*. New York: Columbia University Press, 2019.

Halimić, Enes. *Iz mape Faginovića*. Sarajevo: Bošnjački Institut – Fondacija Adila Zulfikarpašića, 2010.

Handžić, Mehmed. 'Vaz o ulozi muža i žene u braku i njihovim dužnostima'. *El-Hidaje* 1/9 (1937): 145–47.

Handžić, H. Mehmed. 'Važnost vanjskih znakova sa šeriatskog gledišta'. *El Hidaje* 3/6–7 (1939): 80–82.

Henig, David. 'Crossing the Bosphorus: Connected Histories of "Other" Muslims in the Post-Imperial Borderlands of Southeast Europe'. *Comparative Studies in Society and History* 58/4 (2016): 908–34.

Henig, David. *Remaking Muslim Lives: Everyday Islam in Postwar Bosnia and Herzegovina*. Urbana: University of Illinois Press, 2020.

Hertzog, Giles. 'Sarajevo je dobro razmislilo'. *Oslobođenje* (1 March 1995): 9.

Heschel, Susannah and Ryad, Umar (eds). *The Muslim Reception of European Orientalism: Reversing the Gaze*. Abingdon: Routledge, 2019.

Heuberger. Valeria. 'Die Pilgerfahrt nach Mekka von Muslimen aus Bosnien-Herzegowina unter österreichisch-ungarischer Herrschaft (1878–1914).' In *Bosnien-Herzegowina und Österreich-Ungarn, 1878–1918*, edited by Clemens Ruthner and Tamara Scheer, 193–210. Tübingen: Narr Francke Attempto, 2018.

Hirschler, Konrad. *A Monument to Medieval Syrian Book Culture: The Library of Ibn Abd al-Hādī*. Edinburgh: Edinburgh University Press, 2019.

Hoffmann, Stefan-Ludwig and Franzel, Sean. 'Introduction: Translating Koselleck'. In Reinhart Koselleck, *Sediments of Time: On Possible Histories*, trans. and ed. by Sean Franzel and Stefan-Ludwig Hoffmann, ix–xxxi. Palo Alto: Stanford University Press, 2018.

Huber, Valeska. *Channelling Mobilities: Migration and Globalisation in the Suez Canal Region and Beyond, 1869–1914*. Cambridge: Cambridge University Press, 2013.

Husić, Aladin. *Hadž iz Bosne za vrijeme osmanske vladavine*. Sarajevo: El Kalem, 2014.

Ibrišimović, Nedžad. 'Kako da opišem hadždž, kada sam ja gledao samo svoje Bošnjake (odlomak iz hadžijskog putopisa Ruhani i šejtani inspiracija)'. *Stav* (16 August 2018). https://arhiv.stav.ba/nedzad-ibrisimovic-kako-da-opisem-hadzdz-kada-sam-ja-gledao-samo-svoje-bosnjake/ (accessed on 27 August 2021).

Imamović, Mustafa. *Bošnjaci u emigraciji: monografija 'Bosanskih Pogleda' 1955–1967*. Zürich: Bosniak Institute, 1996.

Izetbegović, Alija. *The Islamic Declaration: A Programme for the Islamization of Muslims and the Muslim Peoples* (trans. unknown). Sarajevo: n. p., 1990.

Izmirlieva, Valentina. 'The Title Hajji and the Ottoman Vocabulary of Pilgrimage'. In *Modern Greek Studies Yearbook 28–29*, 137–168. Minneapolis: University of Minnesota, 2012–13.

Jahić, Adnan. 'Obnova autonomije Islamske zajednice u Bosni i Hercegovini 1936. Godine'. *Prilozi* 37 (2008): 95–111.

Jedan Turk. 'Hadž (Razmatranja)'. *Behar* 9 (1906): 98–99.

Joll, Christopher Mark and Aree, Srawut. 'Images of Makkah and the Hajj in South Thailand: An Ethnographic and Theological Exploration'. *Studia Islamika* 27/2 (2020): 205–37.

Jovanović, Tomislav (ed. and trans.). *Sveta zemlja u srpskoj književnosti od XIII do kraja XVIII veka*. Belgrade: Čigoja Štampa, 2007.

Kafadar, Cemal. 'Introduction: A Rome of One's Own: Reflections on Cultural Geography and Identity in the Lands of Rum'. *Muqarnas: History and Ideology: Architectural Heritage of the 'Lands of Rum'* 24 (2007): 7–25.

Kafadar, Cemal. 'Self and Others: The Diary of a Dervish in Seventeenth Century Istanbul and First-Person Narratives in Ottoman Literature'. *Studia Islamica* 69 (1989): 121–50.

Kane, Eileen. *Russian Hajj: Empire and the Pilgrimage to Mecca*. Ithaca: Cornell University Press, 2015.

Karateke, Hakan and Reinkowski, Maurus. 'Introduction'. In *Legitimizing the Order: The Ottoman Rhetoric of State Power*, edited by Hakan Karateke and Maurus Reinkowski, 1–11. Leiden, Boston: Brill, 2005.

Karčić, Hamza. 'Supporting the Caliph's Project: Bosnian Muslims and the Hejaz Railway'. *Journal of Muslim Minority Affairs* 34 (2014): 282–92.

Karić, Dženita. 'Bosnian Women on Hajj'. In *Muslim Women's Pilgrimage to Mecca and Beyond: Reconfiguring Gender, Religion, and Mobility*, edited by Marjo Buitelaar, Manja Stephan-Emmrich and Viola Thimm. New York, London: Routledge, 2021.

Karić, Dženita. 'Online Bosniak Hajj Narratives'. In *Muslim Pilgrimage in Europe*, edited by Ingvild Flaskerud and Richard J. Natvig, 58–69. Abingdon: Routledge, 2018.

Karić, Enes. *Crni tulipan: Putopis hodočasnika iz Bosne*. Sarajevo: Tugra, 2009.

Kargılı, Murat. *Kutsal Yolculuk Hac Hajj/The Holy Journey: Kartpostallarla Hac Yolu/ The Hajj Route Through Postcards.* Istanbul: Kaptan Yayincilik, 2014.

Kasumović, Fahd. 'Prijelazi na Islam u sidžilima sarajevskog šerijatskog suda iz prve polovine 19. stoljeća'. In *Identitet Bosne i Hercegovine kroz historiju*, edited by Husnija Kamberović, 215–37. Sarajevo: Institut za istoriju, 2011.

Kasumović, Ismet. *Alī-dada Bošnjak i njegova filozofsko-sufijska misao.* Sarajevo: El-Kalem, 1994.

Kasumović, Ismet. 'Rukopisi djela Ali Dede Harimije Bošnjaka na arapskom jeziku'. *Prilozi za orijentalnu filologiju* 38 (1988): 153–75.

Kasumović, Ismet. *Školstvo i obrazovanje u Bosanskom ejaletu za vrijeme osmanske uprave.* Mostar: Islamski kulturni centar, 1999.

Kateman, Ammeke. 'Fashioning the Materiality of the Pilgrimage: The Hajj Travelogue of Muḥammad Labīb al-Batanūnī'. *Die Welt des Islams* (2020): 384–407.

Kateman, Ammeke. 'In Moroccan Pilgrims' Own Words: The Hajj Journeys (1321 AH [1903–4]) of Muhammad bin ʿAbd al-Kabīr Al-Kattānī and Muhammad bin Jaʿfar Al-Kattānī in an Age of Steam, Imperialism and Globalization'. *Qira'at* 13. Riyādh: King Faisal Center for Research and Islamic Studies, 2020.

Kātib Çelebi/Hajji Khalīfa. *Kashf al-zunūn ʿan ʾasāmi al-kutub wa al-funūn.* Bayrūt: Dār ʾiḥya⁻al-turāth al-ʿarabī, 1941.

Katz, Marion Holmes. *Body of Text: The Emergence of the Sunni Law of Ritual Purity.* Albany: SUNY Press, 2002.

Katz, Marion Holmes. *Prayer in Islamic Thought and Practice.* Cambridge: Cambridge University Press, 2013.

Katz, Marion. *The Birth of the Prophet Muhammad: Devotional Piety in Sunni Islam.* Oxfordshire: Routledge, 2007.

Katz, Marion Holmes. 'The Ḥajj and the Study of Islamic Ritual.' *Studia Islamica* 98/99 (2004): 95–129.

Kavazović, Osman. *Putopisi hafiza hadži Zaim-efendije Huskanovića.* Tuzla: OFF-SET, 2018.

Khusrau, Nasir. *Diary of a Journey Through Syria and Palestine*, trans. and ann. by Guy Le Strange. London: Palestine Pilgrims' Text Society, 1893.

Kister, M. J. '"You Shall Only Set for Three Mosques": A Study of an Early Tradition'. *Le Muséon* 82 (1969): 173–96.

Knight, Michael Muhammad. *Muhammad's Body: Baraka Networks and the Prophetic Assemblage.* Chapel Hill: The University of North Carolina Press, 2020.

Koldžo, Đevad. *Putopis s hadždža 2008.* http://www.islambosna.ba/putopis-s-hadda-2009-hadi-evad-koldo/ (accessed on 8 August 2021).

Kolegijum autora. 'Ovogodišnje putovanje na hadž'. *Glasnik Vrhovnog islamskog starješinstva u Socijalističkoj federativnoj Republici Jugoslaviji* 29/5–6 (1966): 186–224.

Koselleck, Reinhart. 'Fiction and Historical Reality'. In *Sediments of Time: On Possible Histories*, trans. and ed. by Sean Franzel and Stefan-Ludwig Hoffmann, 10–23. Palo Alto: Stanford University Press, 2018.

Koyagi, Mikiya. 'The Hajj by Japanese Muslims in the Interwar Period: Japan's Pan-Asianism and Economic Interests in the Islamic World'. *Journal of World History* 24/4 (2013): 849–76.

Krejić, Živana and Milićević, Snežana. 'Nastanak putničko-agencijske delatnosti u Jugoslaviji kao pokretača razvoja kulture putovanja'. *Kultura* 161 (2018): 39–51.

Krpo, Muhamed. *Put na hadž (putopis jednog hadžije).* Sarajevo: Štamparija Bosanska pošta, 1938.

Kujović, Mina. 'O prvom hadžu bosanskohercegovačkih muslimana, koji je 1890. godine organizirala Zemaljska vlada za Bosnu i Hercegovinu'. *Glasnik Islamske zajednice* 1–2 (2004): 135–42.

Kulinović, H. 'Pitanje "kadera" ili sudbine. (Po istočnim izvorima)'. *Gajret* 4 (1924): 56–59.

Kurtović, Ezudin. *Putovanje na hadž 1999./1419. hg.* https://znaci.ba/tekstovi/putovanje-na-hadz-1999-1419hg (accessed on 8 August 2021).

Landau-Tasseron, Ella. 'The "Cyclical Reform": A Study of the Mujaddid Tradition'. *Studia Islamica* 70 (1989): 79–117.

Lapidus, Ira. 'Between Universalism and Particularism: The Historical Bases of Muslim Communal, National, and Global Identities'. *Global Networks* 1/1 (2001): 37–55.

Latić, Džemaludin. 'Muslimani moraju kazniti francusko-englesko-japansku pročetničku koaliciju'. *Ljiljan* 4/131 (19 July 1995): 2.

Lavić, Osman. Unpublished bibliography of Hajj manuscripts and published works.

Lazarus-Yafeh, Hava. 'The Religious Dialectics of the Hadjdj'. In *Some religious aspects of Islam: A Collection of Articles*, 17–37. Leiden: Brill, 1981.

Lepenica, Edin. 'Organizacioni aspect obavljanja hadža u SR BiH u fondovima Gazi Husrev-begove biblioteke (1945–1992)'. *Glasnik* 9–10 (2021): 721–40.

Li, Darryl. *The Universal Enemy: Jihad, Empire and the Challenge of Solidarity*. Palo Alto: Stanford University Press, 2020.

Livnjak, Hadži Jusuf. *Odazivam Ti se, Bože . . . – Putopis sa hadža 1615. godine*, trans., intr. and comment. by Mehmed Mujezinović. Sarajevo: Starješinstvo Islamske zajednice u SR Bosni i Hercegovini, Hrvatskoj i Sloveniji, 1981.

Ljubunčić, Hasan. 'Istorija hadža u Bosni i Hercegovini sa putem na hadž u 1954 godini'. *Glasnik Vrhovnog islamskog starješinstva u Federativnoj narodnoj republici Jugoslaviji* 6/1–2 (1955): 42–55.

Ljubunčić, Hasan. 'Istorija hadža u Bosni i Hercegovini sa putem na hadž u 1954 godini'. *Glasnik Vrhovnog islamskog starješinstva u Federativnoj narodnoj republici Jugoslaviji* 6/3–4 (1955): 112–34.

Ljubunčić, Hasan. 'Istorija hadža u Bosni i Hercegovini sa putem na hadž u 1954 godini'. *Glasnik Vrhovnog islamskog starješinstva u Federativnoj narodnoj republici Jugoslaviji* 7/1–3 (1956): 62–88.

Ljubunčić, Hasan. 'Put na hadž'. *Glasnik VIS-a* 4/5–7 (1953): 152–61.

Ljubunčić, Hasan. 'Put na hadž'. *Glasnik VIS-a* 3/8–12 (1952): 262–72.

Ljubunčić, Hasan. 'Put na hadž'. *Glasnik VIS-a* 3/5–7 (1952): 157–66.

Ljubunčić, Hasan. 'Put na hadž'. *Glasnik VIS-a* 1/11–12 (1950): 341–45.

Ljubunčić, Hasan. 'Put na hadž'. *Glasnik VIS-a* 1/4–7 (1950): 130–36.

Long, David Edwin. *The Hajj Today: A Survey of the Contemporary Pilgrimage to Makkah*. Albany: State University of New York Press, 1979.

Low, Michael Christopher. *Imperial Mecca: Ottoman Arabia and the Indian Ocean Hajj*. New York: Columbia University Press, 2020.

Lutfi, Hoda. 'Manners and Customs of Fourteenth-Century Cairene Women: Female Anarchy versus Male Shar'i Order in Muslim Prescriptive Treatises'. In *Women in Middle Eastern History: Shifting Boundaries in Sex and Gender*, edited by Nikki R. Keddie and Beth Baron, 99–121. New Haven, London: Yale University Press, 1991.

Makdisi, Ussama. 'Ottoman Orientalism.' *The American Historical Review* 107/3 (2002): 768–96.

Mašić, Muhamed Seid. 'Arabiji'. *Hikjmet* 6/8 (1935): 238–39.

Matheson, Virginia and Milner, A. C. *Perceptions of the Haj: Five Malay Texts* Singapore, Institute of Southeast Asian Studies, 1984.

Mayeur-Jaouen, Catherine. *The Mulid of Al-Sayyid Al-Badawi of Tanta: Egypt's Legendary Sufi Festival*. Cairo: American University in Cairo Press, 2019.

McGregor, Richard J. A. *Islam and the Devotional Object: Seeing Religion in Egypt and Syria*. Cambridge: Cambridge University Press, 2020.

McLoughlin, Seán. 'Pilgrimage, Performativity, and British Muslims: Scripted and Unscripted Accounts of the Hajj and Umra'. In *Hajj: Global Interactions Through Pilgrimage*, edited by Luitgard Mols and Marjo Buitelaar, 41–64. Leiden: Sidestone Press, 2015.

Mehmedović, Ahmed. *Leksikon bošnjačke uleme*. Sarajevo: Gazi Husrev-begova biblioteka u Sarajevu, 2018.

Meier, Fritz. 'Eine Auferstehung Mohammeds bei Suyuti'. *Der Islam* 62 (1985): 20–58.

Mekić, Sejad. *A Muslim Reformist in Communist Yugoslavia: The Life and Thought of Husein Đozo*. Abingdon: Routledge, 2017.

Meri, Josef. *The Cult of Saints among Muslims and Jews in Medieval Syria*. Oxford: Oxford University Press, 2002.

Metcalf, Barbara. 'The Pilgrimage Remembered: South Asian Accounts of the Hajj'. In *Muslim Travellers: Pilgrimage, Migration, and the Religious Imagination*, edited by Dale F. Eickelman and James Piscatori, 85–107. Berkeley, Los Angeles: University of California Press, 1990.

Meyer, Birgit. 'Introduction'. In *Aesthetic Formations: Media, Religion, and the Senses*, edited by Birgit Meyer, 1–28. New York: Palgrave Macmillan, 2009.

Meyer, Birgit. 'Media and the Senses in the Making of Religious Experience: An Introduction.' *Material Religion* 2/4 (2008): 124–34.

Mikhail, Alan. 'The Heart's Desire: Gender, Urban Space and the Ottoman Coffee House'. In *Ottoman Tulips, Ottoman Coffee: Leisure and Lifestyle in the Eighteenth Century*, edited by Dana Sajdi, 133–70. London, New York: I. B. Tauris, 2007.

Mirojević, Hidajeta. *Putopis sa hadž-a, 1981. god.* N. p.: n. d.

Mujezinović, Mehmed. *Islamska epigrafika Bosne i Hercegovine* 1. Sarajevo: Sarajevo Publishing, 1998.

Mujezinović, Mehmed. 'Sarajevske hadžije druge polovine XVIII vijeka.' *Glasnik Islamske zajednice* 27/1–2, 3–4, 5–6, 7–9 (1964): 42–48, 148–51, 221–28, 333–38.

Mujić, Muhamed A. 'Jezičke i sadržinske osobenosti vakuf-nama iz Mostara (druga polovina XVI stoljeća)'. *Prilozi za orijentalnu filologiju* 25 (1975): 203–25.

Muminović, Davud. 'Organizator hadža inscenirao svoju otmicu'. *Nezavisne novine* (9 May 2009): 4–5.

Munt, Harry. *The Holy City of Medina: Sacred Space in Early Islamic Arabia.* Cambridge: Cambridge University Press, 2014.

Mušić, Omer. 'Hadži Muhamed Sejfudin, šejh sejfija – pjesnik iz Sarajeva'. *Anali GHB* 7–8 (1982): 5–27.

Mušić, Omer. 'Hadži Mustafa Bošnjak-Muhlisi'. *Prilozi za orijentalnu filologiju* 28–29 (1973): 89–119.

Nametak, A. 'Misli uz Euharistički kongres u Zagrebu'. *Hikjmet* 17 (1930): 151–52.

Nevesinjski, R. T. Petrović. 'Iz jedne srbulje'. *Bosanska vila* 3 (15 May 1909): 132–33.

Nikpour, Golnar. 'Revolutionary Journeys, Revolutionary Practice: The Hajj Writings of Jalal Al-e Ahmad and Malcolm X'. *Comparative Studies of South Asia, Africa and the Middle East* 34/1 (2014): 67–85.

Niyazioglu, Asli. *Dreams and Lives in Ottoman Istanbul: A Seventeenth-Century Biographer's Perspective.* London, New York: Routledge, 2016.

Omar, Hussein. 'Unexamined Life: The Too Many Faces of Edward Said'. *The Baffler* 58 (2021). https://thebaffler.com/salvos/unexamined-life-omar (accessed on 30 July 2021).

O'Meara, Simon. *The Kaʿba Orientations: Readings in Islam's Ancient House.* Edinburgh: Edinburgh University Press, 2020.

Pajević, Jusuf. *Hadžijski dnevnik: Autobusom na hadž i hadž u praksi.* Svendborg: published by the author, 2010.

Pavlović, Dragan and Bećirović, Asaf. 'Hadžija u lancima'. *Oslobođenje* (8 May 2009): 3.

Peçevî, Ibrahim. *Tarih-i Peçevi.* Istanbul: Matbaʿa-i Āmire, 1866.

Petersen, Kristian. *Interpreting Islam in China: Pilgrimage, Scripture, and Language in the Han Kitab.* Oxford: Oxford University Press, 2017.

Pruščak, Hasan Kafi-ef. *Nizâmul-ulemâ' ila Hatemil-enbijâ*, trans. Mehmed Handžić. Sarajevo: Islamska dionička štamparija, 1935.

Quadri, Junaid. *Transformations of Tradition: Islamic Law in Colonial Modernity.* New York: Oxford University Press, 2021.

Radić, Radmila. *Država i verske zajednice 1945–1970*. Beograd: Inis, 2002.

Radonjić, Nemanja. '"From Kragujevac to Kilimanjaro": Imagining and Re-Imagining Africa and the Self-Perception of Yugoslavia in the Travelogues from Socialist Yugoslavia'. *Godišnjak za društvenu istoriju* 2 (2016): 55–89.

Rakić, Tamara. 'Stereotipi o arapskom svijetu u srpskim rukopisima (od 1850. do 1940. godine)'. *Književna istorija* 130/38 (2006): 571–78.

Ratkušić, Enes. 'Dva i pol miliona ljudi, iz stotina različitih kultura, stopljenih u jednu misao . . .' *Ljiljan* 3/75 (22 June 1994): 23.

Reinhart, A. Kevin. 'What to Do with Ritual Texts: Islamic Fiqh Texts and the Study of Islamic Ritual'. In *Islamic Studies in the Twenty-First Century: Transformations and Continuities*, edited by Léon Buskens and Annemarie van Sandwijk, 67–86. Amsterdam: Amsterdam University Press: 2016.

Reinhart, Kevin. *Lived Islam: Colloquial Religion in a Cosmopolitan Tradition*. Cambridge: Cambridge University Press, 2020.

Reinkowski, Maurus. 'Conquests Compared: The Ottoman Expansion in the Balkans and the Mashreq in an Islamicate context'. In *The Ottoman Conquest of the Balkans*, edited by Oliver Jens Schmitt, 47–64. Vienna: Verlag der Österreichischen Akademie der Wissenschaften, 2016.

Rexhepi, Piro. 'Unmapping Islam in Eastern Europe: Periodization and Muslim Subjectivities in the Balkans'. In *Eastern Europe Unmapped: Beyond Borders and Peripheries*, edited by Irene Kacandes and Juliya Komska, 53–77. New York, Oxford: Berghahn, 2017.

Ricci, Ronit. *Islam Translated: Literature, Conversion, and the Arabic Cosmopolis of South and Southeast Asia*. Chicago: University of Chicago Press, 2011.

Richardson, Kristina. *Difference and Disability in the Medieval Islamic World: Blighted Bodies*. Edinburgh: Edinburgh University Press, 2014.

Robertson, James M. 'Navigating the Postwar Liberal Order: Autonomy, Creativity and Modernism in Socialist Yugoslavia, 1949–1953'. *Modern Intellectual History* 17/2 (2020): 385–412.

Ross, Danielle. 'Retelling Mecca: Shifting Narratives of Sacred Spaces in Volga-Ural Muslim Hajj Accounts, 1699–1945'. *Religions* 12 (2021): 588.

Ryad, Umar. 'On his Donkey to the Mountain of 'Arafāt: Dr Van der Hoog and his Hajj Journey to Mecca'. In *The Hajj and Europe in the Age of Empire*, edited by Umar Ryad, 185–216. Leiden, Boston: Brill, 2017.

Ryad, Umar (ed.). *The Hajj and Europe in the Age of Empire*. Leiden, Boston: Brill, 2017.

Sajdi, Dana. *The Barber of Damascus: Nouveau Literacy in the Eighteenth-Century Ottoman Levant*. Palo Alto: Stanford University Press, 2013.

Scalenghe, Sara. *Disability in the Ottoman Arab World, 1500–1800*. New York: Cambridge University Press, 2014.

Scheer, Monique. 'Are Emotions a Kind of Practice (And Is That What Makes Them Have a History)? A Bourdieuian Approach to Understanding Emotion'. *History and Theory* 51/2 (2012): 193–220.

Schimmel, Annemarie. *Mystical Dimensions of Islam*. Chapel Hill: University of North Carolina Press, 1975.

Sellheim, R. 'Faḍīla'. *The Encyclopaedia of Islam*. Leiden: Brill, 1991.

Shafir, Nir. 'In an Ottoman Holy Land: The Hajj and the Road from Damascus, 1500–1800'. *History of Religions* 60/1 (2020): 1–36.

Shariati, Ali. *Hajj*, trans. by Ali A. Behzadnia and Najla Denny. Zürich: Indo Oriental Publ., 1980.

Sirriyeh, Elizabeth. *Sufi Visionary of Ottoman Damascus: 'Abd al-Ghanī al-Nābulusī 1641–1731*. London, New York: Routledge, 2005.

Slight, John. *The British Empire and the Hajj: 1865–1956*. Cambridge, MA: Harvard University Press, 2015.

Smith, Jonathan Z. *To Take Place: Toward Theory in Ritual*. Chicago, London: The University of Chicago Press, 1992.

de Sousa, Marco Túlio and da Rosa, Ana Paula. 'The Mediatization of Camino De Santiago: Between the Pilgrimage Narrative and Media Circulation of the Narrative'. *Religions* 11/10 (2020): 480.

Spaho, Fehim. 'Panislamska ideja'. *Behar* 7/3 (1906): 25–26.

Spaho, Fehim. 'Panislamska ideja'. *Behar* 9 (1906): 98.

Spiegel, Gabrielle M. *The Past as Text: The Theory and Practice of Medieval Historiography*. Baltimore: Johns Hopkins University Press, 1997.

Spivak, Gayatri. *A Critique of Postcolonial Reason: Toward a History of the Vanishing Present*. Cambridge, MA: Harvard University Press, 1999.

Subrahmanyam, Sanjay and Alam, Muzaffar. 'Introduction: The Travel Account'. In *Indo-Persian Travels in the Age of Discoveries, 1400–1800*, 1–44. Cambridge: Cambridge University Press, 2007.

Şahin, Kaya. *Empire and Power in the Reign of Süleyman: Narrating the Sixteenth-Century Ottoman World*. Cambridge: Cambridge University Press, 2013.

Šabanović, Hazim. *Književnost Muslimana BiH na orijentalnim jezicima (biobibliografija)*. Sarajevo: Svjetlost, 1973.

Šehić, Zijad. 'Prilog istraživanju turizma u Bosni i Hercegovini u doba austrougarske uprave 1878–1918'. In *Godišnjak Bošnjačke zajednice kulture 'Preporod'*, 302–22. Sarajevo: Bošnjačka zajednica kulture 'Preporod', 2011.

Šehić, Zijad. 'Putovanje bosanskohercegovačkih hodočasnika u Meku u doba austrougarske uprave 1878–1918'. *Saznanja, Časopis za historiju* 2/2 (2008): 69–85.

Šestić, Hasan. *Put na hadž '96 (dnevnik i utisci)*. Bošnjačka zajednica kulture 'Preporod' Zenica: Zenica, 1998.

Šmigalović, Ferid. *Ibrahim a.s. preci i potomci.* Tuzla: published by the author, 2006.

Tagliacozzo, Eric. *The Longest Journey: Southeast Asians and the Pilgrimage to Mecca.* Oxford: Oxford University Press, 2013.

Talmon-Heller, Daniella. ''Ilm, Shafāʿah, and Barakah: The Resources of Ayyubid and Early Mamluk Ulama'. *Mamlūk Studies Review* 13/2 (2009): 1–23.

Talmon-Heller, Daniella. *Islamic Piety in Medieval Syria: Mosques, Cemeteries and Sermons under the Zangids and Ayyūbids (1146–1260).* Leiden, Boston: Brill, 2007.

Tayob, Abdulkader. *Religion in Modern Islamic Discourse.* London: Hurst, 2009.

Taylor, Charles. *Varieties of Religion Today: William James Revisited.* Cambridge, MA: Harvard University Press, 2002.

Taylor, Christopher S. *In the Vicinity of the Righteous: Ziyāra and the Veneration of Muslim Saints in Late Medieval Egypt.* Leiden: Brill, 1999.

Tkalčević, Adolf. *Put na Plitvice.* Zagreb: Tiskom dra. Ljudevita Gaja, 1860.

Tkalčević, Adolfo Veber. *Put u Carigrad: sa četrdset slika i tlorisom Carigrada.* Zagreb: Matica hrvatska, 1886.

T. L. 'Hadžije odmarale u Mersinu'. *Dnevni Avaz* (14 December 2006): 8.

Tofighi, Fatima. 'Religious Rituals as Civil *Hexis*: The Case of Modernist Interpretations of Islamic Rituals among Iranian Pre-Revolutionary Intellectuals'. *Method and Theory in the Study of Religion* 32 (2020): 185–204.

Varatanović, Ismet. 'Sa puta u Meku'. *Jugoslovenska pošta* 5 (14 October 1933): 13.

Varlık, Nükhet and Zens, Robert (eds). *Chasing the Ottoman Early Modern.* Special issue of *Journal of the Ottoman and Turkish Studies Association* 7/1 (2020): 1–253.

Wheeler, Brannon. *Mecca and Eden: Ritual, Relics, and Territory in Islam.* Chicago: The University of Chicago Press, 2006.

Wolfe, Michael. *One Thousand Roads to Mecca: Ten Centuries of Travelers Writing about the Muslim Pilgrimage.* New York: Grove Press, 1997.

Yilmaz, Huseyin. *Caliphate Redefined: The Mystical Turn in Ottoman Political Thought.* Princeton: Princeton University Press 2018.

Younis, Hana. 'Smrtni slučajevi tokom hadža u Mekku kroz primjere iz građe Vrhovnog šeriatskog suda u Sarajevu u periodu austrougarske uprave'. *Anali GHB* 45/37 (2016): 197–217.

Ziad, Homayra. 'The Return of Gog, Politics and PanIslamism in the Hajj Travelogue of Abd al Majid Daryabadi'. In *Global Muslims in the Age of Steam and Print*, edited by Nile Green and James Gelvin, 227–47. Berkeley: University of California Press, 2013.

Zukić, Kemal. *Odazivam Ti se, Bože moj, odazivam Ti se: Putopis sa hadždža.* Zenica: Minex, 2002.

'İklîm-i Hicâz hakkında birkaç söz', *Bosna ve Hersek Vilayeti Salnamesi*, 110–18. Sarajevo: Vilajetska uprava Bosanskog vilajeta, 1892.

'Iz islamskog svijeta'. *Hikjmet* 1/1 (1929): 32.

'Jemen i Hadramaut – arapske države iz hiljadu i jedne noći – u čiju unutrašnjost nije još ušao nijedan Evropljanin'. *Vreme* (14 March 1932): 2.

'Kao žena muslimana na putu za Sveti Grad (Avanture jedne Francuskinje među Arabljanima)'. *Vreme* (10 December 1933): 6.

'Vodić na hadždž'. *Islamski Svijet* 24 (1933): 6.

'Odgovori uredništva'. *Hikjmet* 10 (1935).

'Naše hadžije'. *Bošnjak* 1/14 (1 October 1891): 1.

'Nekoliko pouka iz islamske prošlosti: Predavanje povodom Nove muslimanske godine'. *El-Hidaje* 5/4–5 (1942): 103–19.

'Nezvanično'. *Sarajevski list* (22 January 1897).

'Nove knjige'. *Novi Behar* 11/17–19 (1938): 291–92.

'Turska i hadž ove godine'. *Islamski svijet* 17 (1932): 4.

'Umesto gusarskim lađama i kamilama, naši muslimani putuju na ćabu u pulmanovim kolima, automobilima i brzim lađama'. *Vreme* (5 March 1932): 7.

'Uz naše slike'. *Bosanska vila* 2 (16 January 1889): 30.

'Veliki broj hadžija iz Kine'. *Islamski svijet* 128 (1935): 3.

Mali vjesnik, *Sarajevski list* (11 June 1890).

Mali vjesnik, *Sarajevski list* (5 June 1889).

Mali vjesnik, *Sarajevski list* (30 May 1890).

Mali vjesnik, *Sarajevski list* (30 September 1891).

Mali vjesnik, *Sarajevski list* (17 May 1891).

http://www.prometej.ba/clanak/kultura/prometejske-price-i-pjesme/zuko-dzumhur-kamen-crnoga-sjaja-originalni-tekst-sa-ilustracijama-2956 (accessed on 27 August 2021).

https://www.bir.ba/index.php/vijesti/item/7398-kako-sam-obavio-i-dozivio-hadz-u-programu-radija-bir (accessed on 8 August 2021).

https://www.hadziumra.ba/okrugli-sto-u-susret-mubarek-danima-hadza-hadz-je-na-izvjesatn-nacin-oblikovao-licnost-bosnjaka/?fbclid=IwAR2oe0igw747pHnmZv74ia20UGdJkiu4MnAxeXmSy_scC5WzYG5OQ1T6QOo (accessed on 22 August 2021).

INDEX

Note: *f* indicates figure

Abbasid Caliphate, 42
'Abd al-Ghānī al-Nāblūsī, 67
Abdel Rahim Hadi, 154
Abdul-Aziz, King, 123
Abū al-Qāsim b. Yāsīn, 70
aca'ib, 92
Adā' manāsik al-hujjāj (al-Būsnawī, Ibrāhīm), 68
air travel agencies, 195
Al-e Ahmad, Jalal, 138–9, 182
allegiance, pledging 47
Altı Parmak efendi, 74
Andrić, Ivo, 152
al-Anṣārī, Aḥmad, 34
Anwār al-'āshiqīn (Yazıcıoğlu, Aḥmed Bīcān), 78
al-Anwar Mir Ghadanfar, 36
anxiety, 200
al-Aqḥiṣārī-Pruščak, Ḥasan Kāfī, 34
  Niẓām al-'ulamā ila khātam al-anbiyā (*The List of Scholars Going Back to the Seal of the Prophets*), 34
al-Aqsa Mosque, 163
appearance, 91, 117, 118, 192, 201
  classifying by, 201
  see also race
Arabic language, 24, 25, 64
  on the journey, 75
  travelogues, 118n
architecture, 195
Arnaut, Fikret, 197
art, 65, 67
Asrār al-ḥajj wa-ḥaqā'iq al-āyāt al-Makiyya (*The Secrets of the Hajj and the Meaning of the Meccan Verses*) (al-Būsnawī, Alī-dada), 37
audiences, 24, 72, 211
Austro-Hungarian Empire, 17, 18, 19, 20, 104n, 108
awā'il, 38, 43
awā'khir, 43–4
awliyā, 79–80

al-Badawī, Aḥmed, 79
Bali Efendi, 34
baraka, 57
Bašeskija, Mula Mustafa, 62, 71
al-Batanūnī, Muḥammad Labīb, 12
Bayān fi manāsik al-ḥajj, 68
Bayrāmī-Malāmī, 46
Bebi Dol
  Mustafa, 157
Bedouins, the, 89, 90, 153

Belgrade, 96, 116
belonging, 7, 8
Bikić, Muhamed, 195, 199, 200, 203–4
Black Stone, the, 46–50
blessing, 79, 81
bodies *see* human body, the
borders, 20, 113, 148, 177
Boro-efendi, 73
Bosanska Vila, 107
Bosnia/Bosnians, 8, 180–1, 188, 191, 212, 214
  Austro-Hungarian Empire, 17, 18, 19, 20
  disease, 17
  economy, 143
  European appearance, 118
  exceptionality, 192–3
  Hadžibajrić, Fejzulah, 170
  Hijaz, links with, 170
  independence, 177, 184, 185
  Islam, 8–9, 15–16, 33, 106, 110, 206
  Kingdom of Yugoslavia, 96
  Ljubunčić, Hasan, 142–3
  al-Mukhliṣī, Mustafa, 87–8, 90–1
  Ottoman Empire, 15–16, 29–30, 59
  Ottoman Empire, scholars in, 33–6
  remoteness, 70
  scholars, 33–6
  war (1992–5), 176–7, 179, 183–4, 186–92
  see also Sarajevo
Bosniaks, 145
Bosnian language, 25, 72, 105
Bosnian War/Serbian aggression, 176–7, 179, 183, 191
  maimed bodies, 183–4, 186–92
  visibility, 187
bratstvo i jedinstvo, 7
Brena, Lepa
  Šeik, 157
brotherhood, 133
  unity, and, 7, 8
Brunner, Rainer, 11
burials, 79–80
  awliyā, 79–80
  Gallipoli, 78, 88
  Mecca, 74
  Medina 51, 55, 56–8
  Prophet, 51, 55, 57, 171
  ziyāra, 82
Bušatlić, Ismet, 208–9
al-Būsnawī, ʿAbdullah, 29–30, 31, 35, 59–60, 211
  Kitāb al-yad al-ajwad fī istilām al-ḥajar al-aswad (*The Book of the Right Hand in Touching the Black Stone*), 46–9
  Shāriḥ al-Fuṣūṣ (*The Interpreter of the* Fuṣūṣ), 46
al-Būsnawī, Abdulwahāb
  Manāsik al-ḥajj, 68
al-Būsnawī, Alī-dada, 23, 24, 30, 31, 35, 36–7, 59–60, 211
  Asrār al-ḥajj wa-ḥaqā'iq al-āyāt al-Makiyya (*The Secrets of the Hajj and the Meaning of the Meccan Verses*), 37
  Khawātim al-Ḥikam (*The Seals of Wisdoms*), 37
  Mecca, 35, 36, 37–8
  Mukhāḍarāt al-awā'il wa-musāmarāt al-awākhir (*Lectures on the 'Firsts' and the 'Lasts'*), 37
  Ottoman Empire, praise for, 41–2, 43–5
  Risāla fī bayān rijāl al-ghayb (*The Treatise on the Transcendental People*), 37
  Risālat al-intiṣār li-l-qidwa al-akhyār (*The Treatise on the Victory of the Elect*), 37
  Tamkīn al-Maqām fī Masjid al-Ḥarām (*The Restorations of the Station in al-Masjid al-Ḥarām*), 37–45
al-Būsnawī, Ḥasan Imam-zāda, 30, 31, 35, 53, 59–60, 211
  Dalīl al-saʿirīn ila ziyārat Ḥabīb Rabb al-ʿālamīn (*A Guide for Those Who Want to Visit the Beloved of the Lord of the Worlds*), 51–9, 79
  al-Ilhām al-ilāhiyya fī miʿrāj khayr al-bariyya (*Divine Inspiration in the Nightly Celestial Journey of the Best of the Creatures*), 52
  Tashwīq al-labīb ila maḥabbat al-Ḥabīb (*Inciting a Sensible Person to Desire Loving the Beloved*), 52
al-Būsnawī, Ibrāhīm
  Adā' manāsik al-hujjāj, 68

Cairo, 74, 76, 120–1
  al-Mukhlişī, Mustafa, 89
censorship, 158, 210
Christianity, 132n, 169
cities, 146–7
coffee houses, 62
Čokić, Ibrahim Hakki, 96, 97, 99, 109, 116, 129, 213
  Cairo, 121
  Hadžić, Osman Nuri, 126–8
  'Hajj and Eid al-Adha (*Hadž i Kurban Bajram*)', 132
  Hikjmet (*Wisdom*), 97, 122
  language, 117
  Saudi Arabia, 122
  travelogue, 96, 102, 121, 123
colonialism
  Ottoman Empire, 15–16
  Austro-Hungarian Empire, 17, 18, 19, 20
communities, 75
congresses, 131–2
Covid-19 pandemic, 208, 209*f*
criticism, 21
  Đozo, Husein, 165
  holy places, 121–2, 124
Croatian intellectual elite, 106–7
crowds, 199–200
culture, 184, 209

dalā'il al-khayrāt, 61, 65–7
Dalīl al-manāhil wa-murshid al-marāḥil (*A Guide to the Springs and an Adviser on the Stations of a Journey*) (al-Mukhlişī, Mustafa), 84–92
Dalīl al-sa'irīn ila ziyārat Ḥabīb Rabb al-'ālamīn (*A Guide for Those Who Want to Visit the Beloved of the Lord of the Worlds*) (al-Būsnawī, Ḥasan Imamzāda), 51–9, 79
Damascus, 76
death, 56–7, 69, 165; *see also* burials
desert, the, 197
devotional objects, 32, 83
devotions, 65, 67
diaries, 1–2, 4–5, 133, 203
dictionaries, 196–7
disease, 17, 63, 107–8
  quarantine, 119–20, 148
diversity, 113, 119, 130, 192–3, 198
  Yugoslavia, 141
Đozo, Husein, 160–6, 168
  'Iftar in the Haram-i Sharif, The', 161–2
dream narratives, 175–6, 177–8
dress, 146
Dučić, Jovan, 120
  'Letter from Egypt', 120–1
duty, 68–9, 105, 212
Džumhur, Zuko, 152
  Hodoljublje, 152
  'Kamen crnog sjaja (The Shiny Black Stone)', 152
  Nekrolog jednoj čaršiji (*Obituary to a Small Town*), 152
  'Putovanje po besmislu (The Travel in Nonsense)', 152, 153

education, 5
  Bosnian scholars, 33–6
  Turkey, 146
Egypt, 120
  quarantine, 118–19
  women, 111, 112*f*
  see also Cairo
emotion, 30, 125, 170–2, 180–2, 203–5*f*
emptiness, 212
encounters, 200–1
England, 119, 120
equality, 133
ethics, 69
Europe/European, 99, 108, 192–3

faḍā'il, 38–9, 51, 53, 59–60
Faginović, Mustafa, 65, 67
faith, 130–1, 148–9
family libraries, 202
farewell ceremonies, 114*f*–15
fasting, 175
Fejić, Ibrahim, 141
Fejzić, Fahira, 204, 205–6
'Few Words about the Region of Hijaz, A', 104n
food, 90
friendships, 71, 73, 75

Fuṣūṣ al-Ḥikam (*Bezels of Wisdom*) (Ibn 'Arabī), 29, 46
Al-Futuḥāt al-Makiyya (Ibn 'Arabī), 47

Gallipoli, 78, 88
Gavrankapetanović, Munir, 174–6, 177–9, 186–7, 188–9, 190, 202
  On the Path of Hope and Consolation (*Na putu nade i utjehe*), 175
  Through the Strength of Faith to the Perfection of the Soul (*Snagom vjere do savršenstva duše*), 175
gender, 4, 205–6
  hierarchy, 44
  see also women
genre, 5, 10–11, 178, 201, 211–12, 215
  awā'il, 38, 43
  awā'khir, 43–4
  dalā'il al-khayrāt, 61, 65–7
  diaries, 1–2, 4–5, 133, 203
  dictionaries, 196–7
  dream narratives, 175–6, 177–8
  faḍā'il, 38–9, 51, 53, 59–60
  guidebooks, 64
  Internet, the, 201, 202, 203
  journalism, 95, 97, 102, 104–9, 152
  manāsik literature, 68
  mecmuas, 62, 64
  modern, 25
  premodern, 25
  salname, 104n
  social commentaries, 133
  see also travelogues
geography
  of Islam, 6, 29, 70, 113, 168, 191, 213
  Livnjak, Jusuf 74
Glasnik, 158, 159, 160
God, 174
graves *see* burials
Greece, 116–17
guidebooks, 64

habitual body, the, 186n
Habsburgs, the, 44
hadīth qudsī, 76, 89
hadiths, 14
Hadžibajrić, Fejzulah, 164–5, 167–72, 213
Hadžić, Fadil, 151
Hadžić, Mehmedalija, 179
Hadžić, Osman Nuri, 126–8
  Islam and Culture, 126
  Muhammad and the Qur'an, 126–7
ḥajj al-abdān (Hajj of the body), 69
ḥajj al-aghniyā (pilgrimage of the rich), 69
'Hajj and Eid al-Adha (*Hadž i Kurban Bajram*)' (Čokić, Ibrahim Hakki), 132
ḥajj al-qulūb (Hajj of the heart), 69
Hajj-stones, 114*f*
Hajji (surname), 16
Hajjis, 15–16, 61, 152–3, 159*f*, 181, 189*f*
  exceptionality, 192–3
  futility of, 156–7
  hospitality, 195
  maimed bodies, 186–91
  personality construction, 103
  stampedes, 199–200
Handžić, Mehmed, 111
Hasan ibn Ali, 170
Hasani, Sinan, 141
health, 17, 63, 107–8
heart, the, 48, 69
hegemony, 45
Hertzog, Gilles, 185
  'Sarajevo Thought Well', 185
Hijaz, the, 121–4
  Bosnia, 170
  see also holy places
Hijaz railway project, 124
hijra, 180
Hikjmet (*Wisdom*), 97, 122–3, 132
history, 14–23, 208–9
  movements, 23–6
Hodoljublje (Džumhur, Zuko), 152
Hodžić, Amir, 179
holiness, 30, 38, 77
holy places, 30–2, 35–6
al-Badawī, Aḥmed, 79
  Black Stone, the, 46–50
  Cairo, 74, 76
  criticism, 121–2, 124
  dalā'il al-khayrāt, 61, 65–7
  Damascus, 76
  decline, 125
  depictions, 61, 65

devotions, 65
Džumhur, Zuko, 153–5
faḍā'il, 38–9, 51, 53, 59–60
foreignness of 153
Gallipoli, 78
Hadžić, Osman Nuri, 127
hierarchy, 59–60
on the journey, 73–4
literature, 32
Maqām-I Ibrāhīm, 36, 38–40, 42
material objects, link with, 61–2
modernity, 154–5
Mount Arafat, 135, 156, 198
Ottoman Empire, 38, 41–6, 59
profanisation of, 109
universal values, 36–41
ziyāra 16, 65, 76–81
see also Mecca; Medina
honeymoon travel, 111
hospitality, 195
human body, the, 48, 65, 69, 84, 181
habitual body, the, 186n
maimed, 183–4, 186–92
physical sensations, 204
Hürrem Sultan, 44
al-Husseini, Amin, 136

Ibn ʿArabī
Fuṣūṣ al-Ḥikam (*Bezels of Wisdom*), 29, 46
Al-Futuḥāt al-Makiyya, 47
grave, 80
Ibn Battuta, 32
Ibn al-Jawzī
al-Wafā, 55
Ibn Jubayr, 32
Ibn Saud, King, 135–6
Ibrāhīm, Prophet, 190
Ibrāhīm ibn Muhammad, 67
Ibrišimović, Nedžad, 191
identity, 192, 213; *see also* self, the
IFOR (Implementation Force), 194
'Iftar in the Haram-i Sharif, The' (Đozo, Husein), 161–2
ihram, 184
illustration, 153
imagery, 196
spatial, 7
Imām-zāda *see* al-Būsnawī, Ḥasan Imam-zāda
Implementation Force (IFOR), 194
imprisonment, 116
in-betweenness, 23–6
inclusivity, 112–13
injuries, 199–200
intellectual elite, 106–7
intercession, 56–7, 79
Internet, the, 201, 202, 203
interwar debates, 95–9
Iraq, 141
Islam, 5–6, 125, 129
Bosnia, 8–9, 15–16, 33, 106, 110, 206
communities, 75
decline, 160, 163, 165
diversity, 130
Dučić, Jovan, 120–1
equality, 184
exoticisation, 106, 107
fanaticism, 105–6, 155
future of, 131
geography of, 6, 29, 70, 113, 168, 191, 213
Hadžić, Osman Nuri, 126–7, 128
historic dynasties, 44–5
history, 131
international community, 111–12
Izetbegović, Alija, 181
Kingdom of Yugoslavia, 96
Krpo, Muhamed, 110
limiting, 96
literature, 22
modernity, 101, 133
Mount Arafat sermon, 135
Ottoman Empire, 31–2
Palestine, 138
reformists, 128–9
Reinhart, Kevin, 214
religious fever, 149–50
religious tolerance, 143, 169
ritual emptiness/meaning-making tension, 25–6
schools, 169–70
scrutiny of, 94
shared, 214
soft Islamism, 185

Islam (*cont.*)
spiritual experience, 11
traditionalists, 128–9
unity, 7–8, 110, 118–19, 122, 124, 125, 130–1, 133, 135, 198
values, 7
see also Islamic Community; Sufism
Islam and Culture (Hadžić, Osman Nuri), 126
Islamic Community, 158–9, 194
publications, 158
reformism 159
roundtable, 208–9
superstition, 167
travel, 19, 20, 21n
women 21n
Islamic Religious Community, 96
Israel, 155
Istanbul, 74
Izetbegović, Alija, 166, 176, 179, 181–2, 183–6

Japan, 140
Jerusalem/al-Quds, 162–3, 169
journalism, 95, 97, 102, 104–9, 152
Jugoslavenska pošta, 95

Kaʿba, the, 46–50, 91–2, 125, 127, 200, 204–5*f*
Kamālpasha-zāda, 34
'Kamen crnog sjaja (The Shiny Black Stone)' (Džumhur, Zuko), 152
Karabeg, Riza, 130–1
Kasapović, 63, 71
Kateman, Ammeke, 6n, 12, 101
Khawātim al-Ḥikam (*The Seals of Wisdoms*) (al-Būsnawī, Alī-dada), 37
Kingdom of Saudi Arabia *see* Saudi Arabia
Kingdom of Yugoslavia *see* Yugoslavia
Kitāb al-yad al-ajwad fi istilām al-ḥajar al-aswad (*The Book of the Right Hand in Touching the Black Stone*) (al-Būsnawī, 'Abdullah), 46–9
Kosovo, 194–5
Krpo, Muhamed, 96, 97–9, 102, 103*f*, 109, 110*f*, 213
appearance, 118
Belgrade, 116
government appeal, 116
Greece, 116–17
leisure travel, 111, 116
Mecca, 121–2
social potential, 131
travelogue 96, 123
Kurtović, Ezudin, 201

language, 5, 101, 117–18, 199
Bosnian, 25, 72, 105
dictionaries, 196–7
Džumhur, Zuko, 154
Livnjak, Jusuf, 72
Turkish, 118
see also Arabic language; Ottoman Turkish language
'*lawlâka*' (*hadīth qudsī*), 89
Letopis Matice Srpske (Nedeljković, Milan), 126
'Letter from Egypt' (Dučić, Jovan), 120–1
literacy, 4–5, 100, 139
literalism, 161
Livnjak, Jusuf, 71n, 72–6
ziyāra, 78–82
Ljubunčić, Hasan, 135–7, 141–50, 176
local/universal tension, 23–4

maimed bodies, 183–4, 186–92
Malcolm X, 138–9, 182, 198
Mamluk Sultanate, 42–3
Manāsik al-ḥajj (al-Būsnawī, Abdulwahāb), 68
Manāsik al-ḥajj (Sinanuddīn Yūsuf b. Yaʿqūb ar-Rūmī al-Ḥanafī), 68
manāsik literature, 68
manāzil, 26–8, 71
Maqām-i Ibrāhīm, 36, 38–40, 42, 127, 128
Mašić, Muhamed Seid, 122–3
material culture, 16
material objects, 61–2
Mathnawi (al-Rūmī, Jalāl al-Dīn), 29
meaning 62–3, 101–2, 125–33, 137–8, 180, 212
Đozo, Husein, 161
variety, 215

meaning-making/ritual emptiness, tension between, 25–6
Mecca, 6, 34–5, 50, 106, 198
  al-Būsnawī, Alī-dada, 35, 36, 37–8
  depictions, 61
  Džumhur, Zuko, 153–4
  emotion, 125
  Hadžibajrić, Fejzulah, 170–1
  Ka'ba, the, 46–50, 91–2, 125, 127, 200, 204–5*f*
  Livnjak, Jusuf, 81–2
  Maqām-i Ibrāhīm, 36, 38–40, 42, 127, 128
  modernity, 121–2
  Mu'alla graveyard, 74
  al-Mukhliṣī, Mustafa, 91–2
  postwar imaginary, 148–50
  ziyāra, 81–2
mecmuas, 62, 64
media, the, 22–3, 95, 98, 210
  Internet, the, 201, 202, 203
  isolation, 179–80
  news, the, 104–9, 111–12
  photography, 98, 111, 203
  print, 100, 101, 104–9, 111–13, 115, 116, 158–9, 210
  Turkey, 146
mediation, 101, 214–15
  horizontal, 7
  layers of, 9–14
  temporal, 7
  vertical, 7
Medina, 6, 30, 50–3, 106, 125
  depictions, 61
  Hadžibajrić, Fejzulah, 171
  living and dying in, 56–9
  al-Mukhliṣī, Mustafa, 92
  Prophet, 50, 51, 76
  Prophet, loving the, 53–6
  ziyāra, 82
meetings, 200–1, 213
memory, 144, 184
Mihrimah, 43–4
Mina, 200
minerality, 47–8
Mirojević, Hidajeta, 1–2, 4, 6, 7, 26, 167
  diary of, 1–2, 4–5, 202
  expectations, 12–13
  hadiths, 14
  local/universal tension, 24
  ritual, 7
  umma, 7–8
Mišćina Džamija, 65–6*f*
mobility, 4, 21–2
modernity, 15n, 19, 21, 22, 101, 133, 138, 213
  Đozo, Husein, 161
  Džumhur, Zuko, 154–5
  Mecca, 121–2
  premodern, rift with, 24–5
  Turkey, 145–7
  Western, 155
Morocco, 140–1
Mount Arafat, 135, 156, 198
Mu'adhdhin-zāda al-Mostārī, Aḥmad, 68, 69, 70, 93
  Muḥarrik al-qulūb (*The Mover of the Hearts*), 68–70
Muhammad, Prophet *see* Prophet, the
Muhammad and the Qur'an (Hadžić, Osman Nuri), 126–7
Muhammedan Light, 54
Muḥammediye (Yazıcıoğlu, Meḥmed), 78
Muḥarrik al-qulūb (*The Mover of the Hearts*) (Mu'adhdhin-zāda al-Mostārī, Aḥmad), 68–70, 93
Mukhāḍarāt al-awā'il wa-musāmarāt al-awākhir (*Lectures on the 'Firsts' and the 'Lasts'*) (al-Būsnawī, Alī-dada), 37
al-Mukhliṣī, Mustafa, 26, 73, 75, 84–92
  Dalīl al-manāhil wa-murshid al-marāḥil (*A Guide to the Springs and an Adviser on the Stations of a Journey*), 84–92
Mulabdić, Edhem, 130–1
Murad III, Sultan, 41–2, 44
music, 157
Muslim communities, 75
Muslim fanaticism, 105–6, 155
Mustafa (Bebi Dol), 157

al-Nāblūsī, Abdulghānī, 77
Nametak, A., 132
Nasir Khusraw, 32, 81n
nationalism, 8, 19, 96, 121, 185

NATO, 194–5
Nedeljković, Milan
  Letopis Matice Srpske, 126
Nekrolog jednoj čaršiji (*Obituary to a Small Town*) (Džumhur, Zuko), 152
news, the, 104–9, 111–12
1994 delegation, 176–81, 202
  Izetbegović, Alija, 181, 183–6
  maimed bodies, 183–4, 186–92
  Preporod (*Revival*), 182*f*
  visibility, 187
1999 delegation, 194–5
non-Muslims, 100, 101, 107, 108–9, 138
  Mecca, 82
  pilgrimage infrastructure, 20
  see also Otherness

objects
  devotional, 32, 83
  material, 61–2
Omerbašić, Fehim, 194n
On the Path of Hope and Consolation (*Na putu nade i utjehe*) (Gavrankapetanović, Munir), 175
oppression, 119
Orientalism, 101
  consumerist, 157
Otherness, 20–1, 96n, 151, 193
Ottoman Empire, 15–16, 29–31
  bias against, 106
  Bosnian scholars, 33–6
  genealogy, 45
  Greece, 116–17
  hegemony, 45
  holy places, 38, 41–6, 59, 82–3
  Islam, 31–2
  Mecca, 38
  Medina, 38
  praise for, 41–2, 43–5
Ottoman Turkish language, 24–5, 64, 72, 104
  on the journey, 75

paganism, 127, 128
Palestine, 138, 162–3, 169
pandemics, 15, 107–8, 208
People's Liberation Struggle, 143–4
personification, 49
photography, 98, 111, 203
piety, 53, 105, 139, 148
pilgrimage, 3, 6, 61–2
  numbers, 16, 62
pious visitations 77–81; see also *ziyāra*
places
  emotional connection to, 30
  faḍā'il, 38–9, 51, 53, 59–60
  physical attachment to, 29
  see also holy places
politics, 4, 137, 138–9, 140–1
  Đozo, Husein, 162–3
  soft Islamism, 185
power, 45, 100
prayer, 58, 63, 197
  dalā'il al-khayrāt, 61, 65–7
  Livnjak, Jusuf, 81
premodern/modern rift, 24–5
Preporod (*Revival*), 2, 157–8, 159, 160, 182*f*, 209*f*
pride, 186, 187
print media, 100, 101, 104–9, 111–13, 115, 116, 158–9, 210
profanisation, 99
promotion, 68–9
Prophet, the 76
body of, 106n
  burial, 51, 55, 57, 171
  emotions towards, 50
  loving 53–6
  Medina, 50, 51
  ziyāra, 82
Prophet-centred piety, 53
Prophet-oriented belonging 75–6
prostitution, 94, 95, 96
Pruščak, Ḥasan Kāfī-ef, 34
  Niẓām al-'ulamā ila khātam al-anbiyā (*The List of Scholars Going Back to the Seal of the Prophets*), 34
punishment, 95, 98–9, 116, 153
purity, 50
'Putovanje po besmislu (The Travel in Nonsense)' (Džumhur, Zuko), 152, 153

quarantine, 119–20, 148
al-Quds, 162–3, 169
Qur'an, the, 48, 110
translation, 117

Rābi'a al-'Adawiyya, 80n
race, 151, 157, 158, 192, 201
rarity, 210
reformists, 128–9
Reinhart, Kevin, 214
religion, 128–9, 162
Đozo, Husein, 162
popular culture, 157–8
see also Christianity; Islam
religious experience, 11
religious fanaticism, 105–6, 155
religious fever, 149–50
religious tolerance, 143, 169
remembrance journeys, 144
Rida, Rashid, 11
Risāla fī bayān rijāl al-ghayb (*The Treatise on the Transcendental People*) (al-Būsnawī, Alī-dada), 37
Risālat al-intiṣār li-l-qidwa al-akhyār (*The Treatise on the Victory of the Elect*) (al-Būsnawī, Alī-dada), 37
ritual, 7, 9, 40n, 100, 128, 198–200
Bosanska Vila, 107
Đozo, Husein, 162, 165–6
Izetbegović, Alija, 166
meaning, 12, 25–6
Mount Arafat, 135
prominence, 130
timelessness, 12
Tofighi, Fatima, 139
ritual emptiness/meaning-making, tension between, 25–6
Riza, Edhem, 130–1
roundtable, 208–9
Rūm, 87
al-Rūmī, Jalāl al-Dīn
Mathnawi, 29

sacred, the, 32
sacrifice, 70, 186, 187
Safavids, the, 44
salname, 104n
Sarajevo, 62–3, 115
Mišćina Džamija, 65–6*f*
'Sarajevo Thought Well' (Hertzog, Gilles), 185
Sarajevski list, 107–8, 115
Satan, stoning of, 161, 199
Saudi Arabia, 121, 122–4, 135–6, 179, 200
scholars, 130–1
scribes, 68
Šećeragić, Murad, 141
Šeik (Brena, Lepa), 157
self, the, 202–6; *see also* identity
senses, 84, 196, 204
Serbian intellectual elite, 106–7
Šerif, Šaip, 141
Šestić, Hasan, 195, 203
Shamā'il (al-Tirmidhī), 55
Shariati, Ali, 182
Shāriḥ al-Fuṣūṣ (*The Interpreter of the* Fuṣūṣ) (al-Būsnawī, 'Abdullah), 46
shipping routes, 142, 143*f*
significance, 126–33
Šiljak, Safija, 1–2, 4, 12–13, 167, 202
Sinanuddīn Yūsuf b. Ya'qūb ar-Rūmī al-Ḥanafi
Manāsik al-ḥajj, 68
6 January Dictatorship, 96
slavery, 94, 95, 96
social class, 31, 62–3
social commentaries, 133
sociability 130–1
socio-cultural factors, 3, 4, 5, 13
soft Islamism, 185
spatial discourse, 59; *see also* places
spatial imagery, 7
spirituality, 11, 162
timelessness, 12
unification, 120
stampedes, 199–200
state, the, 4, 114
borders, 20, 113, 148, 177
control, 17–18, 20, 115–16, 137, 158, 167
farewell ceremonies, 115
Izetbegović, Alija, 183
organisation, 19–20
religious monopoly, 176

State Security Administration (UDBA), 174
stereotypes, 89–90, 96
stoning of Satan, 161, 199
Sufism, 34, 46, 69, 101, 168–71
  objections to, 164–7
Suleyman, Sultan, 45
supernatural, the, 81
superstition, 167
surveillance, 4, 104, 113, 115–16
  Austro-Hungarian Empire, 17, 20
  disease, 17
symbolism, 25–6, 180, 183, 212
  ihram, 184
Syria, 196

Talmon-Heller, Daniela, 77
Tamkīn al-Maqām fi Masjid al-Ḥarām (The *Restorations of the Station in al-Masjid al-Ḥarām*) (al-Būsnawī, Alī-dada), 37–45
technology, 4, 22, 100, 102
  Hijaz railway project, 124
  Saudi Arabia, 123, 124
tekkes, 167
texts, 65, 67–8
textual elements/forms, 13–14
Through the Strength of Faith to the Perfection of the Soul (*Snagom vjere do savršenstva duše*) (Gavrankapetanović, Munir), 175
Tih Banī Isrā'īl, 88
timelessness, 12
al-Tirmidhī
  Shamā'il, 55
Tkalčević, Adolfo Veber, 106
Tofighi, Fatima, 139
tourism, 18, 19, 20, 22, 109–11, 150, 213
  Vahida controversy, 157–8
tradition, 44, 49n, 149
traditionalists, 128–9
transformation, 100–3
transport, types of, 18–19, 21, 124, 142, 180, 195, 198
travel, 4, 6, 63–4, 92–3, 113
  air travel agencies, 195
  arduousness, 70, 71
  devotional objects, 83
  documents, 20, 177, 194n
  friendships, 71, 73, 75
  honeymoon, 111
  Islamic Community, 19, 20, 21n, 194
  on the journey, 73–6
  leisured, 111
  local conditions, 90
  local populations, 89–91
  Otherness, 20–1
  Ottoman Empire 16
  pious visitations 77–81
  places and senses, 83–92
  places of highest importance, 81–3
  postwar, 194–5
  protection, 177, 194
  recuperating, 76
  routes, 73–4, 85, 141
  setting off, 71–3
  transport, types of, 18–19, 21, 124, 142, 180, 195, 198
  war, 18, 180
  world, the 212–14
  ziyāra 16, 65, 76–81
  see also travelogues; tourism
travelogues, 10–11, 63–4, 71, 102, 103, 120, 166–7, 210, 211
  Al-e Ahmad, Jalal, 182
  Čokić, Ibrahim Hakki, 96, 102, 121, 123
  diversity, 130
  Đozo, Husein, 165
  Dučić, Jovan, 120–1
  Džumhur, Zuko, 152–7
  Gavrankapetanović, Munir, 177–9, 186–7, 188–9, 190
  Hadžibajrić, Fejzulah, 165, 168–72
  Hadžić, Mehmedalija, 179
  Hodžić, Amir, 179
  as ideological reassurance, 137
  illustration, 153
  Krpo, Muhamed, 96, 123
  language, 117–18
  late publication of, 167
  Livnjak, Jusuf, 71n, 72–6, 78–82
  Ljubunčić, Hasan, 137, 141–50
  Mirojević, Hidajeta, 1–2, 4–5, 167, 202

al-Mukhliṣī, Mustafa, 84–92
Shariati, Ali, 182
Šiljak, Safija, 2, 13, 167, 202
Varatanović, Ismet, 95–6, 109, 123–5
Yugoslavia, 137, 141–50, 151–8
Žiga, Jusuf, 179
Turkey, 116–18, 145–7, 195, 196, 213
Turkish language, 118; *see also* Ottoman Turkish

UDBA (State Security Administration), 174
ulama, 22, 33, 64, 139, 213
graves, 80
Kingdom of Yugoslavia, 96–7
umma, 7–8
universal/local tension, 23–4
UNPROFOR (United Nations Protection Force), 177
unscripted reflections, 199–200

Vahida controversy, 157–8
Varatanović, Ismet, 95–9, 109, 123–5, 144
Variola Vera (Marković, Goran), 107
visibility, 187
Vreme, 95

al-Wafā (Ibn al-Jawzī), 55
war, 17, 18–19, 176–7, 179, 183, 191
Bosnian War/Serbian aggression, 176–7, 179, 183–4, 186–92
maimed bodies, 183–4, 186–92
visibility, 187
water, 90
wealth, 111, 113
women, 4–5, 91, 205–6
Džumhur, Zuko, 153, 155
Egyptian, 111, 112*f*
European, 108
mobility, 21
modernity, 21
al-Mukhliṣī, Mustafa, 91
Vahida controversy, 157–8
ziyāra, 77
world, the 212–14
writings, 210–12

Yazıcıoğlu, Aḥmed Bīcān, 78, 88
Anwār al-ʿāshiqīn, 78
Yazıcıoğlu, Meḥmed, 78, 88
Muḥammediye, 78
Young Muslim Movement, 1, 166, 174–5, 176
Yugoslavia/Yugoslav, 7, 66, 135–8, 150, 166
bureaucracy, 142
emigration, 141, 144–5
first delegation, 141–2*f*
Izetbegović, Alija, 181–2
NATO, 194–5
postwar delegations, 140–8
race, 151
state enemies, 144
tekkes, 167
travelogues, 137, 141–50, 151–8
UDBA, 174
Young Muslim Movement, 1, 166, 174–5, 176

Žiga, Jusuf, 179
ziyāra 16, 65, 76–83; *see also* pious visitations
Zukić, Kemal, 201

EU representative:
Easy Access System Europe
Mustamäe tee 50, 10621 Tallinn, Estonia
Gpsr.requests@easproject.com

www.ingramcontent.com/pod-product-compliance
Lightning Source LLC
Chambersburg PA
CBHW070326240426
43671CB00013BA/2377
* 9 7 8 1 4 7 4 4 9 4 1 1 3 *